Blameless

Death Was Never The End,
It Was My Beginning.

HAVANA BOOK GROUP LLC.
HAVANABOOKGROUP.COM

HAVANA BOOK GROUP PUBLISHERS LLC
43537 RIDGE PARK DRIVE
TEMECULA, CA. 92590

FROM THE LIBRARY OF

Kassidy Brewer

Prologue

In this story, we are going to learn about Kassidy Brewer and the incredible testimony that happened to her. The tragedies that happened to her drew her so close to God that He continues to work through her due to the enormous faith that has developed. When tragedies happen, we tend to look back at our life and lives and reflect. You will also get Kassidy's perspective of the events that led her to pose the question, "What if it's my last day on earth with my loved ones?" Her story was witnessed by family and friends and is a testimony of faith, determination, and perseverance. Like it is said, this is God's story that happened to Kassidy that her friends and family observed with hope. So, relax and envelop yourself into each account that developed a relationship made in heaven.

Kassidy Brewer

Waking up

Did you know that there are around eight different stages to a coma?

Still considered very fragile, I was loaded into an ambulance. My family couldn't use the word "home" as they tried countless times to take me home from the hospital, but it always resulted in a dreadful surgery or something serious. They said to use the simple word shopping, "let's go shopping" when speaking of going home! Everyone knew it was just a code word. And excitedly, it worked. Each and every nurse and doctor became giddy with excitement and anticipation for sending me to go home in the one-hour ambulance drive.

Pulling up to the house, it was extremely nerve racking for everyone, not knowing what the future holds and fear of making a major mistake. Just as we were settling, countless safety precautions were unbuckled from the ride. Then the true miracle happened. That's where the miraculous story of our dog Penny licking me in the face, causing me to remember most things from that point on, comes into play.

There's something about dogs that's completely captivating and can put any situation into perspective once they're a part of it. There's a reason "dog" is spelled "God" backwards. Dogs have a sense of quietness and gratefulness about them. And that can only be revealed in love, goodness, personality and relationally, much like the characteristics of God. Their love for you is unconditional!

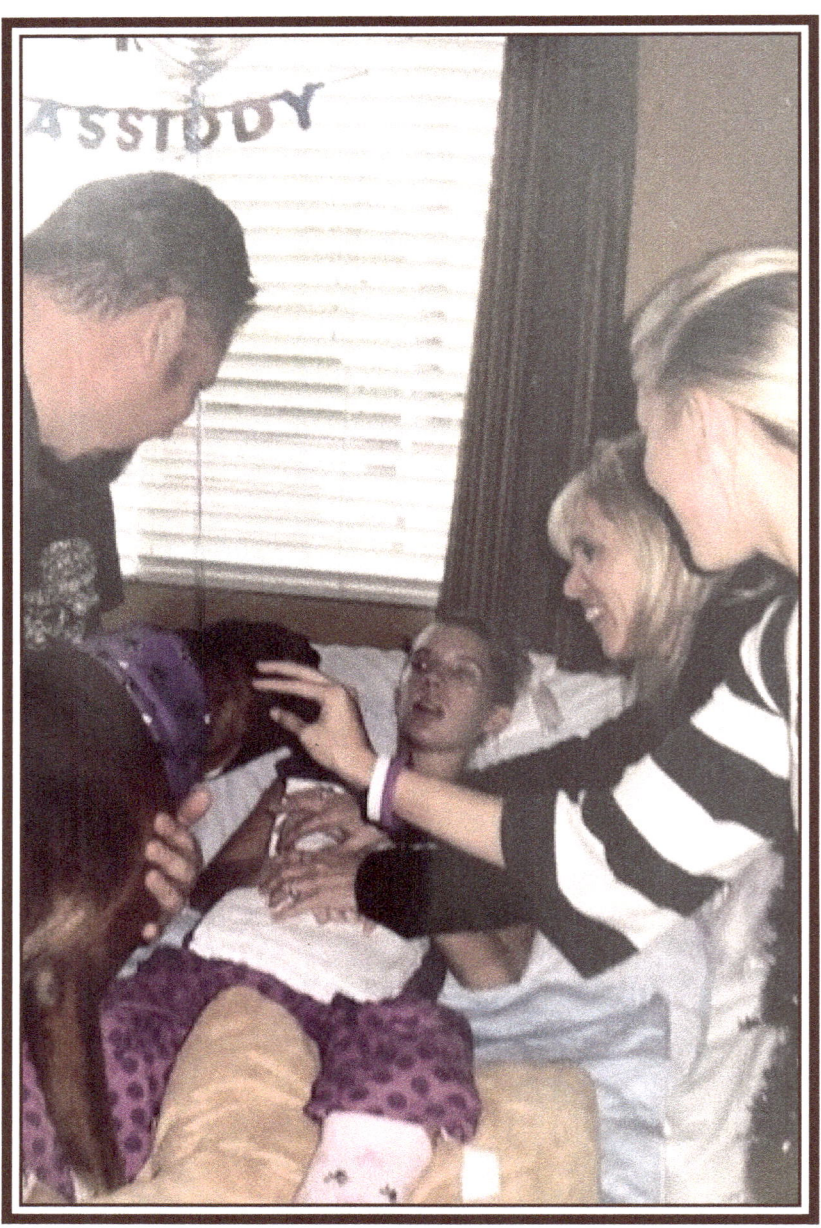

Chapter Overview

Chapter 1

The story of Talitha Cumi

We all have something that propels us to be the best we can be. It's out there, we just need to diligently search. But on the other hand, it's also very joyful and relaxing to just sit back and be entertained by the presence of life. In that instance, a tendency to watch life fly by can take over. Which can result in complacency.

In Mark 5:40-41, the Bible tells us the story of a little girl dying. Jesus comes along and speaks the words "Talitha Cumi" which is translated, "Little girl, I say to you, arise." She does arise and Jesus commands that someone should get her something to eat. The story of the little girl, so close to death was my experience as well. While being played out in a little bit different sequence, my voyage relates. Near-death experiences and God's healing hands are always something to pay attention to. Like the little girl in distress, my near-death experience brought me to God's healing hands. When I was touched by God, I went from death to life.

Blameless

Reading Job one in the Bible, He was and is the ultimate blameless man. The Hebrew word blameless is different from what the English word is. The English word for blameless would be without fault. But the word blameless actually has a Hebrew meaning, "to be complete." Speaking of one's integrity, Job did this. He was a man who followed after God and turned from evil. He did admit that he was not sinless to where I assume there was some humility there as well. Despite the Sabeans raiding his oxen and killing all and using the edge of the sword, killing much of his servants, Job knew that God gave, and God can take away.

Another trial he faced moments later, was regarding the fire of God, referring to the result of knowing Him. Light is a signal; fire is a source. The fire of God came and burned up Job's sheep and another portion of his servants. Then, moments later, the Chaldeans raided Jobs' camels to kill them and took out yet another portion of his servants. Jobs' pride and joy was his livestock along with his countless servants. But that was all taken away. And to top it off, Job had 10 children, and they were all under one roof when a mighty wind came and a building collapsed on all of them, killing all. Yet, Job remained blameless in God. He was shocked and angry yet praises God in the only way he knows. "Naked I came into this world, naked I shall return."

This story is yet another great correlation. For Job suffered countless hardships in a short period of time. However, he was aroused with fury and exasperation, he chooses to praise God with what he does have instead of what he lost. His faith grew stronger with his multiple trials. And that's exactly what took place in mine as well. I went through this difficult chapter of my life with a self-willed attitude. But at about the four-year mark was when Yahshua really started to transform my own will over to Him. Now, all I live for is the Holy Spirit in me. I began to realize that I was saved for a purpose greater than my own. Fully giving my soul, mind, and body to the one who created it.

Now, knowing the meaning of the Hebrew word blameless, the title hits a little different, doesn't it? I was blameless in death because this near-death experience didn't just happen. It was blameless, there was no cause. Theres no one to blame. I'm complete from this incident because I was in the arms of the Father. Within His grasp. He knew that I still had purpose here on earth, so He released me and said that my work here isn't done.

Endless Hope

My ultimate desire is to try to explain hope. Not only hope here on earth, but the hope that is to come beyond what you see. The hope of seeing the light at the end of the tunnel, despite your circumstances. Choosing to be the light apart from your situation. In Hosea 4:6, you hear the word contend. That's just another word for saying, compete to be the high authority. And Jesus commands us not to contend or to rebuke one another.

For example, when we are trying to be a competitor with our neighbor, it's as if they're not important. Likewise, if you win, you have the authority over that individual. But if we actively team up with one another, you end up going further in the long run instead of achieving victory yourself. And no one wants to do anything by themselves, so why not join together? When a person tries to get authority over another, they are attempting to get control of the situation. And who are the best ones to put you on the right path? Yahshua Himself.

Who does he speak through? Pastors and Priests. So ultimately, you're in competition with a priest. Reading on it states that, "you shall stumble in the day." This word stumble is talking about how we can fall or teeter totter at the drop of the hat. When a person is led in their own strength, they seem to waver from this idea to that idea, whereas when we are stable in Christ, our strength comes from Him alone. That will cause our stumbling to be used for His glory and His glory alone. In the instance of gaining knowledge, our stumbling can be used as a stumbling block or a hurdle, or our stumbling can be used to edify Christ.

From knowing where we came from to where we are now, is part of our stumbling hurdle that we chose to overcome with Christ by our side. Using the strength that Christ handpicked in you and for you. As a person rejects knowledge, they're rejecting Christ. And as verse six states, that if we reject him in the sight of others, He will ultimately reject us. He says, that one of the priorities that Christ lays is not to reject Him. In other words, bring Him praise in all situations. Why would you reject your creator? All that you have comes from Him alone.

Life changes can pivot you.
Pivoting is a part of life. You're not going to like me when I say this, but so are those trying times. Those times of affliction where we think we're the only person going through a problem in life. Where the world seems as if it's a long, dark hallway that leads nowhere. Part of life is to acclimate to what's unseen. We must become so well-rounded in the fact that transitioning from a victim's mentality to a victor's mentality comes with ease. It's called being flexible and learning to adapt to the environment. Essentially, we need to work on being like a chameleon with adaptations to thrive. Humans may not have the physical abilities of chameleons, but we do have the ability to shift our perspective to the outcome of a situation. And that's what

pivoting is all about. Seeing the situation for what it actually is yet anticipating and praying for hope.

While we are all called to be exiles in our own type of way, whether that be to something you're not familiar with, to go somewhere new, to get outside of your comfort zone, whatever it is, the Father is going to be right beside you in your efforts. This not only brings Him glory because it's in His power but when we edify Him and choose to give Him the glory, that's what truly warms His heart. Doing something, we didn't know was possible is like being those exiles like Abraham and Sarah in the fact that they had to lean on their faith to pull them through. Much like our difficulties, when we take the leap and just do the dang thing! Leaning on the Father needs to be our first response or MO, in the fact that we can't do life in our own strength. And that's just what these two did in their distinctive calling.

I can recall those moments of being an able bodied, carefree teenager who didn't have a care in the world, had a rebellious nature, wanted instantaneous results, going through life like any other pre-teen. I always had the most fun times when I was around my friends having pre-teen fun with peers and operating under my parents' stature. There were times of joy and times of self-inflicted "emotional" sadness that took place.

But facing death head on didn't seem as if it would be in the cards for me. I had the best life. Going from every tiresome sports activity to middle school life to chilling with friends, I didn't really stop to slow down and understand the day-to-day activities. But maybe a child is only supposed to have fun growing up. At the end of middle school is when not just my life, but everyone in my family had an eye opener. A life shift that would alter us for the rest of our lives.

Now, knowing these times of fun can easily come and go, it's all based upon my perspective of what's to come. See, I faced the reality of living life to the full in a body that operated like every other teen, to having to think about every decision of whether it would propel me forward or halt my recovery.

Chapter 2

Exiles can be used for much more than we think

Due to Abraham and Sarah being exiles, God was using it to show their obedience toward him. The Father already knew that obedience was in Abraham and Sarah, it was just up to them to choose to obey. Now, because Abraham and Sarah did choose to obey, He made their journey comprehendible. They were in the hands of God, as foreigners in the land, they would soon be set free and to experience all that Christ has for them. Similarly, we have the same choice. Maybe it appears different, but we have that picking to go this way or that way. It's a black or white experience. There is no grey matter. Much like there's not a lukewarm movement for Christianity. It all starts in the mind. It's called faith. Trust. Believe.

Fully Embrace Life

Personally, I've found that because of my traumatic experience, I've discovered my true purpose. My true identity. And although it's far from your typical vision of the question, "how do you see yourself in twenty years" kind of answer, it distinctively has Christs name all over it. So, if you ask me, what matters most to you?" My answer is simply, hope. Hope, that there's more beyond your sufferings. More than meets the eye. Obviously, we have no control over the future, but in a slight way, you do. Because again, the choice is yours and Christ knows what your future holds.

By choosing to have respect, integrity, determination, resiliency, self-control and seeing the Father in every area we take part in. Not conforming to our insecurities but deciding to take them head on. When it comes to transparency and being vulnerable, I don't hide. I literally can't! But you know what, people value transparency. If that implies that I show up completely, 100%, who I am, that's exactly what I'm called to be. Embrace who YOU'RE called to be.

In that, what also lights me up is helping those that have a hard time helping themselves. Of course, it's nerve racking to pinpoint someone and ask to buy their meal. Little acts like that are small gestures anyone can do. It's not going to feel comfortable on your part but are we called to live a life of comfortability or to help out those that need it? To pray for them. To be joyful in a world full of animosity, strife and push back. We all need a little help. Be that person that illuminates light and joy.

We have that ability to be the light to everyone around us. And as the darkness tends to flee from the light, if you really pay attention, sometimes the light can attract darkness. Those ungenuine manipulators are referred to as wolves in sheep's clothing. But we can't improve without awareness, right? The whole objective is to seek out tactics that draw in darkness and to not take part in those. But never avoid them at all costs because again, trials produce character. I, first-hand, can tell you that trials are definitely not fun, but they are part of life and taking them on is part of the challenge.

So, in that case, what means the most to me is to fully embrace that this life was never promised to us to be perfect, to have confidence, courage and to let go of expectations. Because with our expectations comes assumptions, and you know what they say about assumptions! To get rid of the fear that's not letting you let go of the voices that make us feel insecure. What's making you hold onto that insecurity? Is it Shame? Guilt? Rejection? What if we just chose to embrace our flaws and uniqueness?

My Upbringing and Family

Playing, jumping, skipping, laughing is what every young kid does. We also make mistakes and learn from them. That's precisely what I did growing up and continuing to do! My parents met in a small city called Valley City, North Dakota. They fell in love, got married, and a few years later, had my sister Dani in 1986. Enjoying the time of having a family of three, they decided to add another addition to the family. In 1991, Lexi came into the world, bringing more joy to the lives of Kevin and Donna Brewer. They agreed that the two daughters were plenty. Well, a couple of years later in 1994 was when the day of the terrifying Northridge Earthquake happened, and to her surprise discovered she was pregnant, again!

It wasn't clear to anyone of why this happened, but they knew it was a gift from the Lord. Nine months later I was born. A healthy, 8 lbs. 13 oz., lengthy, stick-thin, baby girl. There you have it, 3 daughters in one household. Sounds pretty chaotic to some people, but we learned, I'll stay out of your way if you stay out of mine! Looking back at my baby photo albums, I wasn't just a blonde-haired baby like most of you could imagine, my hair was white, white as snow. White hair with glaring blue eyes!

From my age of one to four is when my family was in their more adventurous season of life. I always say, "they had the most memorable times that I don't remember." But with every child they had, it got harder and harder to go places. There are a lot of stories that would be very exciting to tell you, but I was too little to give you any details!

Us kids had a somewhat "normal" childhood. Moving from California to Ohio was quite a journey. I was only four years old at the time, but moving a family of five across the country doesn't sound like a thrill to me! While we were in Ohio, we all made some lifelong friendships we still keep in contact with today. After a short year, we moved back to California to this little town called Murrieta to this wonderful, white, tract home. We didn't know anyone or where anything was in the town, but the Lord kept us where we were for a purpose. Numerous memories were shared and made in that house. Where the Shepherd leads, the sheep follow!

You're probably thinking, wait, how does this relate to Mark 5:40-41? Just keep reading and I'll explain!

Christmas time at the Brewer household was always special. We were the type of family that did everything differently. Still to this day, we open our presents from the family on Christmas Eve then on Christmas day we wait at the top of the stairs in anticipation to find what was left behind. The Lord gives us multiple gifts in life, daily. Ones we want and ones we don't want. Either way they're a gift you don't want to exchange! I started preschool in Ohio, and when we moved back to California, I was promoted to first grade.

We met the nicest lady who had a horse ranch. After talking for quite some time, she was truly a genuine individual. She happened to offer me and my best friend Niki riding lessons! We both love animals and were so adventurous so that decision was a "no brainer"! Niki was not only someone I went to grade school with but was my neighbor who lived three houses down from me.

We were inseparable! We would set up a big tent in my backyard and lay blankets, pillows, and hangout in there all day, then at night we would camp out in it. It was like a home away from home for us. Not caring that the ground was totally concrete; that didn't stop us. We were determined and always up to do something fun! Together a lot, school was a place where we could have our own space and our own friends. Going to the same school for a whole year, I built lots of friendships and learned new skills.

I went to a small public school for kindergarten and first grade. A newer school closer to where I lived was built, to where I ended up going there for second and third grade. Third grade was when I really started to develop my own cognitive and social skills. That's when the light bulb went on! I can do this. By being the naturally kind and thoughtful leader that I was by character, we all develop, grow wings, and find passions in life. Now was the time.

Around this age, I started enjoying surfing with my dad and sister, Lexi. We would snorkel, go tubing and surf on those nice warm summer days. We'd pack a lunch and a blanket and make a day of it! Growing up, only my immediate family was here in California. No Uncle or Aunt or even Grandma and Grandpa. Just us. Everyone else lived back in North Dakota and Michigan. But hey, we all turned out just fine! Since we had no relatives nearby, we invested our time in sports. My dad was involved with his competitive triathlons. Boy, do I have lots of stories from just those alone. Sitting out on the trunk of our car, we entertained ourselves with a sandwich and played games. Those were the good ol' days, so much fun. Traveling around from city to city and state to state. It was like a never-ending road trip. Where to next?!

At the time, we had a Boxer named Penny. She went with us ninety percent of the time. (You'll come across her again in my story.) That was the beginning to my crazy adventure of running! My trips to triathlon events with my dad ignited my love for running. Next to that, there's Lexi who was on the traveling Volleyball team and loved the sport. She was this 5'8'' chick who was a good girl at heart but gnarly with a Volleyball! Now Dani is nine years older than me to where she was focused on work and schooling. And on top of that, I was playing Elite Soccer traveling from here to there too.

Soccer was another passion of mine. I began playing around the age of seven and carried through until I was about eleven. Getting to the travel level of soccer, I really formed a bond with all of the girls on my team. We were definitely sisterhood at that. Running around a field, kicking a ball into a net is what brought me joy at that time. We'd take part in banquets, parties, outings, and anytime we could get together. It's almost as if God was handing me a life to be enjoyed to the fullest at such a young age. The Brew Crew (my last name is Brewer) went from here to there, to all over the place. It was exciting and we never knew what was going to happen next. I have no idea how we did it all!

When I was seven, I went to a horse camp with my Girl Scout group. Of course, my best friend Niki had to be a part of it with me! Going there taught us motivation, self-determination, doing things for ourselves and lots more. That camp was another major eye-opener. Selective in my interests, whatever got my undivided attention was something that really captivated me. And horses were one of those. The horse that I effortlessly rode was named Rusty. Rusty and I had a bond; unquestionably he was my true love.

I even had a birthday party, and my family surprised me with a visit from him in the front yard of our tract house! I still have this bedside decorative figure, that I got for my birthday of a horse with a young girl, and it says, "Girls first love." However, simply taking them for trail rides was not only peaceful but would challenge me to think of how good things don't come with doing easy things, and that's what started me on the path towards barrel riding. Barrel racing is what you see on TV. When the riders sprint on their horse around a barrel without knocking it over then sprint to the other barrel and try to get a record time. It was a challenge, and it was exhilarating! I'd do that over and over again until I couldn't. That was probably when I was living my best life.

At nine years old, my cousin and I went to a bike shop to get something fixed. They told us it would be close to an hour's wait. So, we walked outside and saw a couple doors down there was a Taekwondo studio. Taekwondo comes from the Korean word, tae, "kick," kwon, "fist or punch," do, "the art of." I was very intrigued by it, and we got more information. The next day, my mom and I called to set up an appointment. That was when everything changed, for the better!

Everyone didn't think that I would stay for only a couple of months. But... I stayed in for quite a number of years when I got my first-degree black belt! Overcoming that goal was a dream I thought I could never imagine. That moment in my life was quite a memorable time. Going from working in the office to beating up two boys at once, I've learned to use my surroundings, the knowledge I consumed and a karate chop that will send you flying! Don't mess with Kassidy! Proving people wrong is a fun hobby I thoroughly enjoy! Words cannot describe how much I would suggest Taekwondo for any age.

It was then in 2004 we took a family trip to the Caribbean, St. Maarten. Was that a blast! The plane ride alone was a gorgeous sight. Clear blue waters, transitioning from clear to aqua to blue, takes you to a whole different state of relaxation. We stayed at a resort that had an infinity pool overlooking the beautiful ocean view. They had something fun to do all the time. But we got out of the little square that we were in and explored a bit. We rented these Rhinos (almost like jet skis but bigger) and went into the deep waters to snorkel. Seeing lots of fish and sea turtles was a stunning sight to see. Then, 2007 was a year of more great events. We went to Oahu, Hawaii. That was a trip never to be forgotten. The oceans were lovely and warm! Time to be an official tourist. It was time to explore the island and check out what's around. Day after day, we debated if we wanted to go see the island or go to the beach and accompany those warm, blue waters. Sight-seeing the Pearl Harbor ship was very historical and interesting.

Going into middle school was a big deal. I was nervous, intimidated, anxious, and questionable. At that tender age, heading into "big kids' school" with more classes and a different schedule seemed daunting to say the least, but I was up for the challenge. I got acquainted with my classes, schedule, friends, and thankfully I had a good group of friends that I went through all of it with. As time passed, we soon became our own identity and transitioned into meeting new friends, having different interests. I am the type of person that gets along better with guys. Just for their company, I felt like I didn't have the pressure to have an opinion toward everything. It could've been in my head, but that's how it was, and they were all my good pals. I'm not a fan of the drama that girls come with, so I gravitate more towards males.

That's when I discovered that I adored running. Cross country to be exact. My running adventures turned into running fast for "the mile" at school. I traveled to different cross-country meets at different schools. Even took on the turkey trot every November and ended up in the top three! Looking back, those were the days. It was more of the experience and the people that made it so exhilarating, but the running was fun too! But believe it or not I did not have any hick-ups or pressure in my head due to running for so long, the only red flag we were always curious about was why my face turned beat red. Not like the typical red that you get from exhaustion but literally beat red. We could not figure that out. But I typically turned beat red, so it wasn't alarming at any rate.

Chapter 3

Life before the incident

I was no different than your average troublemaker child. I'd swim in my friend's pool, hang out at movie theaters, go to the beach, you name it, skateboarding, I did it. Middle school was definitely an eye opener as to the many possibilities of becoming my own individual and making more minor choices on my own in life. Nearing the end of my Eighth-grade year., my best friend Felicia and I went on our 8th grade field trip without either of our parents to New York and to Pennsylvania.

It was the end of March 2008, and I had my incident later in August 2008, which was another miracle in itself! If you can picture two teenage girls amusingly traveling across the country, walking the freedom Trail, paying our respects to fallen soldiers, touring around the Yankees Stadium, taking a ravenous ferry ride to see the Statue of Liberty, standing in front of the gigantic White House to touring the marvelous Hersey Chocolate Factory (My Favorite!). We did all that plus a lot more. Being on our own was nerve racking at first, but then we got used to it and knew it was a once in a lifetime experience.

Going to a considerable number of concerts, rocking out was part of who I was. Being silly and a young rebel, I would just listen to the music, pondering what life would be like if I were in their shoes. Two of my best friends Cheyann and Felicia went with me to the Del Mar fair to see my favorite band at the time, Paramore for an early birthday gift. We had a blast and being barely teenagers, got into trouble (but in the most fun, innocent way!) Unknowing what the future holds, we all lived in the moment and had a blast, living our preteen years!

In May of 2008, one of my dad's work partners invited all of us to go camping and hang out on his yacht with him. Our answer, "heck yea man!" We all had the best time. For gratification and pure enjoyment, we were able to use our friends' RV. There was my dad, my mom, Lexi, her boyfriend Travis, Penny, and myself. Travis and Lexi were and still are inseparable. He went everywhere with us. And it is a major part of my story as well. But things got a little strange on my part. We have the exact picture where everyone is having a great time, yet I was on the sidelines tired, squinting, and just out of it. We didn't think anything of it because I was thirteen and I was going through hormonal fluctuations, and everything was an effort at that age. So, we made the most of it and kept living our lives to the fullest.

Being a pre-teen isn't the easiest routine. There's so much to understand yet I don't know how to start. I was that type of kid that was respectful, had integrity, but did have moments of wanting to punch a wall or scream until the birds flew away. It was a fact of life, people get mad, they get fed up. But we all still have a moral obligation. Over time I've learned that it's not the world's job to tiptoe around your triggers. It takes time, diligence, and practice to understand we need to work on improving our own life and confidence in who we are to see that our human traits aren't perfect but one step in front of the other and moving in a forward direction is worth taking.

Don't get me wrong, I had hopes, dreams of the future. To be completely honest though, I never really pictured myself as a 30-year-old working lady. My brain was kind of at a standstill in middle school. I couldn't really ponder beyond that. And maybe that was a protection mechanism unsure of what the future would hold. I'm not sure. But what I know now, looking back, I sure am grateful for the chaos and trials in life that leave me questioning. Where would we be without the difficulties in life? Character is built in trials! But what teenager understands that right?

I was just living day to day. Yes, I had my Taekwondo experience but take into perspective, I was a pre-teen that was figuring out life and who I was. Life as a middle school gal definitely was fun. It's the time that you're not a babe in elementary school but you're not an older high schooler. You're smack dab in the middle. Where I got a little more independence yet have a backbone to rely on. And believe it or not, that time was ordinary. Looking back, I was unaware, but God was giving me the calm before the storm.

Felicia's perspective
(My good friend, like a sister to me)
We were inseparable: longboarding through the suburbs, swimming until our fingers wrinkled, and spending every dollar we had on sour candy and Mexican food. We'd skate around in our bright-colored skinny jeans, blasting Avril Lavigne, Flyleaf, and Paramore on a small battery powered speaker. We built a dream world of our own, one where there was never a dull moment, never a time when we weren't coming up with something new and ridiculous to do.

The wholesome fun we shared wasn't the only thing that made Kassidy different from other teenage friends, by twelve years old she carried herself with maturity and confidence most people never find in a lifetime. She wasn't afraid to speak her mind, to stand up for herself, to try something new. She was disciplined, determined, and so full of life that it was impossible not to be drawn to her. A black belt in Taekwondo, fearless and full of fight—Kass had this way of making everything feel bigger, like the world had no limits. I admired her more than I ever told her back then.

Intro to my family's perspective

My family and friends' point of view states more of what my loved ones went through and how it impacted them. I had the entirety of mentioning what I went through and how different avenues will help but now I want you to hear everything I don't recall. Other stories are so impactful in the sense, when we hear from another angle, our perception changes. Things start to become more real to where we can look to our Father for further clarification. So, in that case, let me ask you, have you ever questioned the meaning of life? The purpose? Why are you here? I'm right there with you. I believe we all have a reason for hope; it's just up to us to figure that out. To stay in our lane and live our life, not our brothers,' not our sisters,' not our parents,' but ours. Our own. Remember, you only live once but we die every day. "When our focus is turned onto death, we start to pay attention to life! "

Matthew, Mark, Luke and John speak from different perspectives.

I won't doubt that I have come a far way. But it didn't always play out that way. Many of the juicy details happened when I was in a coma. And the Father remains to keep them silent as my knowledge of Him grows stronger. In this case, I wanted to reach out to my family members and get their perspective on this incident as well. Just like in the accounts of Matthew, Mark, Luke, and John stating their different perspectives on the same story. We all went through the same story, but all of us experience something very different and go through different barriers and obstacles in our fight to make it through. Each of us endured numerous ups and downs, but through it all, we knew where we stood. Countless of the stories I personally cannot recall because I was out of it, that's where I want to bring my family in to share of what they went through too.

Families' perspective of life before the incident

Mom's perspective.
Kassidy Dawn Brewer, born August 30, 1994. Kassidy was the last of the Brewer girls, she was tiny, but fierce. She was a strong-willed, tender-hearted kid. She loved life, her love and passion for horses at a young age was enduring. Kassidy's development was normal. Kass was extremely confident and sure of who she was at a young age. She was a great student and had a lot of friends. Kass started riding horses at 6 years old with Ms. Heather. Rusty, the beautiful rust colored horse quickly became Kassidy's first love. Kass rode horses until she was 9 years old. She was a natural cowgirl, this tiny girl on top of this strong - tall horse. It brought her peace and tranquility.

Soccer was a sport that Kassidy excelled at, playing in local leagues, and quickly moving up to travel soccer. Her natural athletic ability was pretty impressive.

Kassidy and I stopped by "ATA Taekwondo" in Murrieta one afternoon, as we sat in awe of the athletic ability of the students training in self-defense. Kassidy decided she'd like to give it a try, I personally thought after three weeks she would have had enough; however, Mr. Robles made a huge impact on Kass. He proved to Kassidy how strong she was not just physically, but mentally. He taught confidence, strength, leadership, commitment, dedication, goal setting, respect and so much more… His energy and devotion to each student was astonishing.

She tested for her first-degree black belt at 12 years old and became a leader, teaching and assisting lower colored belts several days a week. She truly found her passion. At 12 years old, Kassidy mentioned a swooshing sound in her head, it didn't happen a lot, but she thought it was necessary to mention it. Months later she mentioned it again. I told her I thought it was time for us to contact her Pediatrician. I didn't make it a priority, only because it didn't appear to be urgent. I still beat myself up for not following through.

Kass continued to do well in school, she ran Cross Country her Middle school years, she loved to run, I would make it to her Cross-Country meets, but noticed with each race, her face would be bright red with beads of sweat, after a cold drink of water and a cool down, her face would be a flesh color and back to normal. I didn't give it much thought after Kass cooled down. She was promoted from eighth grade June of 2008, with excitement and anticipation for High School in the fall. She couldn't wait to start 9th Grade, as her sister Lexi would be a Senior at Vista Murrieta High School in Murrieta. They were looking forward to being together in High School for at least one year before Lexi graduated from High School in 2009.

Dad 's perspective:

The world became a better place on August 30th,1994 when we welcomed Kassidy Dawn Brewer into the world. It quickly became evident that this was a high spirited, high energy, feisty little girl! Kass became the third girl in the clan, and her two big sisters simply loved "playing dolls" with their new little sister, with Kassidy being their own live, little doll. She never had any shortage of attention in the house, with the two older girls carrying her around, pushing her in a stroller, feeding her, but never changing her diapers!

Kassidy's journey from birth to age 13 was nothing short of a miracle. As her father, I find it hard to put into words just how proud I am of the remarkable young woman that she has become. From the very beginning, Kassidy was destined to be extraordinary. Kassidy entered this world on a bright summer morning, her arrival filling our lives with immeasurable joy. From the moment she opened her eyes, there was a spark of curiosity that was impossible to miss. Even as a baby, she was determined to explore the world around her, always reaching out for something new and exciting. Her inquisitive nature was evident as she grew, and she quickly developed a love for learning that set her apart. As Kassidy grew into a toddler, it became clear that she possessed an innate athleticism. She was always on the move, running, jumping, and climbing with an energy that seemed boundless.

Her strong, agile body allowed her to excel in any physical activity she attempted. Whether it was learning to ride her bike without training wheels at an early age or mastering the monkey bars on the playground, Kassidy's athletic prowess was truly impressive. But it wasn't just her physical abilities that stood out. Kassidy was incredibly smart, a quick learner with an insatiable thirst for knowledge. By the time she started school, her teachers marveled at her ability to grasp new concepts with ease. She was always eager to participate in class, asking thoughtful questions and challenging herself to understand things deeply. Her determination to excel in her studies was matched only by her love, which opened up entire worlds for her to explore. Kassidy's independence shone brightly as she navigated her early years. She was never one to follow the crowd; instead, she carved her own path with confidence and grace.

Her private nature sometimes made her seem reserved, but those who took the time to get to know her discovered a deeply thoughtful and compassionate soul. Kassidy valued her alone time, often retreating to her room to work on a new project. Her creativity knew no bounds, and she was always coming up with inventive ideas and solutions to problems. Despite her independent spirit, Kassidy had a strong sense of empathy and kindness. She was the first to offer a helping hand to a friend in need and always looked for ways to make a positive impact on those around her. Her caring nature endeared her to everyone she met, and she built lasting friendships based on mutual respect and trust.

As Kassidy approached her teenage years, her determination and strength only grew. She embraced new challenges with enthusiasm, whether it was joining a travel soccer team, earning her black belt in karate at age 12, or participating in science fairs. Her love for learning expanded beyond the classroom, conducting
experiments, or volunteering in the community. Kassidy's curiosity about the world and her place in it was truly inspiring. She has blossomed into a strong,
capable, and compassionate young woman, possessing a rare combination of intelligence, athleticism, and kindness. Her journey has been marked by a series of small miracles, and one huge miracle with that one being a testament to her incredible spirit and determination. Kassidy's story is one of growth, discovery, and the boundless potential that lies within a curious and independent heart.

My middle sister Lexis' perspective:
We moved a lot as kids because of dad's jobs. Southern California, Chicago Illinois, Mason Ohio, and back to Murrieta California when Kass was five. Kass and I are 3 years apart, so we were in the same school for a short while in elementary school. I always looked forward to the day when we'd be in the same school again, that would be her freshman year of high school and my senior year!

My childhood memories with Kass mostly consist of her and I always in the pool together. We would spend our entire summer break swimming with friends, blasting Bob Marley or The Eagles or Journey. I think our family would agree that those were the soundtracks of our childhood. I literally can taste our famous strawberry pineapple smoothie we made every single summer day when I play Bob Marley's Legend soundtrack, it transports me right back to the good ol' days.

Kass was always the jokester, the quiet silly little sister. She could sit and play with her horses and barn for hours. She was always sucking her thumb. We would go school shopping, and they'd have the hardest time finding clothes that fit her because she was so dang tiny and long. Waist size of a 3-year-old, length of a 7-year-old. She loved and still loves rearranging her room and spaces. We always got along, unless one of us took too long in our shared bathroom once she became a pre-teen. She loved the color purple. She's always been very determined and feisty in the best way. She loved playing jokes on people and making people laugh. She was really good at longboard skateboarding. When I started bringing my boyfriend around when Kass was 12 or 13, she pretended to hate him and was annoyed by his silliness with her, but I know she secretly loved skating with him and the way he gave her a hard time as the baby sister.

A few years before Kass got sick, my parents invested in a Marriott timeshare. We were able to travel to Hawaii and the Caribbean. I remember that being the first time mom and dad let Kass, and I went to the pool alone with just us two. I remember thinking how grateful I was to have a younger sis to do these things with. Sure, my friends were my 'life' during those years but that was maybe a moment of maturity when I realized family is everything. My teenage attitude probably didn't show that, but it was true. We made lifelong memories on those trips and did some really cool things together. I'd say that's also where I fell in love with island life.

All in all, life before August 4th, 2008, was sweet. Our parents, God bless them, made it seem easy. Between Kass doing good in school, excelling in karate, hanging with friends, learning photography, and so much more, we would go out for sushi every week, and Friday night pizza with whoever could make it at Stadium Pizza. The girl loved to make money and would save every single penny. She used one of my dad's old cigar boxes and it was filled to the brim with cash.

She was CPR certified very young so she could babysit the neighbor kids to earn money. She even tried to take over my job which was cutting the neighbor's grass. OB Johnson would pay me $130 a month to cut the grass every weekend. At that point I'd started driving and that was my gas and mall money so there was no way I was going to let her take that over! She was just all around always responsible. When Kass got sick right before her 14th birthday, I knew her future would look different. I mourned that for her. Her friends mourned her, knowing the Kass they knew would change.

Before August 4th, our family was tight knit, our days were busy like any other young active family. On the weekends we were in every direction with sports. Dad competed in triathlons and ironman's, Kass was in travel soccer and a black belt in karate, I played travel volleyball, mom was the taxi driver while Dani was running successful companies. Every Sunday there was church in the morning and a family dinner by the pool, usually steaks on the grill.

I vividly remember driving in the car as a family after church a week or two before Kass got sick and all of us talking about how good we've got it, how blessed we are as a family, we're all healthy, how sweet life was. Fast forward a little and that conversation echoed in my head. One thing I will never take for granted from that day forward is mine and my loved one's health.

Felicia's perspective

Then one day everything changed. It was the last stretch of summer before starting high school and the heat was thick, climbing into the nineties. I remember calling Kass that morning, wanting to hang out as usual. She didn't pick up and as the hours passed with no response, I started feeling uneasy. I was sitting in the car outside a store when my phone finally rang. It was her number but not her voice. Her oldest sister Dani was rushed and frantic. "Kassidy had a brain aneurysm," she said. "Please pray."

The days and months that followed were a blur of ICU visits, beeping machines, and unsure prayers. More tubes and monitors surrounded Kassidy than I thought possible. At some point my tears stopped, and for several years I couldn't cry at all. And the questions wouldn't stop. Why her? Why did this happen to the strongest, most determined, most alive person I knew? It felt so unfair.

Here's where my story begins...

Chapter 4

Disappointment made me

We've all faced some sort of disappointment in life. Whether that be the disappointment of minor inconveniences or waiting for something to happen but never does. What if we looked at those disruptions not as a type of derailment but a way of redirection that will put us on a better route. More often than not, we are set in our ways. Thinking that this would be the best way to reach the goal, and when our plan is taken off course, we are bombarded with doubts and fears. Don't worry, that's a complete human response, you're not crazy.

Turning those doubts and fears that I had and gave them up entirely for a life fully submitted to Christ, that's when I began to see Him work.

As middle school was a time for fun and spontaneity, personally I reminisce on the chaos, as I look back at my young life. Again, trials are tragic, but they are a time for growth and learning from those difficulties. Although I did have a great upbringing, my biggest trial was ahead. Like most challenges and hard times, they cannot be prevented but only endured. After you handle those hard times like a boss, you're going to see true growth like never before.

The beginning of the incident
Just a typical day, nothing out of the ordinary. Mornings in August get hot really fast here in Murrieta. My mom and I were

the only one's home. My dad was at work; Dani was getting her hair done and Lexi was at the movies with Travis. My mom was at her desk upstairs and was called in for a meeting at work, but her coworker called and told my mom not to come in for some reason. We didn't know it but that was the first blessing that saved my life because she rarely worked from home.

Her coworker called her directly and told her that they were laying some people off and that she wouldn't want to come into the office. That was the first major blessing in disguise. Mowing the lawn was not my favorite activity to do. But what you got to do you got to do! So, I did. It was hot but I was done. After that I decided to rearrange my room, a monthly routine I loved to do. So, I started moving furniture around, this way, and that way, carefully planning my steps of where to place my bed. That was extremely fun to me.

Finishing up, I began sweating profusely and felt a tingling all over, then at the very back of my head it began vibrating like a cell phone vibrator stuck on the back of my head. It all happened so quickly yet I still remember every bit of it. I ran out to my mom at her desk about fifteen feet from my room and screamed, "Mom my head." Looking at me crying uncontrollably, she looked at my face dripping puddles of sweat. The pupils of my eyes literally dancing up and down and side-to-side. She called my neighbor who was studying to be an EMT.

My mom didn't know what to think so we grabbed a Gatorade thinking I was dehydrated from mowing the lawn, in a panic we scurried to the car. The nearest hospital was about ten to fifteen minutes away. On the way there, about two minutes in the car I yelled, "Mommy help me." "I have to throw up."

At that point, it was serious. Something was terribly wrong. Interestingly enough, I still remember the feeling of my organs shutting down and my light fading away. Internally, all of my vital body systems were failing, and I was unable to function normally.

The four core elements of a near-death experience.

Near death experiences are referred to as having four core elements. After considering the actual event, I've come to realize that I was in fact, in a tunnel. My peripheral vision was definitely narrowing in. It was as if I was wearing fuzzy racehorse blinders to prevent myself from seeing out of my peripheral vision. Things were very covered or fuzzy and my only thought was, "what is happening?" All I could focus on was trying to remain composed, but this was something uncontrollable, something that I couldn't help. At that moment, I was 100% helpless and everyone else was too. That of which, my event was traumatic. It came on so suddenly and happened so quickly. And August 4th turned into complete devastation.

My early memory

As my mom was running through almost every red light, I passed out and was unconscious. My mom turned a sharp turn, and I abruptly fell into her arms. The hospital we went to was under construction. She was confused about where to go so she just went to the entrance and pressed on her car horn. Yelling and screaming for help, several doctors and nurses came running out to help. They quickly got me out of the car and rushed me inside and did a CT scan of my head. We weren't aware of this until later, but the CT scan at Rancho Springs

Hospital hadn't been working consistently, but the Lord was all over the situation, and that day it happened to be working perfectly.

There was some sort of bleed on the brain, so they called the closest Neurosurgeon. He only works two days a week at his Murrieta location. Only Mondays and Tuesdays were his workdays, and it happened to be a Monday. And want to know another blessing? His office was around the corner, not even two minutes away. My mom called my Taekwondo instructor Mr. Robles first because I was supposed to come in later that day to work out. We were personally close to my instructor, so it was no big deal to call him. But this was serious.

When Dr. Spicer, the Neurosurgeon arrived at Rancho Springs Hospital to help, I was already in a room, he turned to everybody and demanded, "everybody out!" He did an Exterior Ventriculostomy on my head and had to shave half of my head. An exterior Ventriculostomy is where he stuck a big tube in front of my skull to drain the buildup of blood. Excuse me for grossing you out, I think it's so cool! But when he did that, we found out later that blood usually trickles out the tube. Mine shot out and they had to close the room after me to sanitize it. Dr. Spicer was stunned and amazed, he had only seen a handful of these cases, and the majority of those patients don't make it out alive. It was beyond doubt, unfathomable for my family.

The time this happened and my birth time.
Here's another miracle, it was said that I finished mowing the lawn at around 12 o'clock in the afternoon. I then proceeded to rearrange my room right after that. Probably around 12:50 pm

is when I ran out to my mom with my head endlessly vibrating. The timing of this piqued my curiosity. I checked back to what time I was born in 1994. Do you know what time that was at? 12:50 in the afternoon. Crazy, right? This was not a coincidence. There was a reason.

Further insight of my early view

My mom then called my dad who worked two hours away and he could not get there fast enough. Then she called Dani who was getting her hair done in town. She and I share this weird sister connection and kept stalling for time. She didn't know why, but the Lord was speaking to her. When my mom called her, she was immediately on her way. Lexi was at the movies for Travis' brother's birthday. And of course, she dropped her phone, and it was on vibrate, when the movie was over, and she found her phone, it had like forty-three missed calls and texts. When she called back, she got the news and was devastated and awestruck.

At the hospital, Dr. Spicer told my family, "I'm so sorry, but your daughter doesn't have a high chance of survival let alone make the air flight." When he was done with explaining, the hospital staff called the C.H.E.T Team to air flight me to Rady Children's Hospital in San Diego because I was in critical condition. They loaded me in, and my family could not ride with me because there wasn't enough room in the helicopter. Now remember, I'm unconscious during all of this. I'm just telling you the stories that I've heard. On the way there, my mom made phone calls to friends and family everywhere, letting them know and asking for prayer. Friends that lived hours away jumped on the freeway, breaking over 100 MPH just to be there. And before the helicopter even arrived people were there waiting. The Lord has so many tricks up His sleeve to bring us all together as one for His good despite circumstances.

When the helicopter landed, I was taken in to have an MRI of the brain and was diagnosed with a ruptured brain AVM in my brainstem and cerebellum. I was then rushed to the Intensive Care Unit. When we first arrived at Rady Children's Hospital, we had this doctor that told my parents he knew what the end result looked like. More times than not, when a patient is admitted to the hospital with a ruptured brain AVM, most of the time they don't make it out alive. But what we said is "you don't know our God. "Let's just say, never go on scientific research, stay in the faith, and watch the miracles take place.

As I went through countless stories, not only because they happened to me but because I long to remember them. I pray that the Father will reveal what He wishes to in His time. "The journey is all about patience and resilience, not less." Patience in recovery and the patience of understanding. However, I do continue to ask, seek, and knock at the door of His heart like it says in His word of Matthew 7. And in doing so, Yahshua brings knowledge to my understanding of knowing Him better.

Maybe, just maybe, He is using this experience of me not knowing the full picture of what happened, to draw me closer to Him and to share of His goodness. To make His ways a more intimate kind of way. It's a way of having to be more reliant on Him and to gather info and facts from others. Like I said, I remember everything before the incident and everything after but those four/ five months that I was in a coma, I hardly recall. To where I have to rely on friends and family. But then again, that draws me to have a better relationship with them as well.

So, the way that I see this tragic event, I see it as a way to seek family and friends' understandings and perspectives and to be in pursuit of Christ's own heart. His wisdom far exceeds mine, He sees what I do not so why wouldn't I chase after His wisdom?

It's not the satisfaction of going and doing things, it's the satisfaction of doing something on your own.
I find that we crave the neurotransmitter dopamine way too much. And not the authentic dopamine type, the artificial, enhancing type. If you aren't very familiar with dopamine, we can get it naturally when we are creative, overcome obstacles, work through, or do certain tasks on our own. That's where this saying comes from in the picture. Going and doing things is great until we grow tired and weary. That's when we need more of the Father. To lead us and guide us like never before.

In comparison with the Holy One in relation to equality, in Isaiah 40:25-31, we find that there's none to compare but to the Father. He is the holy one. And holy means, sacred. Devoted to God. In conjunction with that, it's in our respect to see who created these things. While we are disciplined to His compassion, "through His might and His massive strength," in reference to all that He declares. We can try to decipher His love and how His deeds are to be honored, yet when we attempt to understand, His works cannot be understood.

While He somehow brings strength and energy and endurance to the weary, He invigorates us all when our reliance is in Him alone. That goes for our strength in every area that we need it. Strength in waiting for the smallest of small desires of our heart, the Father knows and understands our longing. Even those little gestures of hope seem to lift you on wings like eagles' wings to soar. And while they may be endless and tiresome at the time, placing our hope in Yahshuah alone invigorates us in a way like no other. When that trust is set, our endurance and faith will keep us going to the end. He elevates our feet to be feet like a gazelle. Swift, mighty, quick. And that's how I view the picture of our renewed bodies. We hear about having the most majestic, beautiful setting to inhabit, and I can't wait to actually live there! This is exactly how I see it.

Chapter 5

The miracle in the early stages of the incident

My Mom's perspective:

Monday, August 4th, 2008, was another HOT summer day in Southern California, I was working at my home when a client called to cancel our 1:00 PM appointment. Kass was up early to mow the grass and do her chores, she finished mowing and went to her room to get ready for the day, moments later Kass came out of her room confused and stumbling, saying "MOM", I walked over to her quickly noticing the pupils in her eyes dilating and bouncing up and down, her body was beaded with sweat and her arms and legs were posturing.

I guided her to her bed, laid her gently down on the bed to process what was happening. I grabbed a cool washcloth and called my EMT friend Lisa, who advised me to grab a Gatorade to hydrate Kass and rush her to the hospital. I was able to guide Kass to the car, when we drove down the street, she said she had to throw up, I rolled down the window, she threw up... her last words were "HELP ME MOMMY." Little did I know they would be her last words for a very long time, she knew she was dying. This is Kassidy's last memory, her last word. How could I not save my baby? As her head laid gently on the car door window, I knew time was critical, I continued to call out to her, but there was no response. We were at a Red light (of course), I was helpless, so I literally screamed out to God, "Please Help me, Lord."

He prompted me to accelerate, to go through the red light, then before my eyes, the Lord parted the road, opening up a path on the busy street, we hit every red light. I made a sharp right turn at which time Kassidy flew into my Right arm, lifeless and limp. I knew at this moment this was URGENT, and time was in my hands. I'm her mother, I had to save her. I was confused and shaking. I arrived at the hospital, only to notice construction crews pouring cement on the road to the Emergency Room. I had to make a split-second decision; I quickly turned left into the main entrance of Rancho Springs Hospital. I screamed "HELP ME" to a man standing by the front entrance. He quickly ran to the front desk and asked for help.

Instantly I heard the "CODE BLUE" intercom blaring throughout the hospital, within seconds several Doctors and nurses came running to the passenger side of the door. The calm Doctor asked several questions as to what Kassidy's symptoms were before arriving. I was direct and shaking, as my girl was lifeless on my right arm. I didn't know what to do, I was helpless, scared and alone. The medical team swiftly put Kassidy on a gurney and wheeled her to the CT machine, one of the nurses guided me to the ER department to wait for Kassidy. In my head, I thought she would walk back to me and say, everything is okay mom, let's go home. I was calm but pacing with anticipation. I was in prayer, talking to God, asking Him for guidance, protection, and answers.

Not long after, the Doctor quietly asked for me to sit down and look at Kassidy's images on the computer monitor. He showed me the "massive" bleed she had in her Cerebellum of her brain; he told me to prepare myself. I looked at him and quietly said, "He must be mistaken, this is not the image of my healthy daughter. I was confused, trying to process what was happening. Kevin was on his way from Torrance, over an hour away. I called Danielle, her oldest sister, and asked her to get to the hospital asap, Dani arrived first.

They brought Kassidy back from the CT scan to a private room in the ER, she was intubated. I didn't understand the severity of what was happening. Soon a nurse came in and explained that they would be inserting a catheter, I still didn't understand why... Danielle and I went through a million scenarios as to what could have happened, possibly she got hit in the head at Taekwondo? The Doctor shared with us that a helicopter from Rady Children's Hospital was on its way. The CHET team would arrive at any time; it was evident that Kassidy was in need of a top tier at the Children's Hospital that was equipped to take care of her critical needs.

Suddenly the door flew open, it was the Neurosurgeon, Dr. Spicer yelling **"GET OUT," get out NOW."** Danielle and I literally ran out the door, knowing then how urgent the situation was. Little did we know Dr. Spicer shaved a portion of Kassidy's hair to perform an exterior Ventriculostomy, a tube that is inserted to the center of her brain to relieve the massive bleed. As he inserted the tube, a mass amount of blood flew over his shoulder onto the wall behind him.

After what seemed like minutes, Dr. Spicer walked out of the door, looked at Danielle, Kevin and I and said that there is NO way she was going to survive, that it was a massive bleed, she wouldn't make it to Rady Children's Hospital in San Diego. I looked over at Danielle and she fell to her knees, Kevin covered his face in disbelief and tears, I reached out my arms, made a full circle, internalizing everything that was happening and where I was. Not one person in the ER was critical, WHY my baby girl. It wasn't fair, WHY LORD, WHY is this happening. Is this even real or is this all a dream? We followed her gurney to the helicopter; never did I think we'd ever have to experience this moment in our lives. How on earth do you say "Goodbye" to your 13-year-old... She was a healthy girl not even an hour before.

Minutes later the CHET team from Rady Children's Hospital arrived, a team of five nurses, respiratory therapists and doctors arrived to take Kassidy away. What do you mean there is no room on the helicopter for her mother to go? The CHET team assured us that they would take good care of her, that they would meet us at Rady Children's Hospital just an hour away. We had to say goodbye to Kassidy, not knowing if she was going to be alive or not when we arrived.

It was terrifying. Was I dreaming, someone please wake me up from this terrible dream, this can't be happening...

We each drove our home separately, my car had a stream of throw up on the side of the passenger side of the car, we couldn't drive it to the hospital. I called my brother from North Dakota, also known as Uncle Kevin to the girls, their favorite uncle, and my best friend. Thank God he picked up the phone, I screamed out to him, "Kevin, it's Kassidy, she's just had a brain bleed, she was just taken away on a helicopter to San Diego." He immediately helped me to catch my breath and talk it through.

I realized that Kassidy was supposed to be at Taekwondo later that afternoon, I had to call Mr. Robles, I was able to leave Mr. Robles a voice message to let him know that Kassidy wasn't able to make Taekwondo that afternoon because she had emergency brain surgery, she was on a helicopter to Rady Children's Hospital in San Diego. We arrived home in a panic, not sure what to do, pacing in circles. I grabbed a few things. We had to wait for Lexi, she was on her way home from Ontario, we were getting impatient, but she finally made it. We all hopped into the Vespa truck and drove the quiet ride to San Diego.

We made it to the hospital and parked out front, our friend Mike Kozakowski was the first one to the hospital. He had already talked to a nurse who saw that he was out front a little frazzled. Mike witnessed Kassidy's helicopter landing on the roof of Rady Children's Hospital. The nurse quickly directed our family to a "meeting room" on the third floor of Rady Children's Hospital. Dr. Meltzer, a Neurosurgeon at Rady met with our family and gave us the news that after an extensive MRI they found that Kassidy was born with an Arteriovenous malformation in her cerebellum and brain stem, that the bleed was massive, that she also had an unusual amount of feeder veins, the possibility for another bleed was imminent.

We looked at each other, with blank stares. We had a million questions of course, as to how this can just "happen," he explained that Kassidy was literally a ticking time bomb, her chance of survival was ZERO! WTH, absolutely NOT we said. He handed me papers to donate her organs as we stood in the hallway, I pushed them back and told him that we brought the "Ultimate Physician" with us, that we need to give her at least three days.

A nurse guided us to Room 336 to unite us with Kassidy, as we entered the room, as we entered the room Kassidy was hooked up to a ventilator, and machines to keep her alive. She was peaceful, glowing, her skin was like silk, angelic really... We gathered around her and mourned, not knowing how long we had left with our baby girl. We immediately prayed over Kassidy, begging God to give her life, for her to be healed. We gave God the glory for being with us as a family. We cried out to God to save our Kassidy. We promised the Lord that we would use everything for HIS glory, that Kassidy's story, even if this was the end, her life would be celebrated.

Kassidy laid like an angel, a tube protruding from her head with blood being extracted and draining with her hair half shaven. She has a breathing tube in her mouth with a piece of tape over her upper lip to keep the tube in place. She's tan, her skin is flawless, her blond hair is like silk. We all comment on how beautiful she is, laying there, lifeless. We feel the presence of the Holy Spirit instantly, the room is quiet, the air is pure, we didn't blame God, we weren't mad or shaking our fist, we praised Him, we honored Him.

Within the first hour of being at the hospital, friends began arriving, in pure disbelief, that something like this could happen to a 13-year-old, HEALTHY girl. They flooded the PICU waiting room, embracing each other, and praying. That's all we needed was prayer and lots of love. That first evening, nurses allowed everyone in to say their final goodbyes to Kassidy. There must have been twenty-five or more people praying the blood of Jesus over Kassidy. A few dear friends said they saw "Michael the Archangel" over Kassidy's bed, others felt the presence of the Holy Spirit in Room 336. It was evident that Jesus met us there, that we were not alone. We cried out to God together in one accord. We felt the Holy Spirit's presence, also Michael the Archangels healing hand in Room 336. We held hands, we embraced, we were encouraged as the body of Christ. We were the Church.

Around midnight, our dear friends Russ and Sue Muscarella, along with their son Russell and a dear friend Star showed up, we moved Kassidy's limbs and prayed over her. Star, a lifelong friend of our dear friend Russ, was a peculiar man, dressed in white linen and Jesus' slippers we called them; however, they were white converse tennis shoes without the tongue, laces neatly cris crossed. He spoke with a deep, slow voice. Star didn't say much, you could tell he was focused solely on Kassidy and the Holy Spirit that was evident in Room 336. Star didn't leave the left side of Kassidy's bed for 15 hours. His intercession of prayer believing in Kassidy's Miracle was just what we needed. We believed God sent Star to us. We were truly honored to have him as a part of our team.

The following day - August 5th, they hooked Kassidy up to an EEG to make sure she wasn't having seizures, praise God she didn't have one seizure. I was tired and alone with Kassidy. I leaned into her ear, I told her that this wasn't funny any longer, it was time for her to get up and get ready for High School registration. All of Kassidy's friends would be registering for school today, she was so looking forward to her first year of High School, to being with her sister Lexi, who would be a Senior. I was still in denial, still in disbelief that yesterday ever happened.

The nurses came to us asking if we would like to have access to the Ronald McDonald House across the street to be close to Kassidy. To our surprise, this was a FREE blessing for those who had children in critical condition. I said to the nurse that we would be honored, but that we would only need it for a few days, and we would be out of here. She looked at me with sad eyes and walked away. I wasn't equipped with clean clothes, not to mention a toothbrush. The girls, Kevin, Travis, and I didn't leave Kassidy's side, we didn't want to miss a moment, just in case Kassidy woke up.

The next morning, Denise Schiel, a sharp Nurse practitioner, as well as Dr. Bradley Pederson, Director of the PICU, and Dr. Sandeep Khanna stopped by Room 336, they assured us that they would be with us every step of the way. I can't tell you what an amazing team of Doctors and nurses at Rady Children's Hospital we encountered. We knew God sent them to us. They were with us every step of the way.

Kassidy was extremely critical; every day seemed like a week. So many tests, every minute of every day was a roller coaster. Kassidy developed pneumonia 104-106 fever. A nurse brought in a rotation bed for Kassidy to keep the fluid in her lungs moving. The bed would rotate every hour. Medication, cold clothes, a cooling pad, and a rotating bed was in full swing in room 336. We didn't stop praying, we continued the fight, as we knew this was extremely serious.

CaringBridge was a wonderful tool for us to be able to stay connected with family and friends. We weren't able to receive a lot of phone calls with everything happening, therefore CaringBridge was our refuge. We were able to share with the world what was happening in Room 336. Some days there would be 3-4 posts, asking for specific prayers, as well as giving an update for that particular day. It was truly a roller coaster of emotions. We thank God to this day for all of our prayer warriors. The love and devotion from friends, family and strangers was unbelievable. People were able to write on the CaringBridge page, specific prayers and how their families were praying. It meant the world!

Kassidy experienced many infections, CT scans, x-rays, medications, MRI's, fevers, EEG's, ventriculostomy tubes, ventilator. This has only been the first couple of days. We're exhausted, but our Kassidy is holding on, she's fighting strong, just like Friday night fights with Taekwondo. She was a FIGHTER; she's winning the fight. Travis Rosene was a HUGE part of our team. Lexi and Travis had been dating for over a year now.

Rady asked for family only, but we adopted Travis as our Son, he was blond like the rest of the family, so he fit right in. It wasn't until later that the nurses realized he wasn't Kassidy's brother, but Lexi's boyfriend. We giggled and the nurses turned a blind eye. Travis wasn't walking with the Lord at the time, but after witnessing a miracle, Travis is now reading the word of God and believing in Kassidy's full and complete healing. We are so proud of Travis, as he is now our beloved Son-in-law. He's been with us every step of the way and we love him dearly.

A little snippet of my Dads view.
It would be impossible to convey the otherworldly experiences that took place during the weeks and months following the Kassidy emergency. We firmly placed all of our hope and prayers in God's hands from the moment that Kass became ill, up until this very day. That said, it was never an option for us.

Our entire family are strong Christian's who rely completely on God's grace in all that we do.

From the moment that she became ill, we prayed a very simple prayer. **"God please save this child. We know that you have already determined the outcome, and we will trust that your will be done, not ours. We accept in advance that your will is perfect, even if we do not fully understand it."**

It wasn't always easy to say that prayer, namely because as human beings we are selfish. We want what suits us, in our timing, always. As Christians, we come to know that this is not the case, even when it hurts. There were so many ways that this was revealed to us during Kassidy's trial. That said, the total, overwhelming presence of God in that room was there. More amazingly, it was present and evident to people who did not even know us. Nurses, doctors, housekeepers, and even some friends who by their own admission did have a personal relationship with Jesus Christ. God was there among us. He presented himself in many ways, so let me list just a few of the experiences that took place in and around Room 336. Read on to learn more.

My Sister Lexi 's perspective on the very beginning stages of the incident.

It was a day like any other day for a 17-year-old girl on summer break, weeks before starting her senior year of high school. I had a job working for my boyfriend's parents, so on this particular day we were making a delivery about an hour away and decided to see a movie. I remember the feeling I got once we got out of the movie theater and saw that I had seventy-eight notifications on my cell phone. The panic feeling when you know something bad has happened and you are about to find out.

I don't remember who I spoke to first, but I believe it was our friend and neighbor who was a paramedic and had to break the news to me, all while Travis drove the work truck in traffic on the side of the freeway as fast as he could to get me to my family. My ears rang when I heard, "It's Kass. It's bad. AVM. Life flighted to Rady." I remember the only thing I kept repeating "what do you mean?" I remember running inside our house and I could tell right away this will change all of us forever. Our family is not complete without Kass. We jumped in the car, our family and my boyfriend, Travis. We drove the one hour drive down the fifteen freeway not knowing if my sister made it to the hospital alive or if she died on the way.

The weight of the news was heavy, but the presence of the Lord was heavier and so evident. We pulled to the front of Rady Children's Hospital not knowing where to go, and there was a friend of ours just waiting there for us to pull in so he could park our car, and we could run in. Seconds mattered. We were ushered into a room, a room no family wants to ever find themselves in, where a team of doctors went over what's happened, statistics of her dying in the first few crucial hours, chances of her having another brain bleed in the first few weeks, she could be a vegetable, keeping her alive on life support, etc. They left the room to allow the news to sink in.

When you're inside the hospital walls, most people would agree that time is infinite and meaningless. Day and night, days and weeks turn into one another. The first night in the hospital was the night that changed me forever. I saw our people show up. I saw strangers come in and sit and pray and cry for hours. I saw my boyfriend feel Jesus' presence for the first time. I saw nurses turn a blind eye when we broke every rule of having 20+ people in her ICU room 336 to circle her in prayer. I felt supernatural peace. I felt adrenaline, not knowing we were heading into a marathon for our family that would last months and consist of many highs and many lows.

It was summer break and 2 weeks after she got sick was high school registration. We had been looking forward to that day, the time finally came when we'd be in the same school. I'd be able to drive her to school, show her around campus, get our ID pictures taken, get all of our books. I had to go to registration day alone, I remember being tired and angry I was there alone. I was either sleeping at the hospital or driving home late at night to and from San Diego every day. Things were still on a day by day, hour by hour basis with Kass' health. I think she had had three surgeries by then and her viability was still questionable. I remember making up my mind at my senior year registration day that I won't be going to school that year not knowing what that'd look like. I didn't care. Nothing mattered but my sister's life.

Life rapidly changed after that day. Your loved one almost dying permanently alters your inner gauge of importance. Life kept moving outside of the hospital walls. Dad had to go back to work driving to LA every day and back to San Diego at night to be with Kass and mom. Mom didn't leave Kass' side for the first few weeks. I eventually had to go to the first day of school without Kass. I lasted 2 weeks then enrolled in an independent studies program. This allowed me to do my homework at Rady's. I needed to be there to support Kass but also and maybe more importantly be there for mom since Kass was snoozing away. Eventually Kass was sent home in a coma-state.

Mom and I learned a lot, nurses would come for home visits once a week and we'd be annoyed because we thought we changed her G-tube and did feeding and dressing changes better than they did. Haha. We would slam the door behind them and continue talking to her as if she was the same Kass. We would switch off on taking night shifts when she had to have G-tube feedings and medications every 3 hours. We put the hospital bed in the middle of our home, and she was the center of it all. I was so happy to help, I truly did not want to do anything else.

Mr. Robles' perspective on the initial event of my incident:
He's more like an older brother than an instructor and we still keep in contact till this day.

There are moments in your life that mark a distinct image in your consciousness, for me finding out about Ms. Brewers image is one of those moments. I clearly remember teaching at the studio, for reasons I can't and won't try to explain I had a feeling that I should check my cell phone, I walked off the studio training floor and into my office to check my phone, as I picked it up I saw I had a missed call from Donna Brewer, Ms. Brewers mother and there was a voicemail from her. I listened to the voicemail and to my shock it was Donna explaining that Kassidy wouldn't be in today, that she has a medical emergency and was being flown to Rady's Children's hospital in San Diego, she said she didn't know what my beliefs were but If I had any belief in God to please pray for Kassidy.

Even writing this today, so many years later I can still hear and feel the absolute pain, devastation, and fear in her voice. It is something that will stick with me for the rest of my life and something that I pray I never hear from another parent for as long as I live. I kept that voicemail on my phone for years and years after, I remember shocking Donna and the producers of the TV show, more on that later, when I said I still had it, and they were able to record it and use it in the show. To this day I don't understand why Donna felt she needed to call me to tell me that Kassidy wasn't going to be there, but the fact that she did gave me a feeling that perhaps I should go be there to the hospital to be there for Kassidy and her family, in hindsight I believe that call made me feel like more of a part of their family than I previously believe I may have been.

Whatever the reason was I remember running to my car with one of my other students that knew and loved Kassidy, and we were off, I called Donna while I was on the way down and asked if I could come and was told in no uncertain terms that I was family and of course I could come be there for Kassidy, them and maybe even myself. Arriving at the hospital I found my way to Ms. Brewer's family, the state of shock, the tears, the questions all linger with me to this day, We didn't know a lot of what was going on and why and I remember Donna asking me if Kassidy had been hit in the head or anything the days before in Taekwondo training, the idea that there was a possibility that it could be connected to her training absolutely terrified me, it took me a while to come to the realization that her mom was simply in a massive amount of pain and confusion and simply looking, hoping for an answer.

I was allowed to go into the room and see her and for the second time in one day I had another one of those moments that is forever etched into my memory, there in the bed seemingly connected to a million different cords and machines was Ms. Brewer, the happy go lucky sometimes spicy young girl replaced by a little girl fighting for her life, the sight was almost more than I could bear, I so desperately wanted her to wake up, to say Hello Mr. Robles and get back to helping in class and training for her 2nd degree Black Belt.

But I knew that wasn't to be, and it seemed like for the moment the doctors and staff didn't expect much if anything to happen, I remember talks about how we should all prepare for the worst, and it's then where I learned one of the most beautiful lessons about us as human beings, in the worst of times, with love and hope amazing things could happen, I saw her parents absolutely refuse to accept those things as truth. Kassidy... Ms. Brewer... was a fighter and she was in the fight for her life, I drove home in silence with one of my students, trying to hold back the tears. I couldn't fully understand what I had experienced that day, seen, what I bore witness too. In hindsight it was the beginning of a new chapter where I got to know Ms. Brewer better, to see even more amazing things and learn more than I could have ever imagined.

Mike Sullivan's perspective. He is like my uncle/brother who is always supportive in whatever we're doing. We see and involve him and his daughter like family! He has been with us on this whole journey.

I was enlisted in the Navy and currently on month 1 of a 5-month deployment. My then wife sent me a message explaining the incident and a link to the CaringBridge site that was created for

Kass. My thoughts were first and foremost…is she okay. After that, honestly, I figured Kass would be just fine. She is a fighter and comes from a family FULL of them. But it did immediately affect my heart. I was incredibly sad and that was a first for me. I didn't really know where that came from. I was never able to visit the hospital due to being gone.

Sue Muscarella's perspective. She is our good friend who's like a second mother to me.

My recollection of our initial notification of your AVM took place late in the evening August 4, 2008. Your mother called me to inform us that you were taken to Rady Children's hospital due to some kind of brain bleed and that you were in ICU. I immediately called our adult children, RJ and Brittany, to inform them and ask for prayer. RJ's immediate response was that he wanted to call our family friend, Star Gioli, whom he knew was a "spiritual healer." Star lived in Idyllwild, CA.

Star told Russell that he wanted to go to the hospital immediately. At that time, I called Donna (Kassidy's mother) and asked permission to bring Star to the hospital to pray over Kassidy. Donna asked Kevin and since the Doctors were not giving Kassidy any hope of surviving, they both were receptive to inviting a stranger to join them in the hospital room to pray over Kassidy. It was about 10 PM, so we packed up and headed to meet Star in Temecula and drive to the hospital with him.

When we arrived at the hospital we were allowed admittance, which surprised us since it was near midnight. Star immediately touched Kassidy and began silent prayer. He asked all of us, Russ Sr, RJ, Donna, Kevin, and me to lay hands on Kassidy and join in prayer for her miraculous healing. He also asked us to move her legs and arms gently. After a time, the nurse came in and asked us to stop the movement, but Star continued silent prayer over Kassidy for the next 12 hours never leaving her bed, not even for a bathroom break. He was literally a vehicle for God's healing hand upon Kassidy.

I had asked him on the way to the hospital if his gift of "healing" was a blessing or a curse. He said it was both…. He took it as a calling that he could not walk away from when needed.

Russ Sr, Rj, and I left the hospital around 5 am while Star continued his prayers.
Our relationship with the Brewers has always been like "Family." We committed to walk alongside them during this health crisis and were privileged to be given access to Kassidy and the family during the next four plus months while she was in the hospital recovering. There were so many people who were part of this inner circle of healing and support. Bringing meals for the family, sitting in the waiting room listening to healing Spiritual music, praying, and loving on the Brewer family. It was an honor to witness the miracles that happened during her stay at Rady's hospital and then once she returned home.

I watched my dear friend Donna live at the hospital watching over her daughter every hour. Even living at the Ronald McDonald House for months. She never left Kassidy's side and made sure that she was covered in prayer before every procedure was done.
Watching Lexi and Travis bring peace and serenity to the room through music and soft loving words was so beautiful. Everyone had a role from Danielle to Kevin as well.

I truly believe that many souls were saved as they witnessed this miraculous story of healing occurring right before their very eyes. God truly has used Kassidy's story to change lives eternally.

My good friend, Kenzie's perspective.

My parents sat me down the afternoon of Kassidy's incident to share with me what happened and answer any questions I had. They told me as delicately as they could but with as detailed as possible to paint the picture of how serious things were. They shared with me that Kass was in a coma and the outcome was ultimately unknown, but not optimistic. They told me we would go to the hospital the next day to see her and the family but encouraged me to be ready to say my goodbyes.

The moment I got to see Kass in the hospital for the first time, I wasn't sure what I felt or how to process everything, but I remember being a bit surprised with the sheer number of machines and tubes attached to my tiny friend, who looked somehow even smaller. I was told Kass could still hear despite being in the coma, so I decided to ignore all the physical stuff and talk to her about our friends, the day/weekend, school, and how much I loved her. I held her hand and told her how much I wanted her to fight and stay strong but shared I would be more than understanding if it was all just too much.

My family and I went to the hospital every day we could. My parents shared with me what tests were being done and what the hopeful results would be. As time went on and a few things changed, I was told things may be coming to an end; but in the spirit of Kassidy, this was the exact day she made the slightest improvement, and the end could absolutely not be called. From that day forward, there were incremental improvements every day; things were slow, but against all odds, they were moving in the right direction.

Chapter 6

What the doctors said

At that horrific moment, when I was still at Rancho Springs Hospital in Murrieta, I was given a zero percent chance of surviving on the air flight to Rady Children's Hospital. After I arrived at Rady, my family showed up a few hours later where they were greeted with a nurse in the parking lot to take them up to a conference room with the neurologist. Trying to get a grasp of what's taking place, what they found. What is going on? And when we arrived in Rady my family was given more grim news.

While being in the conference room, they were faintly told what an AVM was and what it entails. AVMs are typically hereditary or congenital, and mine happen to be both, but we had no idea that it was there in the first place. Congenital disorders are commonly present from birth, and hereditary disorders are transmitted from parents to their children through genes. Surprisingly, my Great grandpa died of an aortic aneurysm and my Grandpa had a stomach aneurysm that they were keeping an eye on but was nothing to be concerned about.

Living life second by second, we were assigned a neurologist that didn't have the best bedside manner. One of the first acts he did was hand my parents papers to donate my organs. Also speaking that if I do make it, there will be severe brain damage due to the location in the brain. Now at this point, my family was shocked and numb by the unknown of what was going to happen. These words of assuming the worst are not what they needed, they needed a glimpse of hope.

Despite what science said, they held onto their faith. What God has already made known. So, with this frightful, boot-rattling news, my family continued to politely persist in the faith that they have. They courteously let them know that they don't need any negativity right now. If you research any ruptured brain AVM, the odds are slim to none, and any sort of brain damage is highly likely. They were told over and over again that I likely would not talk, walk or speak again. And plus, while you're at it, lay aside any purposeful movements that she'll make. "She'll basically be in a vegetative state long term."

In the instance of Mark 11: 24-25, it says that faiths authority allows the believer to speak directly to the obstacles of life. As we exercise our faith, we can see issues at hand as impossible or too much to where we just brush it off. But what if we were able to address the problem like we were in search of hidden diamonds? Relentless. If Yahshua is above all and knows all, wouldn't He help us along our paths? Yes, it's called the Holy Spirit.

So, my family ended up firing him and requesting a new neurosurgeon. Whenever you have that feeling of darkness and disbelief, fall back on your faith. You will always be guided to the path God has for you.

This new neurosurgeon, Dr. Michael Levy, has had many years of experience and research under his belt and is still like my brother to this day. We love him. And do you know what, he walked into the room and said, "eh, just give her a year, she'll be alright." That's exactly what my family needed to hear, the physical words of hope! And in any situation, hearing those words of ambition is like a breath of fresh air to the circumstance. Dr. Levy is a vascular neurosurgeon who specializes in AVMs and after he showed up, we were on a whole new track of healing and hope. That's when we started to discuss embolization's. Embolization was a way to prevent the flow of blood within the rupture using imaging guidance. Going through the femoral artery up to the brain.

Though my family was in a state of distress, they continued to persist with the only source they knew to count on. They all had their moments of completely falling apart but remained with the hope that I will be completely restored in Yahshua. Much like Job, not only my family but I too, had everything taken away. Things were completely shaken up. Life was caving in; that's exactly what people saw from the outside. But when you can truly fathom faith, anything is possible. Death or life, deliverance is His.

The miracle during the incident
It all started in room 336, that's where the countless number of miracles began. Walking into that room, each person that entered stated that they could feel the presence of Christ as they walked in discouragement of the unknown. Unquestionably it was a grim time for each individual, but my family kept the environment extremely positive and didn't allow for any negativity or doubts to enter.

While I was in the ICU, I was on sixteen different vials of medication and doing tests and sorts. Doing some research, they say that you only survive on eight to nine vials. But God sustained my body to take on all sixteen. The doctors pronounced I was in a non-induced coma and to hope for the best. But they didn't know who was on our side. This gives me chills just talking about it, the ICU was a powerful place. We had thousands of people all around the world praying for hope, praying for a miracle.

Looking back to the four core elements of a near death experience, another one of the elements is, encountering spiritual beings. Now, even though I did not personally experience a spiritual being, each and every individual that walked into room 336 during my incident, mentioned that they could personally feel the love of Christ all around. Plus, one person that came said that he saw a massive angel standing over my bed. He referred to him as Michael the archangel because as stated in Jude 9, the Bible refers to archangels as angels who stand in the presence of God. Michael and Gabriel were most commonly known as archangels, but Spiritual beings are known to come in any form, shape, or size too. This all took place on August 4, the initial date of my incident.

I was administered a Peripherally Inserted central catheter, which is known as a PICC line. It was known to administer fluids, medications, or nutrients directly into my bloodstream. The PICC line was inserted through a vein in my upper chest, kind of above my heart. This allowed for long-term access to the bloodstream. This type of line was often used for antibiotics, antifungals, pain management, hydration, and blood draws. . In spite of my heartbreaking comatose body, I was being poked and prodded from left and right. In the ICU only pillowcases or hospital gowns were allowed. A nurse hand drew on a pillowcase this beautiful piece of artwork to drape over my lifeless body.

Due to the unbearable diagnosis and tragedy of a ruptured AVM, there were plenty of innuendos that came about. But relying on Yahshua's' healing power was the route that we were determined to stay on. With any type of brain injury, the autonomic nervous system (ANS) is always deeply considered due to how the brain impacts our bodily functions, the ANS is our automatic responses that occur in our body. Like breathing and especially our heart rate. Both of which were a deep struggle for me at the time. So, on August seventh, the doctors made the quick decision to do an electrocardiography (ECG) test to measure my heart function. everything came back great, and there were no issues with that. A few days later, on August twelfth, they did another test due to my heart signal and my brain signal, and they configured that the signal between my brain and my heart were overly confused.

The very next day, nurses carried on taking action due to my blood pressure dipping at an unacceptable pace. They had placed a probe in my heart to measure the amount of blood intake I was getting and to measure my heart function overall. We all knew that the connection between my heart and my brain was somewhat disconnected at the moment so they somewhat predicted this would happen, but they weren't sure how intensive it would be.

They figured this would've happened, but mine was a little worse than they were hoping for because of the location of the bleed. The probe would easily measure my cardiac efficiency. Just take into account, again, my physical heart was not damaged, it was the brain not telling it to do its job. The probe was left in for a day or two and then was removed as soon as possible.

Reverting back

Have you ever seen a pre-teen wearing a diaper? In a dis functional and nearly departed body, it still operated with many contraptions no man should go through. Being in such a grim situation, I still went to the bathroom. I had to wear a diaper for quite some time and continued to wear it until ortho rehab. My family was so focused on helping to keep me alive that changing a diaper didn't even matter. It was just another step in the process.

In ortho rehab, one of my simple yet functional goals were to get back into my skinny jeans. Because what 14-year-old doesn't want to be like everyone else? A teen in diapers wasn't my most appealing look so every bathroom trip I made, I was awarded a quarter. That quarter was put into the bathroom bank jar. I'm the type of person that gets motivated by money. Every chance I got was an opportunity to get closer to my goal! With a lot of hard work and determination, Christ took that diligence and helped me to hit my target!

Speaking about this today really brings a lot of humility and vulnerability because what teen do you know of that had to experience that? It definitely broadens my understanding of what people have to go through to get to where they are. Christ created the human body to be able to endure so many tragedies, and everyone goes through something different. We all have a story, this is mine.

Checked heart function and the silly sad slap.
As I remain in my siesta state, many times I had these involuntary movements that caused a giggle to everyone around me and looked up with a glimmer of hope. One early evening, while everyone was winding down for the night, or, to put things into better words, here's the exact story that I took out of one of my CaringBridge entries from August 8.

"While Travis fell asleep on the railing at her bed last night, she (as in myself) slapped him in the face. It made us all happy even Travis laughed. We just want her to get up and karate chop all of us." And because times were so delicate, there were only allowed two people in the room due to infection and the probe happening. Things were changing moment by moment, everyone was on their toes, waiting to hear of the many miracles, the ups, and the downs.

Reflecting on Mark 5:40-41
And this is a description similar to the "Young girl in distress" in Mark 5:40-41. It just goes to show you that when God speaks life and healing over a body, there's no stopping Him from completing His actions. It's almost as if we need to look at hardship from two different angles. One from a heavenly perspective and one from real life. Even if this ruptured brain AVM did kill me, I would've had my healing because it would've brought me to meet my creator and taken me from the pain and discomfort I've had to tirelessly endure. But because it didn't, and now I'm thriving, I'm still considered blessed due to being able to spread His joy and His life.

Like I always say, healing may not always be physical, healing is more mental than anything. I have definitely learned a lot through this experience, and it makes me marvel at how we all go through our own trials in life. It doesn't even have to be a near death experience like mine, it can just refer to someone going through a devastating, life altering challenge. I think of this "child in distress" as someone who is helpless, as someone who needs and desires to be completed, and rescued in any way, any form. Completed by God the Father. And while healing may come in all different shapes and forms, knowing it came from God, is a direct miracle.

Renewed patience and endurance through patient trust
Am I the only one that struggles with endurance and trust? I went through a period of time where mine was tested with trial after trial. It taught me patience, like never before when I was going through it all, I just wanted it to be over. In those times, I always think back to how Jesus round the desert for forty years. It's hard to comprehend being in one place for that long, but it happened. And we have to understand the fact that people in those days lived far longer than they do nowadays and typically our trials seem like they last for forty years!

Now because endurance means the action of enduring an unpleasant situation or process without giving way, we can see that patience is going to have a hard time playing out in this situation. Why? Because we're having to remain hopeful during an unpleasant time and no one likes unpleasant, uncomfortable times. People crave comfortability. But it's comforting that we really see growth. Just like it is said that with being in that state of patient endurance, you will develop patient trust in your reliance of the Father to meet your every need.

In Greek wording, confident trust is the word teen Parisian which means boldness. Developing a dependency on God the Father to care for us is to have the need for boldness and confident trust. So, if individuals look at you and think you're ignorant or are in denial of reality, all I say is yes, confidence may come with ignorance, but it's all measured on your motive. Why are you taking the action in the first place? Live in the matter of leading in love. Just like Yahshua did to freely give us His liberty. He placed His confident trust in the arms of His Father.

You are capable of so much more than you expect. Think back to that time when you were so afraid to do something, and after you finished you thought to yourself, that wasn't so bad. Now it might be your new favorite thing! In that, you had to exercise your patient endurance muscle and in turn, your patient trust muscle was developed. Patient confidence was built as a form of trust.

You might be that type of person that has to test every boundary for yourself? Maybe you're the type that is a rule follower and a perfectionist. But I think that most of us hold a balance of some sort of both. Sometimes those hopes and dreams get shattered because I didn't slow down to involve my Heavenly Father in the process. It was more about getting through and enduring, than actually waiting for His trust in the undertaking.

Reading through Leviticus, this scripture slapped me in the face of how the enemy creeps his way into our life. Practicing divination or sooth sayings is another form of witchcraft prohibited by the mosaic law. It's edifying in a supernatural kind of way to gain achievement in the future. It doesn't sound bad but when you look further into the word supernatural, it speaks of tarot readings and horoscopes. Which is an abomination to our Father. Similar to mediums and familiar spirits, we are to not only distance ourselves but completely disassociate from them.

Just like it's in our human nature to miss the mark and fall for sin, it's the enemy's makeup to speak those dreadful lies into us and encourage us to get further away from our Father. And unlike Christ, the deceiver stands, waiting at the back door waiting to slide into get first place mindset. But like Yahshua states in His word, we only need to enter through the front gate. Because there, we will enter through Him. Going through Him, I know I will have hope, safety, and prosperity in Him. But due to our nature, it's an ongoing battle of wear and tear that we must endure.

We're always going to have those what ifs, those doubts. When I gave up my human life and totally relied on You and Your faithfulness, entering through the front door is what was desperately needed to seek Your divine presence. That's the beginning of patient endurance through patient trust. Acknowledging the reality of what's in front of you but not letting it overcome you is one step in the right direction. I've realized that when I made that choice to enter through the "front door," I started to see shifts of patient endurance not only in my life but the people around me too.

Chapter 7

Family & Friends Perspectives

My mom's perspective in the hospital while I was in a coma.

The CHET team assured us that they would take exceptional care of Kass, and we'll meet you at Rady. They gave us peace. We said our difficult goodbyes and drove home to get to Lexi so we could drive together to Rady Children's Hospital. We finally arrived at Rady, Kass made the helicopter flight safely and had immediate attention with an MRI. A team of nurses met us at the entrance of the hospital where we were brought to a meeting room to meet with the neurosurgeon.

We sat waiting in silence, then the doctor arrived and shared with us that Kassidy was born with an Arteriovenous Malformation (AVM) and that her bleed was located in the cerebellum and brain stem. That she was a ticking time bomb, that her chance of survival was zero. We asked a lot of questions, but still confused like it was all a dream. The doctor handed us papers about donating Kassidy's organs and I pushed them away and said to give her "time," that we brought the ultimate physician with us.

He looked confused as to what that might be, but we knew that the Lord was our physician and healer. We needed time for our Kass. Nurses guided us on the way to Kass' room, 336, she was there laying so peacefully. So beautiful, the room was quiet, the noise of the ventilator was loud and annoying. We felt the presence of the Lord instantly. We gathered around Kassidy and cried for our girl. We prayed and asked God for a healing, for a miracle.

We felt the presence of the Holy Spirit instantly, the room is quiet, the air is pure, we didn't blame God, we weren't mad or shaking our fist, we honored Him.

Within the first hour of being at the hospital, friends began arriving, in pure disbelief, that something like this could happen to a 13-year-old, HEALTHY girl. They flooded the PICU waiting room, embracing each other, and praying. All we needed was prayer and lots of love. That first evening, nurses allowed everyone in to say their final goodbyes to Kassidy. There must have been twenty-five or more people praying the blood of Jesus over Kassidy. A few dear friends said they saw "Michael the Archangel" over Kassidy's bed, others felt the presence of the Holy Spirit in Room 336. It was evident that Jesus met us there, that we were not alone. We cried out to God together in one accord. We felt the Holy Spirit's presence, also Michael the Archangels healing hand in Room 336. We held hands, we embraced, we were encouraged as the body of Christ. We were the Church.

Around midnight, our dear friends Russ and Sue Muscarella, along with their son Russell and a dear friend Star showed up, we moved Kassidy's limbs and prayed over her. Star, a lifelong friend of our dear friend Russ, was a peculiar man, dressed in white linen, wearing Jesus' slippers we called them; however, they were white converse tennis shoes without the tongue, laces neatly cris crossed. He spoke with a deep, slow voice. Star didn't say much, you could tell he was focused solely on Kassidy and the Holy Spirit that was evident in Room 336. Star didn't leave the left side of Kassidy's bed for 15 hours. His intercession of prayer believing in Kassidy's Miracle was just what we needed. We believed God sent Star to us. We were truly honored to have him as a part of our team.

The following day, August 5th, they hooked Kassidy up to an EEG to make sure she wasn't having seizures, praise God she didn't have one seizure.

I was tired and alone with Kassidy. I leaned into her ear, I told her that this wasn't funny any longer, it was time for her to get up and get ready for High School registration. All of Kassidy's friends would be registering for school today, she was so looking forward to her Freshman year of High School, to being with her sister Lexi, who would be a Senior. I was still in denial, still in disbelief that yesterday ever happened.

The nurses came to us asking if we would like to have access to the Ronald McDonald House across the street to be close to Kassidy. This, to our surprise, was a FREE blessing for those who had children in critical condition. I said to the nurse that we would be honored, but that we would only need it for a few days, and we would be out of here. She looked at me with sad eyes and walked away. I wasn't equipped with clean clothes, not to mention a toothbrush. The girls, Kevin, Travis, and I didn't leave Kassidy's side, we didn't want to miss a moment, just in case Kassidy woke up.

The next morning, Denise Schiel, a sharp Nurse practitioner, as well as Dr. Bradley Pederson, Director of the PICU, and Dr. Sandeep Khanna stopped by Room 336, they assured us that they would be with us every step of the way. I can't tell you what an amazing team of Doctors and nurses at Rady Children's

Hospital we encountered. We knew God sent them to us. They were with us every step of the way.

Kassidy was extremely critical; every day seemed like a week. So many tests, every minute of every day was a roller coaster. Kassidy developed pneumonia of 104–106-degree fever. A nurse brought in a rotation bed for Kassidy to keep the fluid in her lungs moving. The bed would rotate every hour. Medication, cold clothes, a cooling pad and a rotating bed were in full swing in room 336. We didn't stop praying, we continued the fight, as we knew this was extremely serious.

CaringBridge was a wonderful tool for us to be able to keep in touch with family and friends. We weren't able to receive a lot of phone calls with everything happening, therefore CaringBridge was our refuge. We were able to share with the world what was happening in Room 336. Some days there would be 3-4 posts, asking for specific prayers, as well as giving an update for that particular day. It was truly a roller coaster of emotions. We thank God to this day for all of our prayer warriors. The love and devotion from friends, family and strangers was unbelievable. People were able to write on the CaringBridge page, specific prayers and how their families were praying. It meant the world!

Kassidy experienced many infections, CT scans, x-rays, medications, MRI's, fevers, EEG's, ventriculostomy tubes, ventilator. This has only been the first couple of days. We're exhausted, but our Kassidy is holding on, she's fighting strong, just like Friday night fights with Taekwondo. She was a FIGHTER; she's winning the fight. Travis Rosene was a HUGE part of our team. Lexi and Travis had been dating for over a year now. Rady asked for family only, but we adopted Travis as our Son, he was blond like the rest of the family, so he fit right in.

It wasn't until later that the nurses realized he wasn't Kassidy's brother, but Lexi's boyfriend. We were grateful that the nurses turned a blind eye. Travis wasn't walking with the Lord at the time, but after witnessing a miracle, Travis is now reading the word of God and believing in Kassidy's full and complete healing. We are so proud of Travis, as he is now our beloved Son-in-law. He's been with us every step of the way and we love him dearly.

It was another eventful day in room 336, on August 26th. Kassidy developed a collapsed lung. Dr. Peterson, our beloved PICU Director, shared with us that it was a concern. He shared with us that the top of Kassidy's brain was intact and working perfectly. The brain stems, our major concern appears to be totally undisturbed. There does appear to be some cellular damage to the cerebellum, but we have time, more time to pray and believe in God's plan for Kass.

This same day, Lisa, a beautiful Pediatric Healing Touch practitioner stops by and asks if she could lay hands on Kassidy. I asked her what it was all about. I shared with her that if it wasn't of the Lord Jesus Christ, I didn't want anything to do with it. Lisa shared with me that she would teach me, and we would do it together, in unison, in prayer. I agreed.

As we stood on each side of Kassidy's bed, we started at Kassidy's feet, one hand on top, one hand on the bottom of her feet, we silently prayed for God to restore healing, blood flow, bone strength. As we slowly went up Kassidy's body, praying for every detail of her internal organs and healing, we got to Kass' head, our hands were on fire, we were sweating profusely, we could feel Kassidy's effected area with our bare hands. My hands were shaking, as I was believing in God for her full restoration and healing.

Just then, the door swung open, I looked out the glass sliding door and there stood about 7-9 Doctors and nurses, with their arms up high cheering, and their eyes as big. Little did we know the Respiratory Therapist was testing Kassidy's breathing on the ventilator. SHE WAS BREATHING ON HER OWN, while we were praying over her!   It scared me for a second, as I took my eyes off of Kassidy, they told me to finish. A few minutes later, Lisa and I looked at each other and smiled. The door flew open once again. The Doctors and nurses just witnessed a MIRACLE! Lisa and I were just a vessel for the Lord.

Minutes later the phone rang, which it never rang before. It was my dear friend Grandma Faye Loop from Monroe, MI. She received a call from a friend from her church that has three daughters. She was praying for Kassidy at the suggestion of Grandma Faye, as she was doing the dishes, she had an overwhelming vision of a mother with healing hands, and that she should call Kassidy's mother to tell her about it. The vision happened at the same time that I was laying hands on Kassidy. God is at work. All Glory to God!

As Kassidy's 14th Birthday fast approaches, we can't help but want to celebrate Kassidy's life. We decide to set aside being sad and worrying about the negative, we are choosing to celebrate. August 30th arrives - **HAPPY BIRTHDAY KASSIDY DAWN**

BREWER!   As you lay there in a coma, we will honor and celebrate YOU... Friends far and near came with cupcakes and food to feed an army. As family and friends sat in the waiting room, it didn't matter. We needed to be together. We laughed, we cried, we honestly didn't know what the future would hold for you. We can't imagine life without you. Our hearts ached, but we continued to trust in the Lord.

September 1st - The PICU team shares with us that Kassidy's breathing tube must be removed in fear of infection. They are predicting that she will need a tracheotomy in order for her to breathe. I insist that she will NOT need the procedure, I don't want Kassidy to have to rely on a trach for the rest of her life, not to mention the scar.
Respiratory Therapists arrive for the procedure and believe that she would breathe on her own. Within an hour Kassidy's ventilator was removed,
KASSIDY IS BREATHING ON HER OWN!   SHE IS BREATHING ON HER OWN!   May God be the Glory! We praise you Lord, we thank you for another miracle.

The medical team shared with us that in order for Kassidy not to have another bleed in her brain, we would have to kill off the AVM, she would need a minimum of four embolization's. This procedure is where they take a catheter from her femoral artery to her brain, release or inject glue to her cerebellum, this procedure would kill the feeder veins to the AVM. This procedure is done at UCSD and would require full medical transfer. We agree with the procedure, but in all honesty, it scared the crap out of us.

For the past few days Kassidy has been experiencing Brainstorms, it is extremely painful to watch, it's as though her body is convulsing every 2-3 minutes, it is, however her brain rewiring, re-firing signals through the affected pathways and electrical circuit. It also releases endorphins and other chemicals. These processes must be relearned. Each time a storm occurs, it resembles a small seizure, with shaking, flexing and obvious confusion for her. Truly heart wrenching to watch. It takes a toll on each of us to watch. This continues for weeks…

September 9th - Kassidy's first embolization at UCSD, all went well during transport. Dr. Pocboz was able to correct one third of the AVM by injecting the super glue into the AVM. The surgery was a success. They do, however share with us that Kass will need additional embolization's due to the multiple feeder veins. Once again, Kassidy is intubated and sedated. We continue to pray and ask God for HIS will and direction. We feel like this was a setback for Kassidy, but in reality, it was a big part of her healing. One step forward, two steps back. The fight continues.

Kassidy was finally extubated on September 9th. We sat her up in a high back wheelchair today and strolled her out into the courtyard. No vent, no meds and lots of sunshine. We haven't had this time together in 36 days. We were giddy with excitement.

September 12th - The Neuro Storms continued with great intensity. I refuse to leave your side, I stroke your face and hold you tight through the storms, as tears roll down my cheek. I wish I could take the pain away. My prayer daily, "Lord you promised that you would never leave me or forsake me, therefore, BY YOUR STRIPES may Kassidy be healed". I would repeat this all day long... I knew God was listening, I felt His presence.

It was another evening in Room 336, a restful evening for Kassidy and I, as I, resting on a fold-out chair with a firm mattress on top. It was my space so I could be right next to Kassidy. Around 5 AM I hear Kevin and the nurse whispering about something. I wake up and ask, "what's going on", Kevin looks at me and says, I think the nurse should tell you. Our darling ICU nurse witnessed a supernatural encounter she really had a hard time describing. The nurse witnessed a small vial of medication thrown at the glass door and tumbled to the ground.

The nurse quickly came to Kassidy's door, slid the door open, as she stood inside the room the light began to flicker, just then a gust of wind whirled past her, the COW (Computer on Wheels) moved. It was over... Just that quickly, it was unexplainable. We listened and believed that the power of death had exited the room, and the power of light and life was exposed. The next day, Kassidy was more active than other days, her eyes were opening, but with no response. We could feel the presence of "LIFE". It's as though there was a huge transition, nothing was holding her back.

September 12th continued- Kassidy is being moved to the step-down floor - Room 130. I'm extremely nervous, as there are 3-4 patients to one nurse. We are used to having a private nurse for Kassidy's apparent needs. I can't leave her side, not even for a minute. I will have access to the playroom and more stimulation, but Kassidy is still in a coma, her eyes are open, but no one is there. It's frustrating and scary. Kassidy begins PT/OT, but honestly, she's not ready.

Lexi and Dani are there to help wash Kassidy's hair and shave her legs. Lexi French braids Kassidy's hair and talks to her. Dani gently wipes Kassidy's face with a warm cloth; Travis plays his guitar and sings a song of praise. His soft voice and guitar fill the room with peace and healing. Kevin writes in the CaringBridge App about what is happening with Kass on any given day. This is our new norm, as long as we're together, that's all that matters.

September 19th - Another speed bump today, they did some testing on Kassidy's voice box and found that her left vocal cord is paralyzed. Not only would Kassidy need this for speaking, but also for swallowing. We pray that the Lord will "wake up" her voice box and heal her.

That same day, she also had a G-Tube surgery, to insert a feeding tube into Kassidy's stomach. This will alleviate the feeding tube through her nose. The Doctors believe it's important to perform a Fundoplasty, to tighten the top of her stomach, in her esophagus so that she will not aspirate. Kass is back in ICU again, intubated after another double surgery. The incision is about six inches long, it's painful for Kass. Another step back, but we pray...

September 23, Kassidy is understanding more and more commands. She is trying to use her motor skills, but it is difficult. She's trying to stick out her tongue. Kassidy is working hard in PT and OT. Kass is waking up more and more and is awake for about a ½ day now, Kass's hands are still clinched.

Kassidy is experiencing an upset tummy getting used to her

feeding tube, as we walk through the hall of Ortho Rehab, she has bouts of wanting to throw up, but because of the Fundoplasty, she is unable to. I quickly learned how to insert a plastic syringe into the button of her feeding tube to release the excess liquid. It's terrifying and urgent. With not having a nurse to assist you, you quickly learn how to handle urgent situations. Little did I know they were training me for going home and doing everything solo. It's okay, God was with me, He never left my side.

October 1st - Another MRI was needed today for Kassidy, the MRI indicates a higher than acceptable level of cerebral fluid, which means that the cranium is not "moving" the fluid through the brain properly, causing uneven pressure in parts of the brain which may be slowing down her ability to shake off the effects of the coma. Doctors quickly decide they need to open a tiny hole in the cranium and insert a tool to invasively open a new drainage path for fluid. Kassidy would need a 3rd Ventriculostomy surgery to drain the fluid from her brain due to Hydrocephalus., We feel like this is a major setback, but it's what she needs in order to "wake up".

Kassidy is now following commands, such as blinking her eyes once for NO, blinking twice for YES. This is now our way of communicating and we are thrilled that she is understanding us. We are back in ICU - ROOM 336, a room where it all started on August 4th. We felt the presence of the Lord, here Kassidy is again intubated and resting after yet another surgery.

After a few weeks, we notice that Kassidy is a little clearer and more responsive during Physical Therapy and Occupational Therapy. The discussion of "GOING HOME" for Kassidy to "wake up" is taking place. Logistically, this is a big undertaking. As we discuss a hospital bed, feeding tubes, nutrition, feeding pole, diapers, wipes, bed pads, bed sheets, medications... It was all so much to take in. I was scared to death, how am I going to do all of this, I'm not a nurse.

With great anticipation, I discuss the issue with Denise (PA), she calmly guides me into purchasing a 2.5" binder with tabbed inserts to categorize each area of health: The first Tab was Medication and dosage, another page for times given and dosage. A page for feeding times and amount of nutrition through her feeding tube, also for water through her feeding tube for hydration. Another page for Doctors notes and phone numbers, another page for journaling. An alarm was necessary to set for medications every 3-4 hours, another alarm for feeding, yet another alarm for rotating Kassidy's body on her hospital bed every 2 hours - 24 hours a day.

HOLY MOLY, How am I going to do this I ask, Denise reassures me that I've already been doing it for the past 2 months. She is a Godsend... What would I have done without Denise? She gave me confidence; she was there for me with every emotion. We just wanted to go HOME, however, there were so many logistics to get Kass home. First and foremost was having her medically stable. She wasn't there yet, she wasn't ready, or I wasn't ready to be a full-time nurse at HOME, not to mention Kassidy wasn't anywhere near coming out of her coma.

There are many stages of being in a coma. We referred to the Glasgow Coma Scale many times. This scale is often used at the scene of emergency or at the ER to measure three main responses: eye opening, best motor response, and best verbal response. These are graded using the numerical system, the lower the score, the more severe the injury. However, this scale does not predict how well a person will recover or regain their functioning.

Response: Score:

Eye Opening:

Spontaneous   1
To speech   3
To pain   2
None   1

Best Motor Response:

Obeys commands   6
Localized movements   5
Withdraws   4
Abnormal bending and flexing   3
Involuntary straightening and extending   2
None   1

Best Verbal Response:

Is oriented   5
Confused conversation   4
Inappropriate words   3
Incomprehensible sounds   2
None   1

Kassidy was at Level 1 - No response. Appearing to be in a deep sleep or coma, does not respond to any stimulus, including voices, sounds, light or touch. We are waiting patiently for her to emerge... We pray; we believe in the almighty's touch upon our girl.

After about 2 months, we see Kassidy at a level 2 - Generalized response. Remains primarily asleep but may respond to certain stimuli. Movements do not seem to have any purpose. Eyes may open but do not focus on anything in particular.
We celebrate the slightest improvements; every day brings new challenges or victories.

October 10th arrives; we are scheduled to go home today. With great anticipation we wait for Doctors and nurses to prep Kassidy for going home. An ambulance will arrive this afternoon to take our girl home! Nurses are prepping me with information about timing on meds, feeding tube, what to watch out for etc.... I was a bit overwhelmed; however, I didn't have a choice. It was to figure it out or put her in a facility. I was not about to put Kassidy in a facility, she needed to be home, we all needed her HOME!
Another embolization was scheduled for a few weeks at UCSD, this would be her 2nd embolization, her 2nd brain surgery, done through a catheter, where they inject glue into the site of the AVM to close off the vessels.

We packed up the room at the Ronald McDonald house, went to the pharmacy to pick up a month supply of meds, along with the feeding pump and formula. As we wait for the transport ambulance to arrive, nurses and doctors stop by to say goodbye. We had an overwhelming feeling that Kass was not okay to go home, she wasn't waking up. Dr. Peterson stopped by, we asked if he could check to see if Kass was 100% to go home, something didn't seem right.

Within minutes Kass was being wheeled to radiology for yet another CT scan. Our intuition was correct; our girl is critical once again. The Neurosurgeon made the decision to take her right away for another Shunt revision, her 2nd shunt revision in one week. WHAT A SETBACK, we are devastated. Hydrocephalus (fluid on her brain) was making her not wake up. This time they will implant a shunt with a drain tube that runs from her brain, outside of her head, under the scalp, then through her neck down to her stomach. This will be permanent. This is Kassidy's 5th surgery since August 4th. We are exhausted and scared for our girl, but we cry out to God and He continues to tell us to Trust Him, so we do.

We are back in ICU, watching the nurses hook Kassidy up to more tubes, machines and again fully intubated, our strength is diminished. In walks an ICU nurse that was one of Kassidy's nurses after surgery #4, just a few weeks prior. She was quiet, with tears in her eyes, she asked if she could pray over Kass, we are elated! We hold hands and allow her to lead us in prayer. We didn't have the strength, but GOD sent us an Angel. We prayed together and embraced. We needed her at that very moment. Thank you, Jesus, ...

The very next day was a new day, the sun was shining through the window, the nurse extubated Kassidy, she was resting comfortably when this same nurse from the night before who prayed with us walks in to share with us that because of the experiences surrounding Kassidy's many stays in ICU, that something has changed. The staff in the "ICU" has been talking, they have decided that based on Kassidy, that they need to incorporate "Prayer" as a reasonable and necessary part of the healing process in the Pediatric ICU.

She went on to calmly tell us that the reason that Kass did not go home today was because of the fact that she needed this fact to be revealed to more nurses on the floor. Nurses were coming forward to join the movement. They decided to call their movement of praying nurses, the PURPLE ARMY, in honor or Kassidy Brewer. We are beyond grateful and realize that God has a plan and a purpose for ALL of this. There are too many miracles, too many impossibilities that give GOD ALL the GLORY. We are in awe... The Lord was using Kassidy to show the world HIS plan and purpose.

You see, Kassidy left a legacy in the Pediatric Intensive Care Unit of Rady Children's Hospital, Officially or unofficially "Prayer" is now in the medicine cabinet at RCH. All Glory to God. We don't know why God chose her and our family. We have a new mission now, everything has changed. We are in awe...

Kassidy continues to rest and heal from her last surgery, we again plan to "go home" the following day, Then we realize Kassidy is not responding to commands, we realize there is yet another SHUNT FAILURE. On August 13th Kassidy is once again undergoing another emergency surgery. What do you mean the shunt is clogged again. We feel defeated and frustrated. How much more can our girl take? This is her 3rd emergency surgery in 7 days. The anesthesia, being intubated again and again, the emotional rollercoaster was just too much for Kassidy, as well as the rest of the family.

This last shunt fail was too much for mom, she just couldn't take it anymore, she took off running down the hallway in tears, not knowing where she was going to go, she was approached by the Rady Chaplin, who prayed and held her, telling her that everything was going to be okay. God was with her. We ask how much more can Kassidy's body take? She is now only 75 lbs.

We are back in ICU, as Kassidy is resting well tonight, as she is sedated and intubated for the night so she can rest. Kass slept most of the following day but opened her eyes around 5 PM, her big blue eyes are like crystals. We are grateful she is waking up, which means, the shunt is working, the fluid on the brain is draining successfully. Thank you, Lord!

Finally, October 16th arrives, we decide that every time we say we are "going home", her shunt decides to fail, so we say, "we're going shopping", which means we are really "GOING HOME". The Physical Therapy girls showed up with leg supports to put on Kassidy's legs one last time to show us how Kassidy can stand with 100% assistance, the braces were on to show us what was possible for Kassidy. We cried and marveled at the amazing team of specialists at Rady Children's Hospital. We had to bring Kassidy home to "WAKE UP" from her coma in order for her to qualify for in-patient Ortho Rehabilitation.

A few minutes later, the Ambulance team arrived to transport Kassidy from the ICU to the ambulance going 15 Freeway North to Temecula, CA - yup, we are "going shopping" or "GOING HOME". Dr. Khanna, our outstanding Doctor who was there every day, arrived on his day off to make sure Kassidy was 100% ready to go home. Dr. Khanna hopped in his car and followed the ambulance onto the freeway. We are so grateful for this amazing Team of Doctors, nurses and specialists.

I was able to ride with Kassidy in the ambulance on the way home. Kevin and the girls were following. We are beyond excited, but also a tad bit scared out of our minds… Kassidy was still so delicate. We arrive at "HOME", with decorations on the outside of the house… Inside the house is a hospital bed, waiting for our girl, with a medicine pole for her feeding tube and water, cases of canned food, for her feeding tube, diapers, wipes.

Pretty much everything we had at our disposal in the hospital room. The EMT's take Kassidy to her new hospital bed in the middle of the living room, there stands Penny, our boxer who has missed Kassidy for the past 3 months. Our family has not been home together in almost 3 months…

Further stories from my Dads perspective:
I belonged to a Christian motorcycle club. When the word got out to the brothers, the entire club rode from as far away as 350 miles to sit and pray over Kassidy within the first 48 hours. One of the brothers was a highly enlightened see-er of things beyond the physical world. Upon entering the room, he calmly pointed out that there was a large guardian angel present. The vision was so clear that it brought him to tears.

On another note, a nurse approached me in the middle of the night as I was writing my daily update on Caring Bridge. She asked if she could ask me a question that was way beyond what was acceptable by hospital standards, to which I said of course.

She said to me, "I've watched you calmly sit here in the middle of the night on your computer. I need to ask you if you've ever experienced any event that can only be described as other-worldly". I responded with a chuckle and said, "of course, why do you ask". She went on to tell me that she was preparing some medication. There was a concern at some point that Kass' body did not like the meds. She told me that the vial of medication that she was going to administer flew off the prep table and went across the room. The nurse was in the hall and actually saw it happen.

Every staff member marveled at the calm in the room. Here lay a now 14-year-old, in a deep coma with no predictable outcome, the air was still, but completely devoid of anxiety and stress. They asked all of us how this is possible, we had a very simple answer. **We're waiting on HIM:** This is not our fight.

There are angels among us. A couple asked to visit. We had no knowledge of them, not a clue who they were. They said that they drove from Temecula to see her and pray for her. As they did, they became overwhelmed with emotion, tears streaming down their faces. When they finished, they just got up and left. Never even knew their names. Months later, I was in Trader Joe's in Temecula. It was that couple, they were there in the store! I made way over to say hello to them. In what was one of the strangest experiences of my entire life, they saw me, and they seemed to look 'through me, not at me. I said "hello", and they responded in a kind way, with "hello". Then……. they made their way down the aisle. It was then I realized that there is a realm of beings that we are not equipped to understand in this life. Most of us call them Angels, and they do appear in the flesh.

CaringBridge – is a website designed to allow people to post updates on people in the hospital, make announcements, and even raise money. There were so many people reaching out from around the country that we chose to use Caring Bridge for the updates. I took an hour or so every night to write an update on her condition. It also allowed me to witness, in my own way and on behalf of the family our complete trust in Jesus. Those short little updates turned into some highly inspired writings that came "through me but were not always from me". Over the weeks, at one point there were over 150,000 hits from all around the world on Kassidy's CaringBridge page. Many wrote to tell us that the writings, the demonstration of complete and total faith in Christ, and the messages had caused them to reexamine their own Chistian Walk and rededicate their lives to God. Many came to Christ for the first time. It was incredible.

The Purple Mustangs – Outward demonstrations of any religion by staff were expressly prohibited at Rady Children's Hospital, as it is most hospitals. As countless nurses watched the unyielding demonstrations of our faith, something amazing happened. Word was out over the hospital of what we were doing in Kassidy's room for the many weeks that we were there. I cannot recall when it happened but one of the nurses came to us to proudly tell us that they had met with the senior management of the hospital and sought permission to openly pray with families as their hearts led them to do. Their position, based on Kassidy's story, was so compelling that the hospital administrators would now allow staff to openly pray with families while on duty!

Mike Sullivans thoughts

I can't say as to anything I "heard" during the coma period. I was not a spiritual person at the time, but I did immediately start to pray to God specifically for Kass to pull through....and a few other things. Never prayed before.... didn't really know how to. And that in itself could be an entire book!!

My good friend Mckenzie Gomes thoughts

The time Kassidy was in a coma felt, and to this day feels, like forever to me. I still wonder how her family dealt with it all with such poise in the way they did. For me, some days were better than others, but I did everything to stay as strong as she was. I dyed my hair purple, her favorite color, and listened to her favorite Christian band to feel close to her. I visited as often as my parents would drive me down, celebrated her birthday in the hospital, and wrote to her as much as I humanly could. I reflected on our memories and times together every day wondering if we would ever get the chance to make more. I remember the first day she was able to come home from the hospital; I visited her in her new downstairs bedroom with decorations spurred about. In a way the time Kass was in a coma is a blur, but every milestone and incremental growth she made stands out with such clarity.

If you can't be a bridge, be a lighthouse.

Surprisingly, we can't be everything to everyone. We have to intentionally space out our energy output. Keep your sight on your goal and continually be in prayer in preparation for what's ahead. Just like the Bible states, Aaron was invited, along with the tribe of Levi to equip oneself, we also need to anticipate and accept the good and the bad. Using acceptance for each event that we face. Sometimes we are going to come into contact with individuals that are going to steer you off course in your ventures but just think, if everything went smoothly in life, would we gain resiliency?

Maybe, just maybe if we looked to Christ, our daily requirements would come effortlessly. If you can't be a bridge of wisdom, be a lighthouse that leads to it! Do you like confrontation? I know of people who are good at it but that doesn't necessarily mean that they like it. Christ put a characteristic inside each of us to where coming to terms and understanding each other is a basic human requirement. So, in the quote, if you can't be a bridge, be a lighthouse is saying that if you can't build a bridge in the conversation gap, at least you can be available to be a lighthouse of reference when they need it!

Shifting my mindset from one that was living life having fun and not caring much of what I was doing to help others succeed to being in a state of reliance on them, incapable of doing anything, I was flat out on my back, unconscious. At that moment in time, I had no capabilities of getting further in life. Advancing to the next step in my 14 years of existence. I was in a coma, everyone was sad, no one was sure of the future. I could not be that bridge to help anyone. They had to help me. But I choose to think of it in a different way.

There were more plans than expected. Maybe Christ didn't want me to be a bridge, but He sure did use my life to be a lighthouse. Because others are running to Yahshua due to that horrifying circumstance. In that time, there was no doubt that it was terrifying and hopeless. At random times I think back to where I was and where I am now. The beauty in a person's life is so precious and can be easily taken. When you find the dainty, small, meaningful gifts every day that pop up out of nowhere you start to question. Question the fact that those little blessings throughout life were not coincidence.

We all have a choice.
The pathways of life are very statistical and laid out straightforward. You can either choose the path of life and light or the path of ruin or darkness. The choice of it all first began in the garden of Eden. There was a deceptive creature that told the humans that a good life could be found by taking this easier path. The path that pointed away from the light.

Sometimes in life, it may seem as if we have a choice. But just remember, the "narrow gate" and "wide gate" that we get to choose. The narrow gate is a more difficult way of life but represents a path of genuine, sacrificial love from the heart. To where the "wide gate", is an easier more destructive path of life that portrays outward righteousness yet hides inner turmoil. The choice is yours, to proudly hide a corrupt heart behind righteous looking behaviors or humbly go after a transformed heart by loving wholeheartedly.

This is why I want to paint somewhat of a picture for you. When one chooses the path of light, referring to life and exuberance, we thrive. But when one chooses the path of darkness, it's talking about the pathway of death. I was teetering between the two as I laid lifelessly, barely relying on life support. I wasn't conscious but as my body rested in a non-induced coma, there were actions taking place behind the scenes. Nothing no one knew about. It was something no human being, no medication could control. This was beyond our ability and powers.

Imagine a young girl helpless of which path to head. The path of life or the path of death. It is a decision that was made from something beyond earth. It's a declaration of what's to come. We may see failure and frustration but if we choose the straight and narrow road that leads to light, our approach at life changes.

We all have that choice. To choose an easy life of misery is also known as the path the deception and darkness or a challenging life that will in turn develop your character if you allow it to, known as the path of authentic, unadulterated light of peace. They're both promenades and avenues that you get to decide on. What choice are you going to choose?

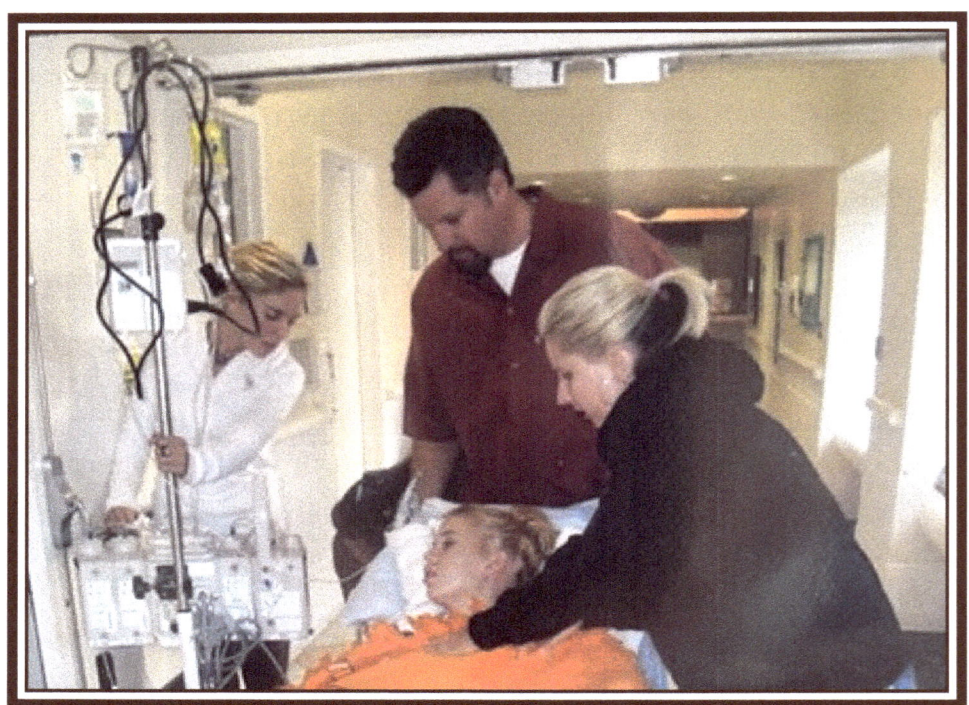

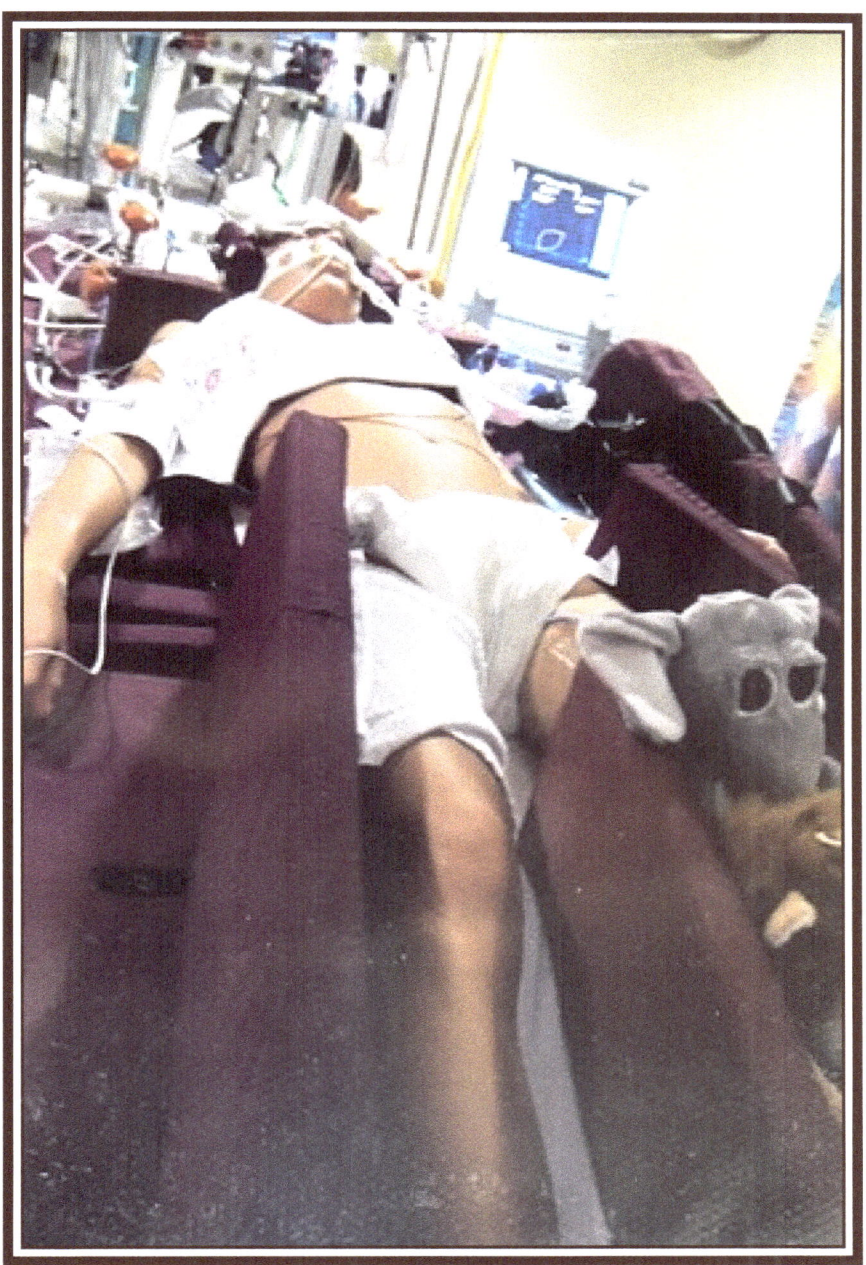

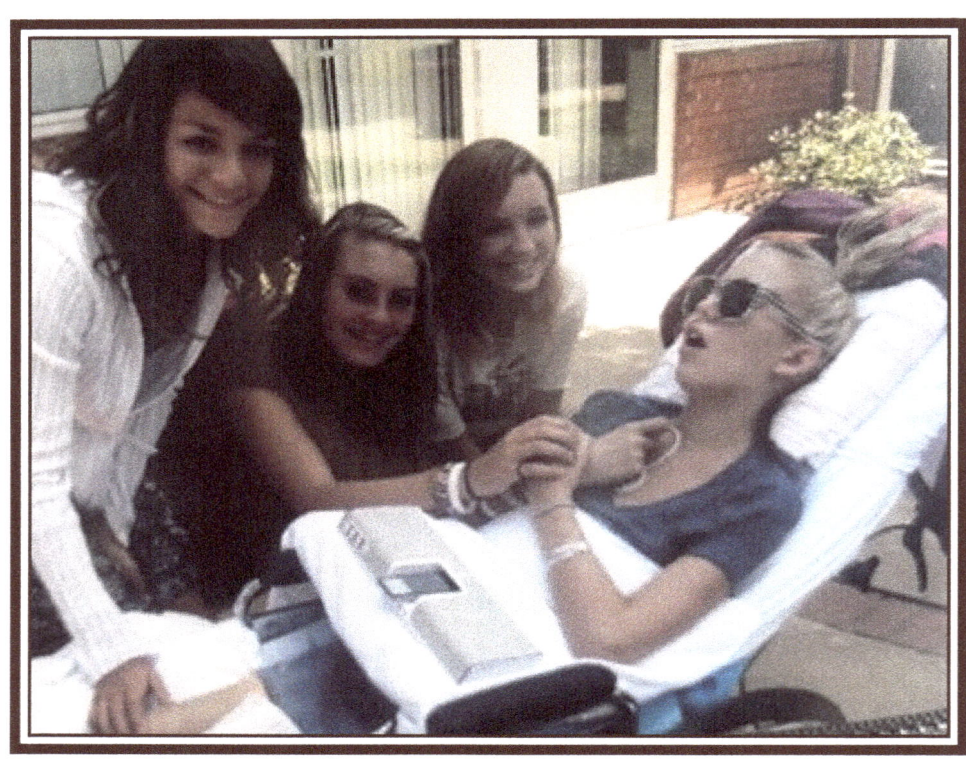

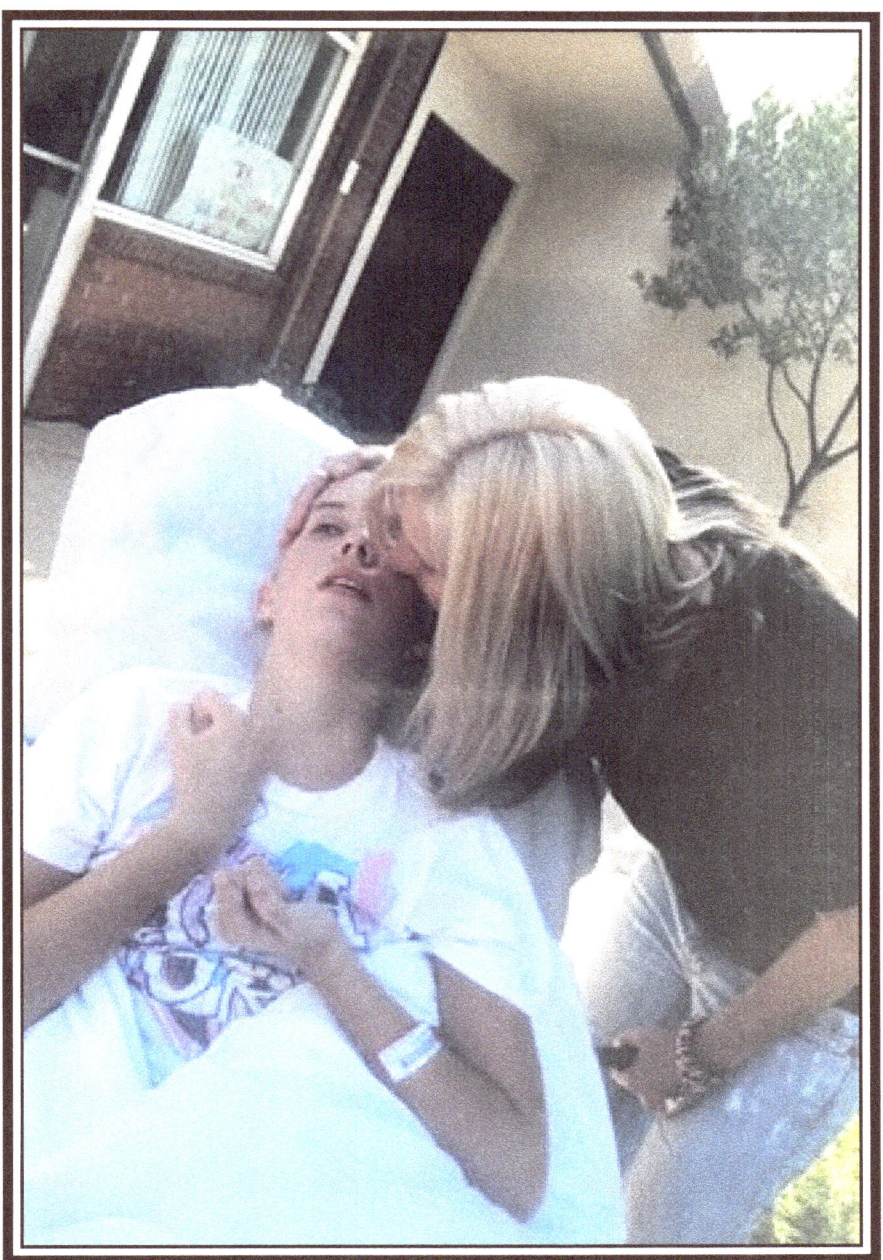

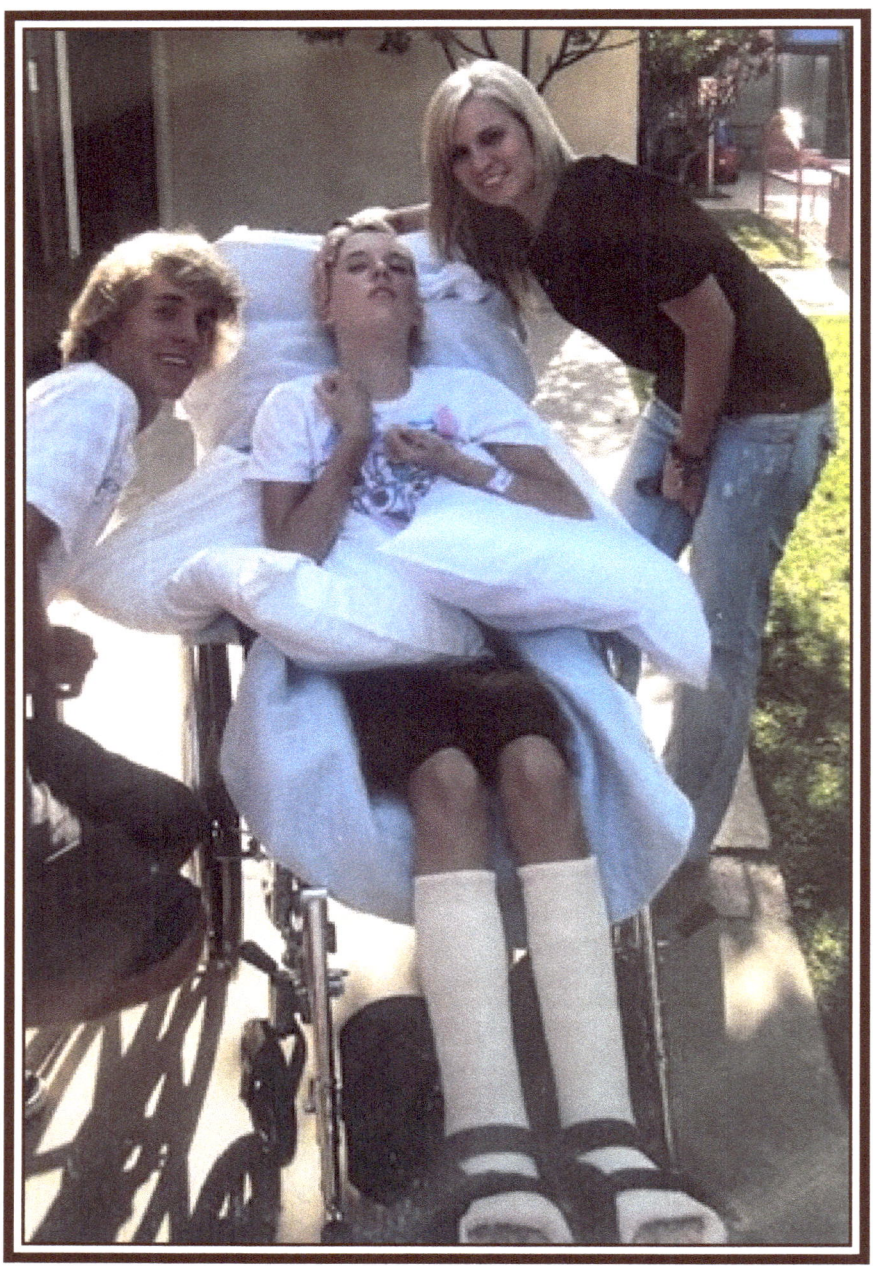

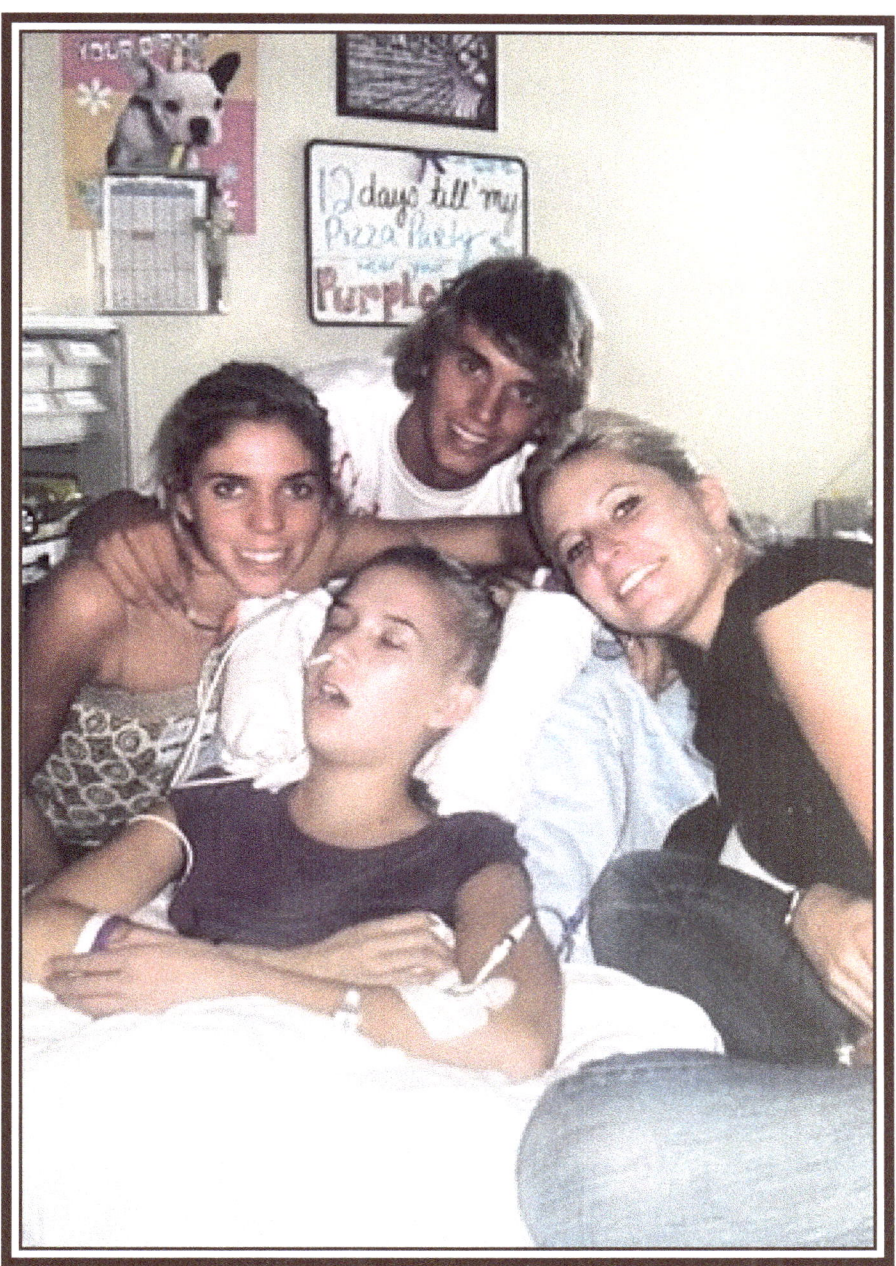

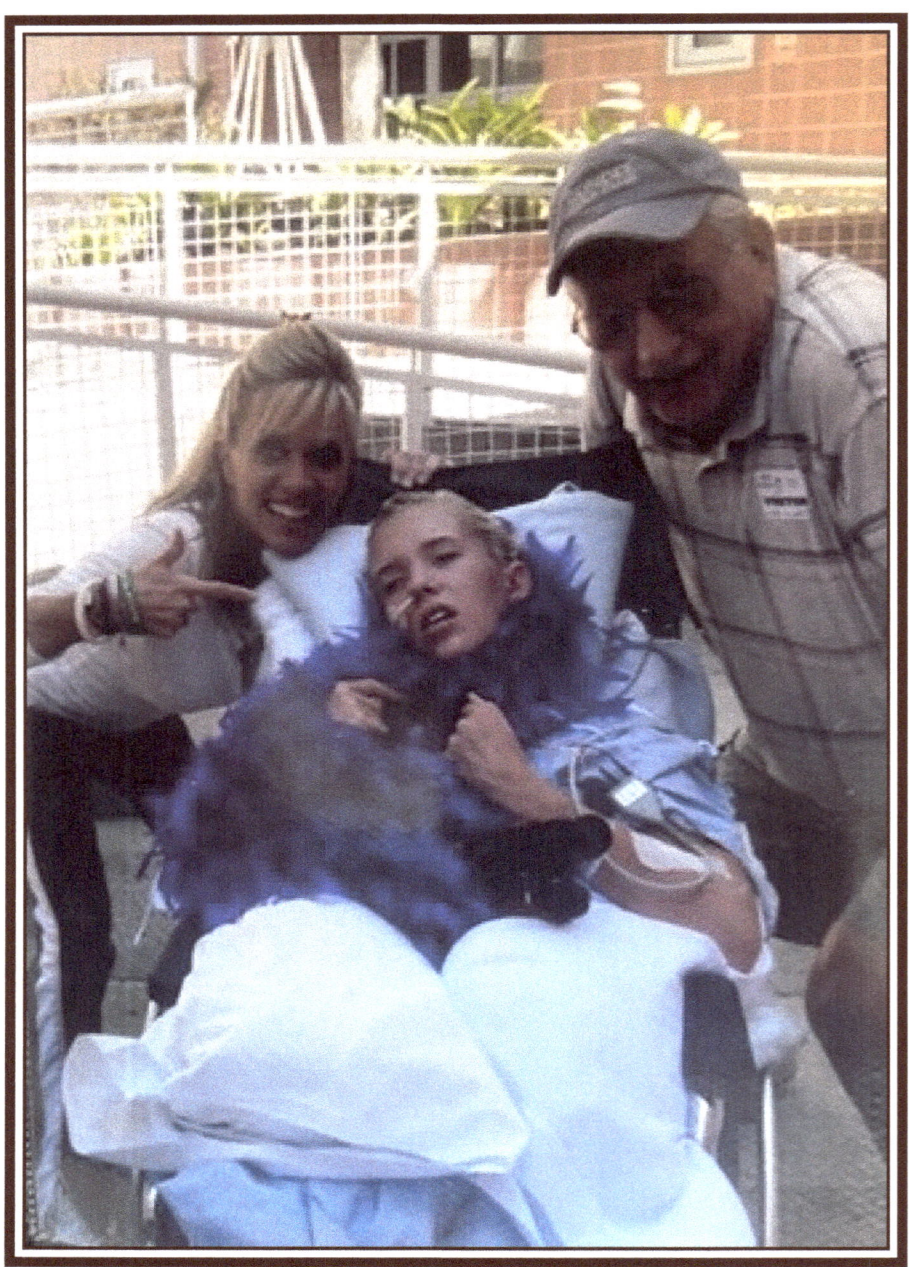

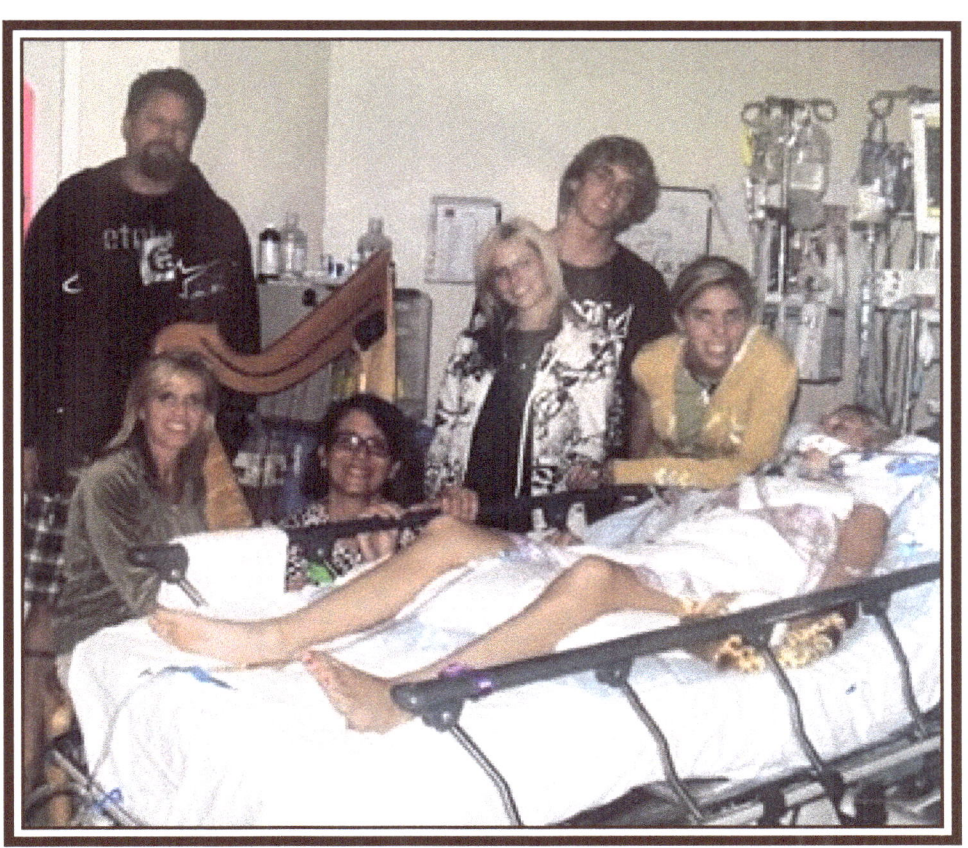

Chapter 8

Experiences In the hospital and Coma

Caringbridge.com was a wonderful reference where the family could post journal entries on "Kassidy 's site", so friends and family all over the world could follow my progress from the very beginning. It was a lifesaver for my family as they were constantly in with doctors and visitors all throughout the day. People were able to write in the guestbook and give Kassidy and the family words of wisdom and scripture and letting them know that people were praying for them. CaringBridge brought on a life of its own, and that is where the "purple army" originated.

The purple army was all of Kassidy 's supporters, and most likely why I'm alive today, from all of their prayers. Thank you, purple army! Thousands of individuals, known and unknown, submitted entries giving their condolences and stating prayers. As my family wrote, **"everyday consisted of several ups and downs but our strength remained."** On a typical day before the incident, I'd write a list of "To Do's" to get things I had to done. Reading through multiple journal entries, on the date of August 7, 2008, it stated that my sisters were telling me, "That I still need to come home and pick up the dog poo!" A chore that was my job to complete. And of course, if it were on my list, I'd get it done.

To keep the miracle train going, often times we hear about these events that take place that seem too good to be true, or unrealistic. But what if they were too good to be true? What if it was an act from Yahshua that can only point to Him and not come from a human perspective? In the very beginning stages of the incident, I was in the desolate, grim part of the hospital called the ICU. Because I was extremely critical. It was a long day, no one got much sleep during that time. Except me of course! My mom slept on the small, couch, pullout bed with a sheet and made it her sanctuary. That specific night was like no other though. You know those super deep slumbers that only come around once in a while that you don't understand why? Yea, that's Christs' hand gently laid upon you, letting you know that it's all going to work out, He is in control, we just need to roll with the punches. There was one nurse on the night shift that was in the room and witnessed this all with awe.

As four A.M. came around, one of many miracles started to happen. In the ICU, they have something known as a C.O.W. (Computer on wheels). While both my mom and I were totally out of it, a glass vial was thrown, and it hit the sliding glass door to my room. The night shift nurse was on pins and needles, as well as other nurses on duty. Unsure of what to do and was in complete awe of what was happening, she entered the room, and the lights began to flicker above her, at which time there was a swish of air that flew past her, the computer on wheels shifted as though someone moved it, but there was no one there. An hour or so later is when my dad came in for an early morning checkup. He and the nurse began informatively conversing back and forth about what took place that night. She was explaining the story in a fearful and excited whisper. During their enthusiastic undertones, my mom was awakened and retold the mysterious story.

All we could do is ponder of what was just disclosed, that it could have been the Spirit of life and death fighting for my body. Since this was defected about of month into my incident, it was obvious that this could only result in two options. Increment vibrancy or coming face to face with my Creator. The following day the doctors, as well as my family, noticed some changes in my awareness. It was as though the Spirit of death and darkness fled the room, and the Spirit of life was fully present. There was a sense of God's healing hand upon me like no other. I was progressively making improvements daily from this point on.

Days passed by slowly and things changed quickly. I always tell people; this is Gods' story that changed my life that my family remembers, and I remember little. Lots of friends and family came to visit. Personal friends, people from school that I really wasn't close with but knew, came to show their support, friends from all over. Their families pitched in and drove them all the way down to San Diego! My family that lived in North Dakota and Michigan and all other states came out to be with my family.

On that initial night, my dad's friend who is a "see'r" came on his Harley Davidson motorcycle to visit. When my parents asked him what he saw, he said "you mean that massive Angel standing behind her bed?" No one else could see it, but the angel was there. That huge Angel happened to be Michael the Archangel who was protecting me from evil. We just kept praying and saying thank you to the Lord for His support through everyone else. But my family was exhausted. From having to cope with, that their daughter might die, to these multitudes of people visiting daily to hardly sleeping on these "beds" to having to commute back and forth. I have no words to express how thankful and grateful I am.

About two to three days in is when everyone was praying over my body, lacking assurance of the physical. When the Father spoke to Travis in His own ways. Very quietly, very intimate. Just him and Christ. Travis stepped back from the crowd of individuals praying and had a moment with Elohim. While stepping back, Travis completely and wholly gave his life to Christ. Right there, he told the Lord that he would follow Him and Him only. Because a miracle is happening before his eyes and Christ is very much involved in this situation.

On another note, remember how I was explaining that I was infamous for dressing, quite unique! Having my own style, wearing Paramore shirts, Bob Marley shirts, colorful pants, neon shades with my iPod speaker following me around wherever we went and when I was in the hospital, they tried not to change that!

Good times call for good friends, which was exactly what happened, and you know who came? About a week in, Niki (still my really good friend) was in Catalina for a summer camp. One of those summer camps that don't come along very often, the kind where you are literally on a boat learning about sea life. It was at that time that she got called to the back of the deck where she was informed of what happened.

She was then released from camp to head back home and go straight to the hospital. Not knowing all the details. I figured a lot had to be going through her head at the moment. She has gone through so much in her young life, now experiencing one of her best friends fighting for her life too, God had a plan through her life with everything she has had to endure. And now, she is a nurse!

Niki's thoughts

Kass was more than just my best friend growing up, she was someone I looked up to with awe. No matter where life took us, even after I moved to a new city, we always made time to visit one another. Her family became my second family; their love and support carried me through so much. Kass was the embodiment of strengths she could take on anything life threw at her.

She was a hardworking student, an incredible sister, a loyal daughter, a gifted athlete, there was no challenge she couldn't conquer. To me, it felt like she could do anything, and do it better than anyone else. It was the summer I spent at camp on Catalina Island when everything changed. I was called to the camp director's office, and they put my mom on speakerphone. I could hear the urgency in her voice when she told me there had been an emergency.

I couldn't even imagine what it was. We had no phones at camp, so I had no way of knowing what was happening, but my heart sank as I immediately thought something might've happened to my grandmother. They rushed me onto the first boat out of Avalon and sent me to Long Beach. When I arrived, my mom didn't say a word until we were in the car. It wasn't until we were driving that she told me, her voice trembling, that Kassidy had suffered an aneurysm. We were headed to the hospital to say goodbye.

In that moment, I couldn't breathe. I had already lost so much at a young age, my father, several family members. But this was different. This wasn't just someone I loved; this was my best friend, someone my age, someone so full of life, someone who never stopped fighting. It didn't make sense. How could someone like Kassidy, so unstoppable, be lying in a hospital bed fighting for her life?

At the hospital, a worker took me into another room to explain all the life-sustaining machines connected to Kassidy's body. They tried to prepare me for what I was about to see, though nothing could have prepared me for the devastation. As I walked into the waiting room and saw her sisters, my heart shattered into a million pieces. It felt like a nightmare. I'd only just heard the news hours before, while they had been dealing with it for days. It was unreal. How could I possibly walk into that room and say goodbye to my best friend?

When it was finally my turn to go in, I couldn't stop shaking as I entered the room. Kassidy was hooked up to machines, and my heart sank. Her dad called me by my childhood nickname, "Sticks." I stood there, holding her hand, telling her how much I was going to miss her. My heart was shattered, lying on the floor beneath me, and I was saying my final goodbye to her. And then... her eyes shot open.

My mind went blank. I didn't understand what was happening, but before I could process it, nurses rushed us out. I remember running back to the waiting room, tears streaming down my face, barely able to speak. I kept saying over and over, "She opened her eyes." I was broken—physically, emotionally, and spiritually drained. I returned to camp, unsure of what was meant to come, not knowing if my friend would survive.

I had just a week left, and all my things were still in Catalina. But when I came home from camp, I found out that Kassidy was still alive, still fighting, defying all odds. I visited her a few more times in the ICU, and then months later, I saw her again in rehab. She was frustrated. She was strong, but her body had to relearn everything. I could see the pain and frustration in her eyes, and it broke my heart to watch her struggle.

But through all of it, she never stopped fighting. She was still my unstoppable friend, the girl who could conquer anything. She clawed her way back from the edge of death, and I knew in that moment, if anyone could overcome this, it was her. She wasn't going to let this break her. She was still the same fierce, determined, amazing Kassidy I had always known. And I knew, without a doubt, she was going to rise again.

The Tilt bed

Inadvertently, I was put on a tilt bed to assist the fluid in my lungs. It was a giant bed that would rotate me every two hours. Little did my family know, the nurses were extremely cautious of what to say to friends and family to where they just said that it was for my lungs. But what was really going on, is that I had pneumonia to where I had extremely high temps around 104-105°. This all took place before my embolization.

But again, symptoms are our body's way of telling us that something is off. And we knew that there was already a major issue to where this pneumonia was part of the process. Nurses were administering medications, getting it under control and taking precautions. Yes, those paramount temperatures could have killed me in the state that I was in, but it didn't. That's yet another miracle of survival that Christ saved me in. Overall, I was on this rotating tilt bed for over a week or more. This "bed," looked like a prisoner's straight jacket but for my whole body. Supposedly, it really helped my lungs, but it was harder for my family to move me and exercise my limbs.

"We tend to think of health and healing as blessings. But God knows that sometimes we don't truly cling to Him until we have true difficulty."

This chaos happened on August 4th, and my freshman year of high school was to begin August 17th. Lexi would have been a senior; Travis would have been a junior and I would've been a freshman. We were equally excited to be at the same school together. But plans changed. While we had that in mind, God had something grander in His perception. Prevailing over the days, and filled with concern, Travis and Lexi both did independent studies in their final year of high school to be available in order to help out at the hospital and at home.

So, laying there in a coma everyone thought I just didn't want to sign up for school. Growing up, I was always the jokester in the family, but this time I wasn't playing around. August is a big month too because August 30th is my birthday. That day was extremely bittersweet and somber for everyone. A few friends even came down to the hospital to celebrate and they brought cupcakes with them too. We weren't going to let this stop us from having a party. My room was already covered with "get well soon" cards, "we love you" cards, and "praying for you" posters. But now cards were overlapping with happy birthday!

Grandpa shaving my legs.

Okay I have to share the story of when my grandpa shaved my legs! Just the thought of it makes me laugh. Obviously, I don't remember, but your body still functions when you're in the worst of conditions. My family wanted to keep things as normal as possible. I was getting a bath one day and being pampered by Gramps the next. Fearlessly he says, "she needs her legs shaved." No one wanted to, they were all nervous, but grandpa said, "gimme the razor." How often do you see a grandpa shaving his granddaughter's legs?

Every Friday, my family started a tradition of having purple Fridays. My favorite color was purple at the time. Everyone was wearing purple to support me and let others know they're there for me too. People were so beyond supportive. Taking me outside for the first time in several weeks had to be very refreshing. For everyone! A great reminder that everything that's happening is temporary. My family was extremely diligent at keeping me limber and stretching out my legs every chance they could get.

The doctors ordered me to start physical therapy with one of their aids but in fact, they didn't know that physical therapy was already taking place in my room with my family. The nurses even had to ask them to slow down a couple of times because it was too excessive! But in the greatest way possible. I was always used to intense exercise with my past of horse riding, running, traveling, soccer, martial arts and all my extra-curricular activities.

I do have to give credit to where credit is due. My family was an amazing support during this trial. I thank them from the bottom of my heart for all that they have done and continue to do. They are the main reason I am where I am today, typically, with hard times like these, someone always gets left out. But, because I was the youngest daughter, Dani was already out of the house, driving, doing her own thing and Lexi had just gotten her license a few months before so that just left me. So, my parents didn't have to worry about transportation for the two of their daughters.

Third element of an N.D.E.(Near Death Experience)

The third element of having a near death experience is having an out-of-body event. I, however, did not experience this phenomenon. Again, my event was more of a traumatic experience, and it all happened so fast, I didn't know what to think or do. I'm still praying that the Lord would reveal that to me in an intimate kind of way. As I stated, I remember everything before and everything after but those four months in a coma, I was down and out. I hardly remember anything unfortunately.

AFO's and therapy

Doctors put AFO's (Ankle-foot orthotics) on my feet to stop them from rising up and keep them flat. AFO's are casts that go on your feet for a short period of time. We used to joke around and call them UFO's! Still in my coma, I was in physical therapy to regain endurance and attempt to hold my head up again. Lots of therapy was done, but we couldn't have gotten through everything without the help of certain doctors and nurses who were by our side each step of the way.

On September 5, I had my first Embolization. I'm not sure how, but the surgeons went through my Femoral Artery to inject glue and a type of chemo to kill off the AVM. The AVM was in my cerebellum and brain stem and the Femoral Artery is on the complete opposite end. CRAZY! Now, this wasn't your typical chemo, it was the type of chemo the only happens for a minute. It was only to help the embolization. And that took place with each embolization I had. I had four in total.

A couple weeks after that on **September 18**, I had a G-Tube inserted to help me eat (liquids of course.)
"A gastrostomy tube, often called a G tube, is a surgically placed device used to give direct access to your stomach for supplemental feeding, hydration or medicine."

That same day was when I also had a Fundoplication done so I wouldn't aspirate and choke. "Fundoplication is a surgical procedure that helps prevent the stomach contents from flowing back up the food pipe, called the esophagus." Basically, they tied off my esophagus, so I wouldn't be able to throw up.

On the day that I was well enough, we went out to the courtyard. It was the very first time of being outside since the actual event took place. My mom, being the mama bear that she is, wanted to learn everything regarding my care. Not having any knowledge of nursing or caring for an ill child, she relied on the Lord for her knowledge. Not knowing what she was doing, He sustained her to carry through. And because of that, she learned how to feed me through my G-tube.

A very intensive practice yet how I got my nutrients. While we were on our way outside, my mom was pushing me down the hallway in the hospital, when I threw up. But remember, I have a Fundoplasty that prevents food from coming up the esophagus, so I ended up violently throwing up through my G-tube. Now, if you can imagine a young girl in a high-back wheelchair, not able to lift her neck, throwing up through her stomach. What a sight. Right?

It was a lot to endure, but by grace we battled through it. As a dear friend wrote in "Don't open your heart and emotions to fear. It can put you on a roller coaster of emotions and it will result in double mindedness, having divided faith, you will begin to doubt the Word Of God and waver." On October 6, I had a third ventriculostomy done, which is a surgical procedure for treatment of hydrocephalus in which an opening is created in the floor of the third ventricle using an endoscope placed within the ventricular system.

On October 10, Dr. Levy inserted a shunt, which tragically failed. Then on **October 13** is when he fixed the shunt. **On November 24**, I had my second embolization done at the hospital next-door. That's where they went through the femoral artery to shoot brain glue and some intense chemo in order to kill off the AVM again. And once again, **on December 2**, I had my third embolization done, all of that with success.

"Let us hold fast the confession of our hope without wavering, for He who promised is faithful." Hebrews 10:23

Believe it or not, that was not the end of my surgery days. I ended up having a few more with the hope to have this body survive. "When you pass through death and allow your inner being to be broken, God overflows that and turns it into new." Weirdly as it is, there is a surgery where you can get Botox in your eye to help with double vision, that's what I did on **January 6, 2009**, with no success. I went on to have three more eye surgeries with the hope of single vision with no success. Sometimes obstacles are put in front of you not to fight against them but to roll with the punches.

All of these surgeries were deeply pondered upon, and thought out by doctors, nurses, family and friends. Sorrowfully, my family went through multiple tragedies every day. It was without a doubt a nightmare, but they knew they had to be strong for my survival and not bring any negativity into the room. The ups and down's that they had to confront on a daily basis was paralyzing due to the countless life and death decisions they had to make.

On the morning of **February 26, 2009**, my family received a call from the hospital stating that I was due to have my fourth embolization and that they had all the nurses and doctors set up and ready for my surgery that Monday. We didn't have time to take into account, pray and prep as needed. We kind of just showed up and prayed for the best. Not having much time to contemplate or view the hindrance at hand, we had to go through with it. Persisting through difficulty after difficulty, my family spent the next hours living with anxiousness and distress. But it was another hurdle that we had to turn over to Christ. Well, Christ has a purpose in everything and though, not known at the time, something greater is always in store.

A great deal of times, we end up playing the blame game when bad things happen. It's part of our human character. But it's not how God wants us to live. He wants us to follow after His character and to live **"blameless."** And as stated, the Hebrew meaning for blameless is **"to be complete."** And while this unexpected surgery snuck up on us, greater things were taking place. Christ had this all under control; it just wasn't in our own authority, so we didn't have any power over the situation.

That surgery ended up causing a stroke in my hypothalamus. The hypothalamus is an area of the brain that produces hormones that control: body temperature. Heart rate. Hunger. Mood. This was exactly what my family was praying against, but it happened. It seemed as if that had set me back ten steps in my initial recovery process. We're not the type of family to sit in pity of what took place, rather than have our time for frustration, annoyance, bitterness, and resentment yet not residing there but moving on. Staying in your pain is one of the worst things one can do because it results and hopelessness and despair.

Then, on April 27, 2009, was when I had the AVM feeder veins completely removed through an invasive ten-and-a-half-hour surgery. Again, they don't get many cases of a massive, ruptured AVM in children. There is a .01% chance of life, so they were very cautious in this tricky situation. With this being a ruptured AVM, which is rare and not very common, this case of mine was one of Dr. Levy's most difficult cases due to almost fifty feeder veins throughout my rupture. To consider, typical AVM's usually have anywhere between eight to twelve feeder veins, mine had close to fifty.

"Surgical removal, or resection, is the surgery type that completely removes the AVM. It's the most invasive and riskiest type. Doctors generally only recommend it for an AVM that has ruptured or has a high chance of rupturing." During this surgery, "The steps are generally as follows:

A neurosurgeon makes an incision in your scalp, removes a part of your skull, and, using a microscope, closely examines the blood vessels in the AVM. With tiny instruments, the neurosurgeon separates and removes the AVM, being careful not to damage any structures around it. Once imaging equipment shows the AVM is completely removed, the neurosurgeon reattaches the bone to your skull and stitches the incision. When you wake up, your healthcare team talks with you to make sure you can understand and respond."

After the surgery was completed, I was so pumped up with pain meds that I honestly felt like going shopping. I wanted to go to Target, to be exact!

On January 30, 2011, I had another eye surgery completed. Then I had an additional eye surgery on August 29, 2011. Not very many people can state that they enjoy the feeling of being under anesthesia. I absolutely adore the initial reaction when you fade away! It's pretty much like taking an extended nap. It's the coolest thing ever. But to be honest, I know that surgery will be taking place and recovering from surgery is never fun, there is a trade-off. The fun part and the not so fun part.

For example, in July 2016 I had a shunt revision. Yes, I got the chance to be put under anesthesia once again, but the recovery of malfunction is never fun on my behalf. Then in January 2019 I had another shunt revision which, soon after that in

February 2021 is when I had another shunt revision. All of these revisions are necessary due to the hydrocephalus on my brain. Keep reading to learn more about my shunt revisions later on. It's kind of like we endure these trials and tribulations for a short time. The cause is always unknown at the time we realize and the time to come. It might be for a short time or for a long time, but there is always motivation behind it.

If you consider the people around, you might be witnessing it. It might be for them to change their lives for the better. To back track, in 2008, I had just graduated Eighth grade. Just gotten my braces off. Just colored my hair for the first time, I looked like a whole new person. Grown-up and mature my life was looking great. Then this happened. During that time that was in a coma, I was on gruesome life support for twenty-nine days and was intubated for almost forty days.

All that time of being intubated for so long started to shift my teeth. Completely relocating all of my teeth that I worked so hard for and endured the pain for two whole years. And if you're wondering why my teeth were so important as opposed to the life-saving medicine that was being inserted into me, I always had a thing with my teeth and still do. When I was finally home and able, I started to wear my retainer again to realign my teeth. and you know what, God completely took care of all of it because you would never know that my teeth shifted or moved at all.

How waves need to break and fall and crash before they turn into new
Sitting by the ocean on a warm, breezy day sounds like a very

enjoyable act, right?! That is, until the breeze starts to pick up and waves become more frequent. But have you ever paid attention to the tiny yet mighty processes of a wave? A wave first needs to be built up and form then it must crash and be built up yet again. And the process continues. It's the ebb and flow, with its cycles and patterns to form something beautiful.

Furthermore, after it collides with stillness, the movements of incremental streams are built back up with uplifting life. Just like we say that there's always calm before the storm, that's exactly what I picture when a wave is being built back up. An interchangeable example of myself, I needed to fall and break in order to be built back up in the knowledge of Yahshua and further understand His miraculous goodness.

A wave doesn't only require change, it requires transformation. Because what goes on in the inside is going to happen on the outside too. A verse that comes to mind is Romans 8:6, which states that "the mind governed by the flesh is death, but the mind governed by the spirit is life and peace." And even though a wave doesn't have flesh, it is still in there, nature to be built up. But waves completely surrender to the earth. And who made the Earth? God. So, Christ is in control of everything that takes place below heaven.

Trusting the tide

Consider reading Hebrews 12:5-11. There we learn about the word chastening which refers to misfortunate events resulting in improvement of the recipient, personally, I like to think of it as constructive criticism. When bad things happen to innocent people, that's when we start to question God's faithfulness and forget His promises as a whole. We have to remember, He doesn't work on our clock but rather His watch. God has the ability to not cause hardship but misfortune in our life due to His love.

You're probably thinking, wait, I thought love is caring for a person and helping them? But what if Christ does do that but in an everlasting way? He ties in His love to an ordinary father's love of his child. And what father doesn't correct his child? Just like we are Christs' child, He causes this misfortune in our life to correct us and put us on the path towards Him, towards His will for our life. Chastening might be enduring to go through at the time, ultimately it brings not only obedience, but love, joy, peace, patience, kindness, long-suffering, and so much more.

As Yahshua states, if we are those that don't endure the chastening, we are not considered to be partakers with Christ. Partakers is another way of calling them companions or partners. To where, those who go through those misfortunate events and follow Him for further improvement will become partakers or partners with Him. Going through the correction or misfortune, it may seem like rebuke but as time goes on and we are trained up in His ways, we begin to see the lasting blessings as a result of being chastened.

Because of the constant depreciation of my survival, I had no chances to fight for my own life, neither did anyone else. This was completely a natural cause that no one could strive. The sole thing to do was to pray and allow God to have the final say. Don't get me wrong, I 100% think that there's a time to grieve, a time for sadness for any misfortunate event. And when a person dies, grievance is at a whole different level. But I had to look at every angle of this event for others' sake too.

If I did die, I'd be in the arms of my Heavenly Father, if I survive, I'll have quite a story to share to use my life to point to You. For my loved ones, they'd lose a daughter but gain an everlasting angel, have peace knowing that they'll see me again, or be ecstatic that I made it but scared for what lays ahead and to have me by their side. There's always a tradeoff to any situation. It's just in our efforts to try to see all of the outcomes.

The fourth core element of a near death experience
And finally, the fourth element of near-death experience is being in a heavenly realm. Unfortunately, that has not come to my knowing yet. I'm still in the process of praying for the comprehension of that and it will be revealed to me when it's time, the Lord knows that there is a time for everything and with everything there is purpose.

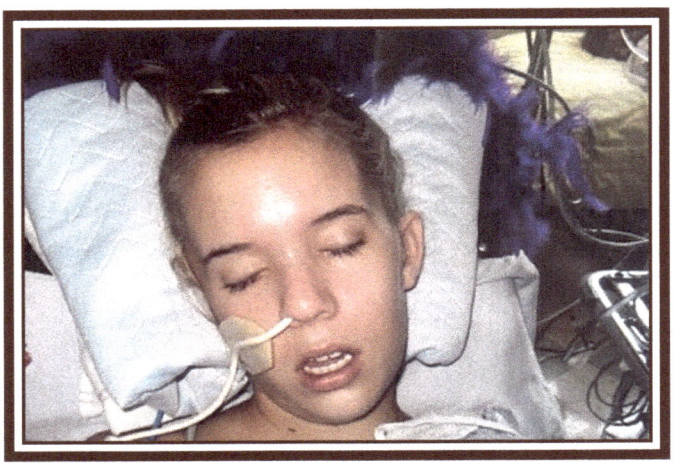

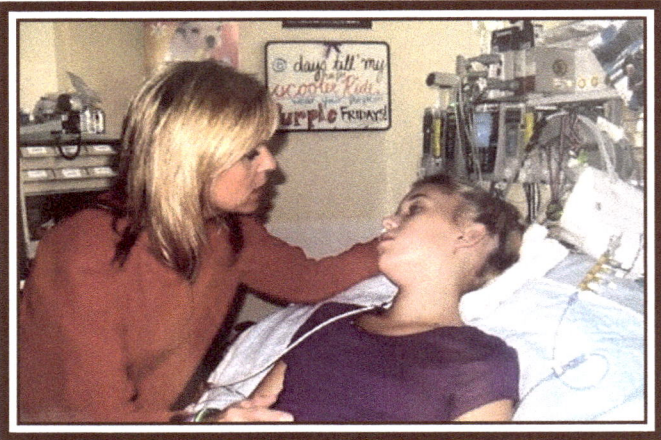

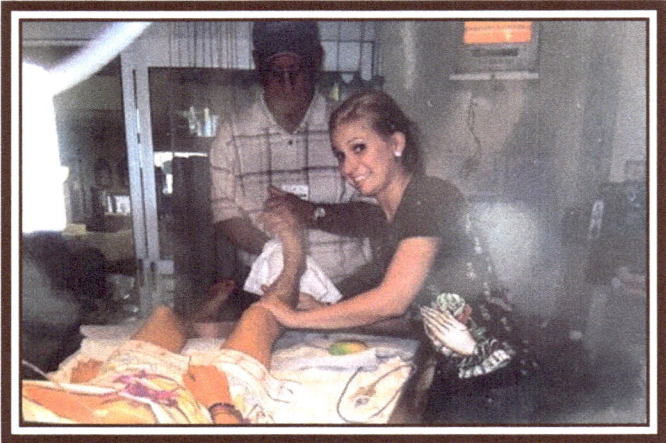

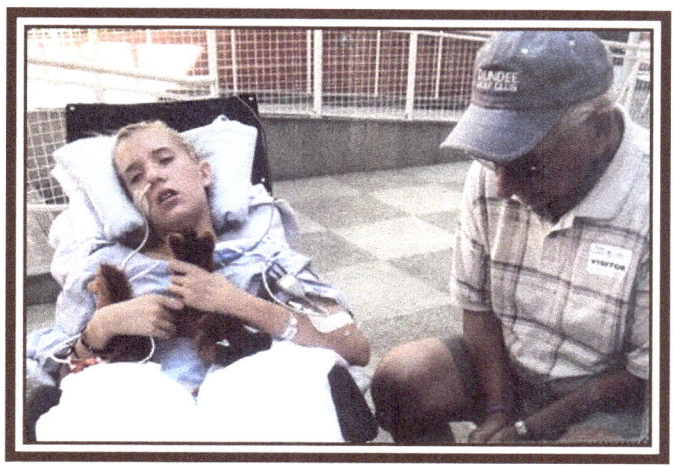

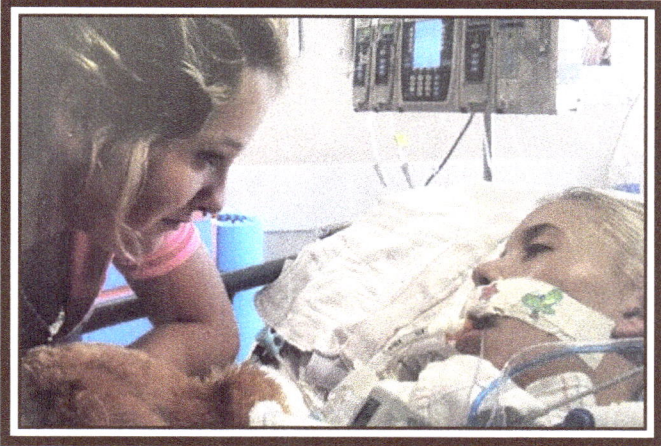

131

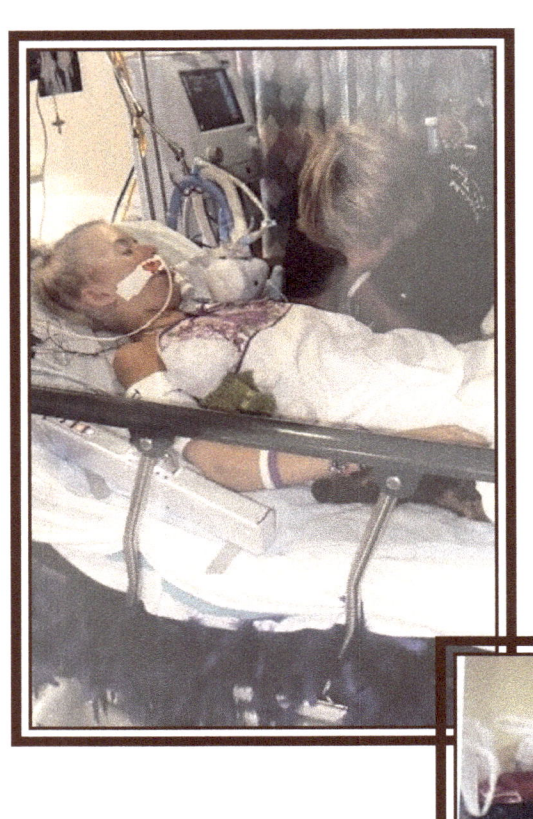

Chapter 9

Penny's story

When I was about seven or eight years old, our neighbor's dog was having Boxer puppies. And we thought, "We have to have one!" Not knowing how much of a difference Penny would have in our life and what it would be like with her in it. She was a straight angel to our family with the impact that she made just a few years later. Though she was a wild puppy, she had her time of maturing and turned into the most wonderful love! We did everything and went so many places with her by our side. Life just didn't seem the same without Penny by our side.

Each of us girls were in a different season of life to where our lives appeared very contrasting, but it all flowed together. And Penny was there through the thick and thin! And because I was the youngest, I was home more, working on homework and playing with friends more that made Penny and I inseparable to say the least. It was pretty much like having a best friend that is stuck by your side. Which made it very strange when I wasn't home for those four and a half months in the hospital, she knew something was going on.

In a CaringBridge entry, it said that almost every night that the typical family wasn't at home, Penny would sleep on my bed. That is such an intuitive process because, though it wasn't the usual individuals' home with her, yet she knew I was the one in distress. How? That's just how God designed dogs. To be in tune with "their person."

Though house pets typically aren't allowed at the hospital, my family kind of made it work! They brought Penny outside of the hospital. Seeing her through the window, which brought everyone some much needed comfort knowing she was there. And it was a sigh of relief for everyone.

When it came time for me to come home, (still in my stage of coma), everyone was giddy yet beyond nervous of what the future would hold. I could just imagine Penny being a ball of energy, happy and energetic, feeding off everyone else's emotions not knowing what's to come. When I arrived home from the ambulance drive from San Diego to Murrieta California, it was a dreadful experience for everyone because any movement of mine could cause a serious life altering injury. So, every minuet maneuver they made was well thought out.

When I was rolled in through the back door, my family lifted Penny up to greet me face to face and when they did, that's when the home healing began happening. She never licked anyone out of manners, but at that moment, that's exactly what I needed. It was almost as if she was sending an angel kiss directly from Yahshua Himself.

Saying, "Your home, I've missed you. I sense you're going through something hard; everyone is upset but I just wanted to tell you that Jesus loves you!" She licked me square in the face and from that point on I started to remember more knowing I was home. Penny was always a curious dog but not to the extent that she could be used as a miracle. Through all the nighttime feedings and bed rotations, Penny was there throughout my healing process for a time! So, in my five-month journey of being in different stages of a coma, it's been a long journey, but Penny has been a big part of that!

But in 2010, Penny's life came to a halt. She was a very healthy, go with the flow kind of dog so we didn't suspect anything. So, when she tragically unknowingly passed away one summer morning, we were all devastated to the core. We were thinking it could've been a stomach tumor, but we weren't positive. It was extremely bittersweet because it was two weeks before my sister's wedding. So, we had to pick up our bootstraps and lament and mourn for a short time then it was wedding party time.

"Humans can't just march into God 's world. So, God will reach out to us using these spiritual ambassadors also known as angels."

Waking up
Going back to that stage of coma that I was in, on my way home, I was loaded into an ambulance (I was still considered very fragile). Oddly enough, I scarcely remember a slight image of the ambulance ride, not knowing anything. Not able to see things clearly. It was as if everything was very bright and fuzzy. All I remember was the ambulance doors closing. Nothing too exciting, just the perception of going in and out of consciousness.

Each and every nurse and doctor were giddy with excitement as they sent me off for the one-hour drive to Murrieta. One of the doctors was so concerned about my care that he followed in his car behind us all the way to the freeway to just make sure everything was going to be okay. Then, pulling up to the house and getting settled, that's when the story of Penny licking me in the face comes into play.

Slowly becoming more coherent. I was realizing how different I was from everyone else. Mentally, physically, emotionally. I couldn't really relate to anyone my age because things like this don't happen to fourteen-year-olds. I was stuck in this body that didn't function and just wanted to hang out with my typical friends without them treating me like an alien. I was much more than that, I'm just healing from a brain injury but I'm still Kassidy.

A dreadful voyage later, many therapies and goals completed, the odds were being overcome. The hard work continued to be in motion and even though it seemed like too much to bear, I kept moving forward because that's what I grew up knowing. Not sapping in what already happened but recognizing that it took place and learning from it in order to move forward.

Loved ones perspectives of waking up.
This is my mom's input:
We lift Penny up so she can see Kass. Penny proceeds to lick her face and Kassidy smiles, her first smile in 3 months. It's as though she knows she is home, later Kassidy shares with us that she knew she was home after Penny licked her in the face. Dogs have a way of making everything better.
We are home together as a family, it feels so good to be HOME.

As a family, we rolled up our sleeves and jumped right in, the routine at home is intense. There is a long list of meds, and of course the feeding schedule, as she is still on an electronic feeding pump that moves formula from a bag, through her G-tube and into her stomach. The bags last a couple of hours then have to be cleaned and refilled.

There is a separate schedule for the medications, which does not coincide with the feeding bag refilling. This leads to no more than an hour or two between schedules, and this must go on 24 hours a day. For us, it's a labor of love and we look forward to the one-on-one time that the process gives us with her.

Lexi made the decision to give up her Senior year of High School to stay home and help me with Kassidy. She meets with a tutor who gives her assignments for the week. I don't know what I would have done without her. Lexi and I take Kassidy to Physical Therapy, OT and Speech a few days a week now. It's a lot to transport Kassidy, as it takes 2 people to lift her into the car. Lexi sits in the back seat with Kass to hold her head in place. I lifted the high back wheelchair in the back of the SUV, along with transporting the portable feeding device and tubes to keep Kassidy fed and hydrated.

We are seeing the results of Kassidy's therapies; she is getting stronger and staying awake longer as well. After a visit to Rancho PT, Lexi and I noticed a neatly folded note on our windshield, it says:

"I was sitting in my car waiting for my daughter to come out of PT when I saw you drive up. I saw something so tender, so beautiful and it touched my heart, and I wanted to share it with you. The picture of REAL LOVE was displayed before my eyes. I saw a team, a mother/daughter team so tenderly taking what I assume was your other daughter out of the vehicle and pacing her in her wheelchair. The love was so evident and so

sweet. I saw you both stroking her face and her hair. I started to cry. That kind of love can only come from Jesus - you were a shining example of 1 Corinthians 13 kind-of-love. This is a note of encouragement... What a blessing you both are and kind words from a stranger hopefully can go a long way. I love this scripture in John 14:27 "Peace, I leave you, my peace I give to you. Let not your heart be troubled, neither let it be afraid". God has great plans for you and your family. "Many are the afflictions of the righteous, but the Lord delivers us out of all of them". Psalm 34:19. What a precious witness you were to me as a believer in the Lord Jesus Christ - how you will let others see the hope that lies within you by your life, example, words, tenderness. Great Job. Keep pointing them to the one that heals, changes lives, restores, forgives, and the one who leads, guides, and directs our every footstep! My prayer for you...
Dear Jesus, please continue to watch over this precious family, help them daily to look to you, the author, perfector and finisher of their faith. Thank you for having equipped them with everything pertaining to life and godliness. They lack nothing. Continue to give them the faith and strength for each new beautiful day you give them. You are an awesome God who is able , more than able to accomplish what concerns them today. Wrap your loving arms around them and let them know and feel your love. In Jesus name, AMEN!"
Mighty Warrior, Annmarie

This is a complete stranger, we saw no one watching us unload Kassidy from our SUV. We never know the examples we can be. We cried all the way home feeling the love from a complete stranger. God is soooo good.

We were able to contact a new Physical Therapist who would be able to come into the home for PT, his name is Chuck, he is also a Black Belt in Taekwondo, they make a wonderful connection. Kassidy responds very well to his firm, but gentle approach.

We have been home for over a week; Kassidy is making great strides:

Speech - Kassidy is still non-verbal.

Arms - Great improvements, she is still not able to have control but trying to lift her arms.

Legs - Kass is purposefully moving her legs with just a little help. Her nerve pathways are starting to open and respond to instructions from her brain.

Head and neck - Her neck is getting stronger every week. She can move her head from side to side.

Sight and Sound - Kassidy is tracking well, we're not sure if there is double vision, but she is watching movement. She can hear and respond to voices.
.

Fine motor skills - This is the last area that will recover. Her bleed was located near the cerebellum, and this is part of the brain that controls: Coordination and movement, gross and fine motor coordination, postural control, Balance and equilibrium, eye movement.

Emotions - Kass reacts to all stimuli. Remember that the top two hemispheres in her brain were not affected in any way. This area of the brain controls our higher functions like memory, personality, thought processing, learning etc. You see, Kassidy is still very much Kassidy. That adds to the frustration. She understands "everything". They refer to her overall condition as being "locked in". She knows what she wants to do, but she cannot make her body respond to the commands from her brain.

Kass works extremely hard every day, she is determined and focused. She tries so hard that she begins to cry. She cries, but she does not stop, she pushes herself so hard during her 45-minute sessions that she usually collapses into a deep sleep as soon as she finishes. It takes every ounce of energy and concentration to complete even the simplest movements. We are so proud of her.

November 24th arrives; we return to UCSD for the second embolization procedure. We are not looking forward to yet another brain surgery for our girl. The procedure involves running a catheter up the femoral artery into the brain. The catheter is guided into the area of the AVM, at which point a medical glue is injected into the bad arteries. This clogging effect will close the bad vessels, which will eventually kill off the AVM.

Again, we kiss Kassidy's forehead and pray over her as she is wheeled away for her 7th surgery. Again, we wait in the waiting room pacing back and forth asking God for another Miracle. There are many risks with Brain surgeries, usually a 50/50 chance of life or death. The odds are too high for us; however, we don't have a choice or there could potentially be another AVM bleed.

The surgery went well; we give honor and Glory to God for his faithfulness.

The ambulance is ready to take Kassidy from UCSD hospital to Rady Children's Hospital about 20 minutes away. We got Kassidy settled back where it all started on August 4th, we're back in ICU again, fully intubated for the night, resting comfortably. They extubate Kassidy the next morning and she responds to commands. We are now communicating with her eyes, One blink for YES, two blinks for NO. It's a total game changer now that we can truly communicate.

Thank God Kassidy is able to go home after a few days after surgery. We can't wait to go HOME. Home is truly the heart of healing. It's a place of refuge and peace, rest and family. We feel love, we feel joy. Thank you, Lord for HOME,...

I sleep on the couch, an arm's length away from Kassidy. I set the alarm every 2 hours to rotate Kass from side to side, so she doesn't get bed sores, start her feeding catheter, as well as new meds needed throughout the evening. I can hear every breath, it brings comfort, it gives her reassurance that I will never leave her side.

We have many friends that are touched by Kassidy's story. A dear friend Charyl Stark stops by to share with us a letter board to test to see if Kassidy is able to spell words on a chart, as Charyl is a special needs teacher in Temecula Valley, she deals with non-verbal autistic children. She shows Kassidy the spelling chart and sure enough, Kassidy is spelling words! We are freaking out with excitement. This means SO much, it confirms that Kassidy's high functioning abilities are in-tact. PRAISE GOD! We use the chart to start communicating with how she is feeling or her immediate needs. Thank you, Charyl, for bringing us great HOPE.

Kassidy continues to do well at all of her Therapies; it is as though her healing is happening in supersonic speed. Every day there was something new, changes were taking place. Now that we can communicate with the chart, it has made our lives so much easier.

Monday, December 1st - I received a phone call from UCSD late that afternoon. The nurse was confirming Kassidy's 3rd embolization for the following morning. I said, "Excuse me", I don't know anything about the surgery. Typically, it's scheduled with the patient then the medical team, transport from UCSD to Rady Children's Hospital, then admitted to Rady Children's Hospital. Well, it looks like everyone was informed except for Kassidy and her family. The entire team was already scheduled, so we couldn't cancel. It's only been a week since her last embolization, Kassidy's 2nd surgery in a week. This is too much to handle...

Kevin arrived home from work, and we made the decision to have the procedure done.
We shared with Kassidy, and she was so upset, she is understanding everything now, as well as having deep emotions. We understand Kassidy's frustration, but we also know the risks if she was to have another AVM bleed. We had to kill off the AVM, we are praying this will be the last embolization surgery.

Tuesday, December 2nd - on the road at 5:30 AM Southbound from Temecula to San Diego. We arrived at UCSD a little frustrated and exhausted from barely recovering from the last surgery just a week ago. The medical team prepares Kassidy once again, this time Kassidy cries with anxiety and fear. We pray together; we hold her tight. The medical team allowed dad and I to join her in the surgical room, we held her hand, reassured her that God is with her and will NEVER leave her and when she wakes up, I will be by her side in recovery. As the gas is administered to her small frame, we watch her fall asleep and melt comfortably onto the surgical table. Kevin and I once again walked away trusting in the Lord with tears in our eyes. We have confidence in the medical team. We're good on both items, it's on, and all we can do is wait and trust.

The surgery went very well, the Doctors tell us that there is a chance they may have killed off all of the AVM, we have an appointment in 6 weeks to confirm, if not they may elect to take one more look at it through the catheter. In the meantime, we will rest and heal.

Back at Rady Children's Hospital Room 325 for recovery. RCHSD a safe place for us, familiar faces, Doctors who have been with us from the beginning. Kassidy has a rough night; her catheter is hurting her. I remembered to bring the alphabet chart, Kass spells out "Catheter", I immediately called for the nurse who removed the catheter. Kassidy was finally able to fall asleep fast. She was extubated the next morning and finally able to go "HOME", to really rest and heal.

Friday, December 5th - We love our purple Friday's, we all dress in Purple for Kass!

Chuck - Kassidy's Physical therapist arrived for an early PT session with Kass. 8 AM is a bit early for all of us, but Chuck had a busy day ahead of him. Chuck knows how to get through to Kass, in fact, Chuck built Kassidy a wood bench to fit in the back of our living room. Chuck is able to use the table not just for sitting, but also for the use of tummy work and exercise ball training.

Kassidy sat at the edge of the bench with Chuck and was determined NOT to work out that day. Chuck was talking to Kass in his low/calm voice and asked, "Kassidy, do you not want to work hard today?" Kassidy with frustration and tears in her eyes said "NO" .... Wait, WHAT, she spoke, her 1st word in 4 months and 1 day! Her deep / low voice was direct and angry, but she stopped and realized what she said. Chuck and I looked at each other with our eyes wide open. I yelled for Lexi upstairs, who was still sleeping.

LEXI... Lexi came running to the top of the stairs, then stumbled downstairs to see for herself. Chuck then asked Kass, "should we stop working hard for today?" Kassidy said "YES" ... We screamed at the top of our lungs with excitement and danced around the room. Kassidy sat with Chuck for a minute to soak it all in, she had her crooked smile. Chuck had tears in his eyes... You see, Chuck and Kassidy had this bond, Chuck pushed Kassidy to the point of talking / walking / eventually walking with a cane. Lexi called everyone to let them know the news.

You see this past Monday; our entire family specifically fasted for Kassidy's voice to be returned to us. God allowed her to find her voice. Today we celebrate! We give God the Glory for his endless Grace and Mercy.

December 7th - Kassidy is now able to verbally communicate, slowly and with a very deep voice. Her throat is sore, but we understand her.

Kass is mentioning that it's hard for her to see, we use a patch and switch it from one eye to the other. This is a part of the cerebellum healing.

Tuesday - **December 9th** - We met with the Neuro Ophthalmologist today, Dr. O'Halloran that Kass's eyes are 20/20 looking forward, but has peripheral vision is double vision and blurry.

Kassidy mentions that her body hurts in different areas, but the doctors reassure us that it is her nerves healing. She's more and more depressed, but that too is her brain healing. She cries a lot at night, but we hold her tight and reassure her that everything will be okay. Dr. Levy thinks it's a good idea to start her on a low dose of Zoloft. Those who have TBI (Traumatic Brain Injuries) require a low dose of antidepressants. Thank God it helps our girl.

Kassidy doesn't like all the attention from others, we are inspired by her display of concentration, dedication, and desire to become whole again. She goes about her work in a very quiet and confident way. She seeks no acknowledgment for her accomplishments, she shuns all attention, and she expects no special treatment. She works hard, to the point where she cries out from frustration and pain. Then she stops and she moves on. We take so much for granted in our daily lives, as did she prior to August 4th. Now we measure victories in increments normally reserved for babies and small children. Sit up, one foot in front of the other, one small bite of pudding, roll over, and so on. For her these are the new units of measure. It used to be improving her 5K time or attaining her next test on the way to a 2nd degree black belt or working late at night to maintain her 4.0 GPA. Today she walked 25 steps with help from mom and Chuck, her PT. These are our new measures of VICTORY!

As we pray daily for God to heal us and make us whole, and to stop the pain and suffering. We are reminded:

- I asked God to take away my habit. God said "NO", it's not for me to take away, but for you to give up.

- I asked God to grant me patience. God said "NO", Patience is a byproduct of tribulations. It is granted; it is learned.

- I asked God to give me happiness. God said "NO", I'll give you blessings - happiness is up to you.

- I asked God to spare me pain. God said "NO", for suffering draws you apart from worldly cares, and brings you closer to me.

- I asked God to make my disabled child whole. God said "NO", Her soul and spirit are whole, her body is only temporary.

This is a true reminder that God is in control and allows suffering to draw us closer to HIM.

Kass has been through a total of 8 brain surgeries and procedures over the last 4 months. God delivered her back to us from death's door, that she may become whole and offer her testimony to the world for years to come. We see our job as nothing more than to help her get to the point that she can take care of herself. She is up to the task, and we have made the decision to dedicate our lives to making it happen.

The plan is to wait for about 8 weeks to allow her brain to heal from the last two embolization procedures.

At that time, they will assess the need to perform one more invasive procedure. At that time, they will assess the need to perform one more invasive procedure to get a final look at the site. The Med team is very hopeful that the combination of past procedures has the AVM neutralized. We pray for this every day. Now we continue the rehabilitation process. Kassidy continues with PT, OT, Speech Therapy five days a week, she works hard and never complains...

My dad 's perspective

Kass was in varying stages of a coma for over 4 1/2 months. The first stages were complete unconsciousness, then transitioning into semi-comatose, then the early stages of being fully alert. Every day brought a small amount of progress and an immense amount of hope. We knew we were getting our Kass back, but honestly we were not sure how long the progress would continue before it hit a plateau.

There were many plateaus on her journey back to health.

In typical Kassidy fashion, every time that she hit a new plateau, she kicked that door in and raised the bar again! Her desire to get her health back was simply incredible. Kass was eventually discharged from the hospital. We brought her home in an ambulance to a hospital bed that we set up in our living room. She was all of around 80 pounds, she had a feeding tube in her belly, very limited movement, and required around thew clock care.

Our family accepted the challenge, and we set out to get her well enough for her to return to Rady Children's Hospital for full-time, in-patient rehab. It was a lot of work for all of us, but no one complained. Why? Because we simply watched how determined that she was to come back. We took our inspiration from her, her hard work, and from our Lord and Savior. He showed us the way. We did our part, Kass did her part, and the Lord was our guide.

My Sister Lexis' perspective
Every few weeks Kass would emerge a little more from her coma. The brain is difficult, and healing is so different for every person. There were stages to her 'waking up' from her coma. Some weeks were really hard and frustrating for everyone, other weeks were joy-filled, and progress was made. Of course, the first word she said (yelled) was "NO" to her physical therapists Chuck and Diana. I remember being upstairs just waking up for the day as a sleepy teen and hearing her deep voice. My mom screamed and I ran down. We celebrated! We had waited a long time for that first word.

A few weeks after that she was approved and had made enough progress to be accepted into a full-time live-in physical therapy place attached to the hospital. We knew this would be very telling in her healing journey and tell us a lot about her future. Mom and Kass moved into their room where they would spend 16 weeks in an intensive therapy program. So many different fundraisers and events were being done by friends to raise money for our family to cover the nonstop hospital bills. Dani, my dad and I would go to all of them while once again, Mom never left Kass' side. Kass was never alone, there was always someone sitting or sleeping beside her at home and in hospital.

Kass had to fight every single day. She had to relearn everything. From breathing, to swallowing, eating, sitting up, crawling, walking, talking, writing, feeding herself. She inspired people from all over the world. Her strength would give us strength. Her drive and fight would give us just that.

I mentioned earlier that her journey was and is a marathon. To this day she continues to fight every day and inspires everyone around her. Something simple for me or you are a large task for her. Her body continues to heal and after 16+ brain surgeries, countless hospital stays, hours upon of hours of therapies, health setbacks, and more, there has been an undeniable amount of miracles and blessings, too many to count, that could only come from the Lord and only Kass could do with such grace. I thank God every day for her life and that He saved her that day! There's no doubt her story has furthered the kingdom of Heaven and in that we rejoice!

Sue Muscarella's perspective:

I remember when Kassidy was released from the hospital. Many friends helped to prepare the house for her return. One friend remodeled the downstairs bathroom to accommodate Kassidy's needs. A hospital bed was brought in for her to sleep downstairs. When she came home, she was quite limited in her mental and physical abilities. Her dog "Penny" was a steady presence by her bed. I believe that Penny was instrumental in reawakening Kass to being home and brought her mentally to a place of calm.

Donna was right by her side 24/7. She had a schedule of her daily med's. Therapists came in regularly to assist with her recovery. She wasn't eating solid food at that time. I remember her getting a taste of "cool whip" from a cake and boy did that get her attention. She wanted more and more, but Donna was so sweet and firm in only allowing her a little (for her own good). I will always remember how patient and kind Donna was with Kassidy from day 1....that relationship has only gotten stronger and stronger over the years. Because of the bond they developed through this trial, Kassidy built trust with Donna unlike any I have ever seen with a mother and a daughter.

Lexi and Travis were a fixture in the house. Lexi home schooled for her senior year so she could help with Kass. Travis would quietly sit by Kass' bed and play his guitar in such a soft and sweet way which truly comforted Kass. The whole family rose up to surround Kassidy with "healing love". So many friends showed up in amazing ways to help. Whether it was to donate food, money or pray, it was such a beautiful story to witness the goodness of people rising up to come alongside the Brewer family.

Our family participated in several fund raisers for Kassidy. The first was at the Vespa dealership in Oceanside. Rustico's Restaurant supplied the food, and many donations were given to raise funds for the Brewer family. You could just feel the love and support that their friends in Murrieta exhibited on behalf of Kassidy. It was a privilege to be a part of Kassidy's recovery just to witness the Faith and love of so many people who wanted to help. Many people came to a "Faith in Jesus" through Kassidy's story.

They witnessed the many miracles that took place that contributed to her healing journey and could not deny the existence of Christ. Another fundraiser took place at Kassidy's Taekwondo studio. I remember Kassidy testing and earning her Black Belt. There was even News Media there to cover the event! Kassidy stayed extremely focused and achieved her goal. I was so impressed by her mental focus despite the crowd of over 150 people there witnessing her testing out.

Donna did not return to work. Her new responsibility was to help Kassidy heal from your Brain AVM. They spent many hours at Rady Children's Hospital in San Diego. I know the doctors and nurses were amazed at the miracles they witnessed on Kassidy's journey. I understand they even changed the protocol in the ICU to include "prayer" because of the miracles they witnessed while Kass was in their ward.

Felicia's thoughts

When I heard Kassidy was waking up, I thought pure relief would wash over me, but I also felt a new kind of fear. No one knew what to expect. Would she recognize me? Would she remember all of our shenanigans? Would she even be Kassidy? Walking into that room, I was terrified. She couldn't speak or hardly move. I didn't know what to say, or how to act. But none of that mattered because she was here. My best friend was alive, and that was a flat-out miracle.

What consumes your mind controls your life

I'm going to let you in on something that has really piqued my curiosity lately. Whatever consumes, your mind controls your life. In the aspect that although we are human, we have to accept the fact that we are going to have hard times in life. That's a fact. They're going to come. It's nothing to fear though, because when you truly understand that Yahshua Elohim has already won, conquered, defeated the enemy who's trying his hardest to take you out.

We can be fully confident that the Father within us will fight the battle on His terms. And once we fathom that fact that Christ has already won the battle, it places a further hope in you to carry through. Because He created you for battle. Not in a literal sense, rather a spiritual one. Our time here on earth may seem like an eternity but who are we to speak of something taking too long? Yes, it's not in our timing but that's another story. What if Yahshua has you where you are as a steppingstone to get you to where you need to be?

Authorized Personnel Only
Personal Autorizado Solamente

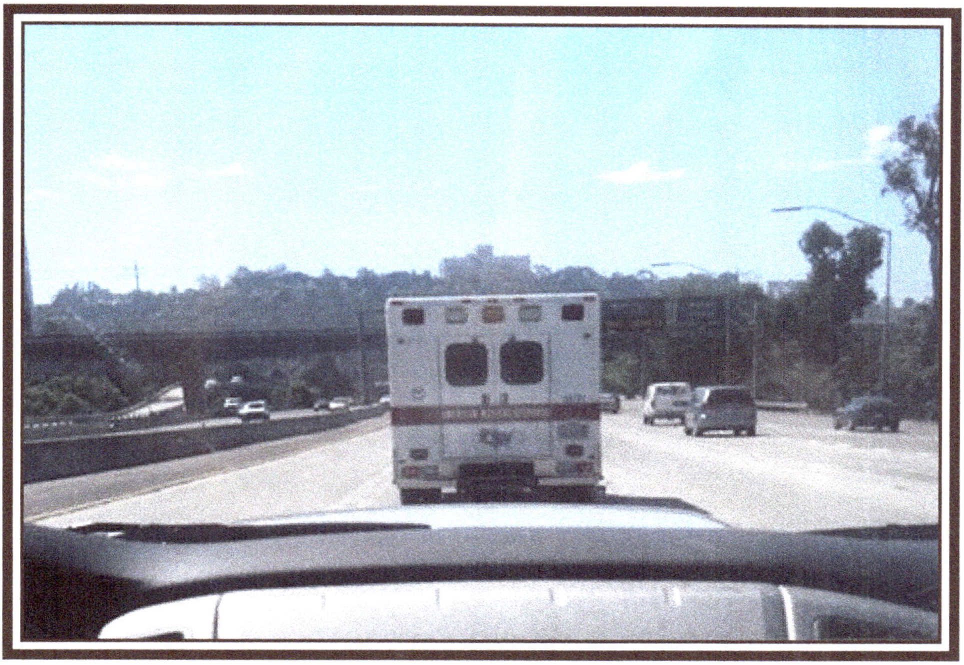

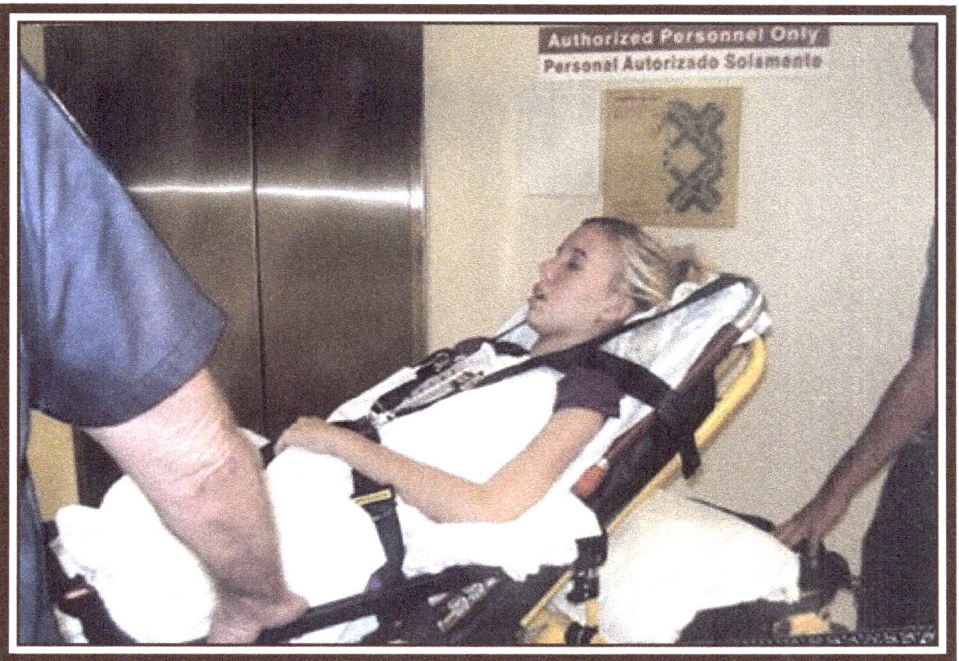

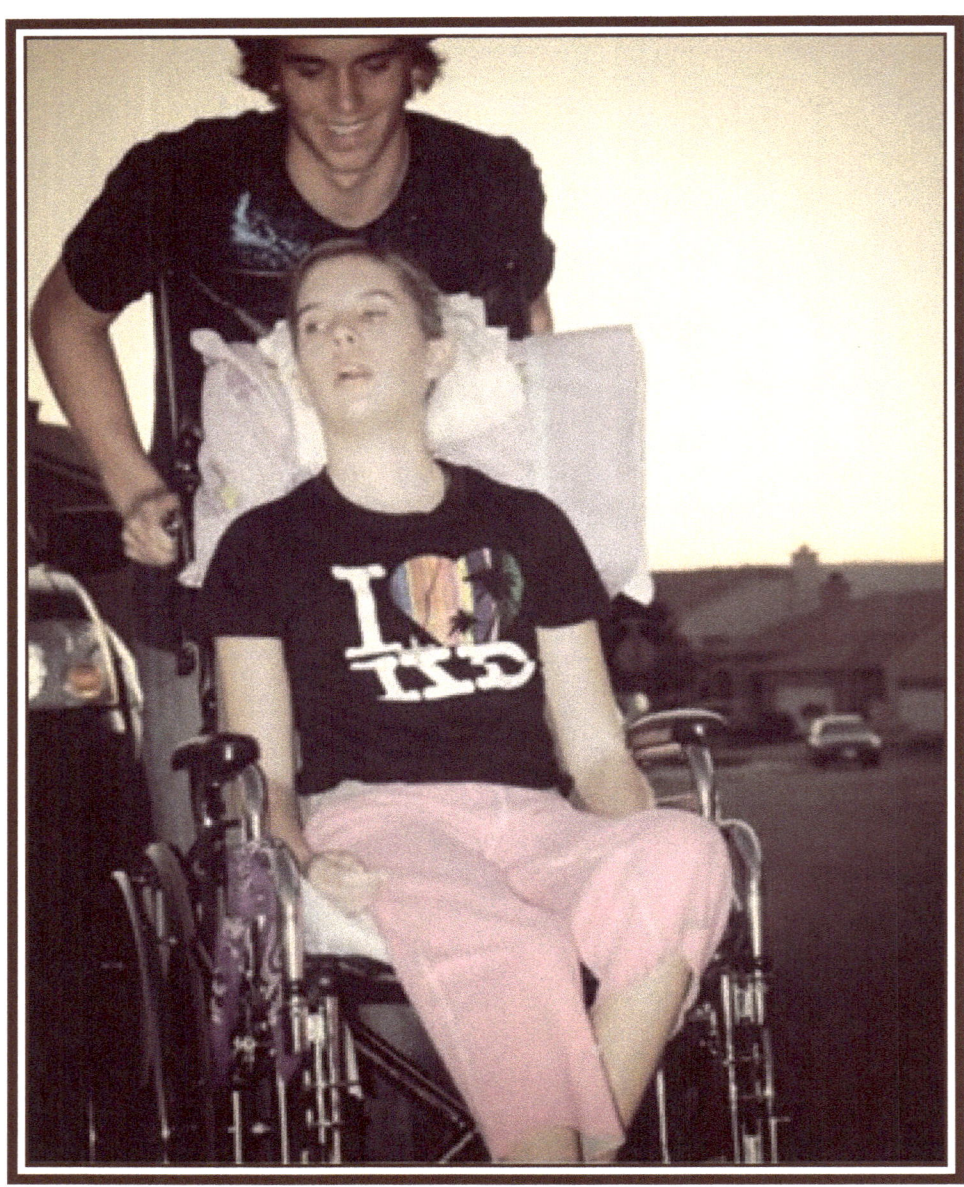

Chapter 10

Scars are more than evidence of trauma;
they're proof of resilience

When my physical scars were very evident and bold, I was quite ashamed of them because of the fact that no one my age had a roadmap on their tummy. I never ended up hiding or trying to cover them up. I had other things to focus on like trying to hold myself up and function as a normal human being. I can remember that with my G-tube, I was extremely fearful of getting that thing out because I had it in my mind that it would hurt taking it out. But that was exactly the opposite of what it entailed.

During one of my surgeries, they ended up taking it out at the same time unknowingly. And to top it off, I have a sweet looking scar to show for it. They call it a second belly button! But I was still fearful of stretching any of my scars, thinking that my insides were going to fall out and it was going to be painful. It was totally understandable to me, but other people just wouldn't understand. It was definitely a mind game. My mindset was altered in a small and significant way, in a way that drastically changed how I looked at not only scars but imperfections as a whole. Scars are more than evidence of trauma. They're proof of resilience.

It reveals strength you didn't realize you had. We need to take into consideration that pain is not just a teacher, it's a sentimental reminder of your ability to withstand adversity. Many times, with adversity comes imperfections and trying your best to get by. It could end in a tragedy; it could end with rainbows and butterflies. But the sole reasoning of it all is the purpose of why you're doing it. Is it to edify you? Is it to edify Yahshua? What are your reasons behind what you do?

Sporadically, I find myself wishing for those scars to reappear. When a scar disappears, it's supposed to be the most exciting thing ever. Right? But I want them to reappear to have tangible evidence of what Yahshua has done. And even though they're not as apparent, having the story to tell of something that was an eyesore to now having to look closely and intentionally, is very relatable to the resurrection. Jesus was here and walked on earth one day. Then He was crucified, thrown into a tomb, and was raised three days later.

See, we all have scars of some sort. Whether they're physical, emotional, relational, scars are scars. They don't go away. They're a part of who you are. This is Christs story in your life. No, horrible experiences are not a walk in the park but learning from them is part of the undertaking.

Deficits I have

After all these unfortunate events, I was left with several life altering deficits from my ruptured brain AVM. Like Vision impairment giving me permanent double vision even after four corrective eye surgeries. Cognitive impairment to where some things I do may not make sense to others, but they make complete sense to me, and I get the job done. Auditory processing disorder, which affects my right ear, I have a hard time fully understanding.

The only outcome is my right ear, meaning that the signal between my ear and brain is broken. Not the hearing part. I also have a rare vascular disorder, resulting in complications with my vessels of the circulatory system in the body including blood vessels, arteries, veins and lymphatic vessels. Also, it left me with balance problems with where I use a walker for long distances. For short distances, we call it "monkeying," because I take a few steps, then bump off of a wall or something or someone, go on my way, do that process again and again until I get to where I need to go.

On the other hand, my stroke is what brought on the Ataxia. That's where you see the constant shakiness on the entire left side of my body. It's very unreliable and causes me to trip or break objects or drop items. It's almost as if I am dancing in my seat because the movement is constant. I get very frustrated with it and everything I do is hard and very defeating but then again, I do whatever works for me and if some people are uncomfortable with what I'm doing, I'm sorry I'm not sorry! That's why I always advocate for, "just being you" because that's exactly what I do. I will only promote what I am proud of.

And when you learn to get past the embarrassment of what other people think, you blossom into a mindset of knowing who you are. That mindset is done out of Yahshua's love when you fully surrender your mind, body, and soul. It will make the struggle that much better. You take them on with ease, knowing that Christ is there to help you along the way. He has already defeated it all, I just needed to focus my mind on Him and let Him take on the issue at hand. I just needed to hand it over to Him in order to progressively see change. Easier said than done, right?

Are you aware that having imperfections is another way that I like to call having prosperous flaws. Those flaws are prosperous because Yahshua takes those imperfections and flaws and uses them for Him. Not for anyone to get the credit but solely Him. Adonai designed every prosperous flaw in you. And because of that, He desires relationship with you. Not only a religious act that you check off of your to do list, but an ongoing, everlasting relationship. He gives me fruitful faith, and I only want to please Him. That is given from obedience through His faithfulness to never leave you. He is not only the way maker of my life, but He directs my steps. Honoring Him along the way, the intense passion of His glory shines in and through me.

When I was going through times of seeing my various imperfections as a burden and shameful, without a doubt I didn't like the new me. But overtime I've realized that it wasn't the one who I didn't like. It was the body that I didn't like. My heart and soul just needed to fully give my life up to its maker. Yes, everything was hard and an effort. From breathing to watching something on TV to talking to someone, having to understand someone talking to me, even thoughts in my own head were hard to make sense of. Everything seemed hard.

Going through life as, "the girl that always had her walker with her," always went through my mind. And when I found "my people" or "my tribe" and they knew that I came with countless tribulations or baggage in my life, many of those individuals stay present with you, because they genuinely want to help you unpack that baggage. They look at your baggage not as an obstacle, but rather they look at it as a challenge to overcome. They will help you.

And that's where finding your tribe comes in. Nevertheless, my walker never slowed me down from living my best life. It was more of a neuro fatigue thing and fatigue in general. Also known as debilitating fatigue caused by the brain, and tiredness of the overall body.

According to brainline.org, neuro fatigue is a decrease in concentration, focus, memory, recall, and word retrieval. This fatigue or tiredness is not the same as exhaustion due to physical exertion, insufficient sleep, or overworking.

"Studies show that because some parts of the brain are injured, the brain of a person with a TBI works harder and uses more brain cells to process information. More brain areas are involved in performing normal activities than pre-injury, which requires extra bypasses in the brain and consumes more energy to complete a simple task or a thought. So, reaction time is slower and requires more energy. Because your brain is still healing, you need to take things slowly. What is most important is recognizing that you are not where you were before your injury and giving yourself the time, patience, and acceptance to heal is crucial."

I have to admit, it did limit me, for several years. Though I sometimes knew my boundaries, when it was time for me to end the day or exit the room, that's exactly what took place. And because that neuro fatigue got me tired for any specific reason, I could only take certain events for a short period of time.

As we read the Bible, it supplies countless stories of noble acts. For example, God uses Abraham and Sarah as a type of exile to be faced with the outlook of a new land. A place of newness that was called upon them. And using their obedience, there's always a blessing to come with obedience to Yahshua. Sometimes we get so complacent in our everyday routine that God brings about change, we may not know reasoning behind it but there's always a purpose in everything.

What Abraham and Sarah went through was a time of discomfort, non-comfort ability that was used for an unknown reasoning at the moment yet was revealed later on. More times than none, we are forced out of our comfort zone for a certain motive and put into unknown territory too. And honoring God is an attribute that I desire. So, taking into account Abraham and Sarah's example of being led into the unknown to restore God's blessing and being obedient is a characteristic I pray for.

This story of Abraham and Sarah very closely reverberates with my story as well due to the unknown territory that I was put in. Their whole life did not drastically change, but they were in a whole new environment. Much like how I had thirteen years, my typical life of being a kid, not having to worry about the details in life to have a whole new mindset and body where everything operates differently.

But Abraham and Sarah encountered a situation in a new land where all they had was the familiarity of each other. When it comes to drastic life changes like these, all we can do is trust and rely on Yahshua for His trust and reliance that everything is going to work together in His timing, not ours.

I've already done enough crying, and that just blurs my vision - even more!

Although my double vision can get in the way of some things, I don't let that stop me from doing and being what the Father called me to accomplish. My progress may have been halted for the time being, but that doesn't mean that it's ended. I don't give up on something just because it's hard or it's not easy. Since when have you ever seen or heard of a victorious person that had an easy life? Never, right? We grow and develop character through trials and tribulation.

And due to that, we view life with new eyes, it may be a challenge to see two of everything, but Christ has lifted that burden to where my double vision is always there, yet it doesn't have a grip on my everyday life. A word of encouragement for those that have had altered vision, speaking of seeing things from a different angle, choosing to see the best, looking for the light at the end of the tunnel. Whatever it may be, we have the choice to choose.

In that case, I'll let you in on my personal secret. Sometimes I have to just step back and laugh at the whole situation, because I've already done enough crying, and that just blurs my vision, even more! It's almost like knowing and believing and seeing there's possibility beyond the storm. Just like the Father doesn't reframe the light from the darkness, He doesn't take away the storm, speaking of the obstacles or challenges, but He contains it.

That's where the challenge of taking life head on to commit to the issue and not back down just because it's hard. Now I know that sometimes you're just over your "challenging days" and you just want an easy break. I fully understand that, but who is there helping you along the way? It's only going to be difficult when you're doing it in your own power. What if there was a chance that it really could happen?

Want to know something most people don't admit or speak about? I pray for challenges. I completely believe that Christ will do something in and through them. Yes, I always have that second thought, "that I'm going to regret praying about this." But then, I slap myself in the face, reminding myself that I have the Holy Spirit in me. I don't need to fear, but to be empowered because He has already triumphed over it. It's the initial empowering feeling that gets me going, then when I'm confronted with difficulty, that's when Yahshua helps me out in the process. It's a team effort.

Having this squad of Yahshua and I, we are invincible together. Have you noticed that the Father doesn't beat around the bush? He's very straightforward in the sense that He quotes everything in a parable but the message behind that parable couldn't relate more to what we're going through at that moment. That's why it's always wise to commune with Him before anything. He already knows the solution it's just in our knowledge and resources to uncover His sayings.

That's the mystery of Christ. He discourages deception and encourages open communication. Just think of a marriage, we need healthy, open communication in order to help it thrive, much like our relationship with the bridegroom. This is also another example of why we should always keep our head on a swivel, because of the deception of the world we live in today.

Like we see, "... leaders can transform themselves into ministers of righteousness..." to where we must be on guard, on the lookout, aware of every move. Not turning a blind eye but not associating with deception. That's where each of us need your help to disassociate from ALL traditions of men. Because it can be the root to deception, weary of false apostles, deceitful workers, transforming themselves into apostles of our Messiah. As found in 2 Corinthians 11:13-15.

In order to completely conquer the assignment, I had in front of me, I had to be able to view the obstacle for what it is. That obstacle was getting through the day. Getting through the day with a mindset that didn't see every movement as burdensome. But setting aside the tears and anger was easier said than done. At that moment in time, all I wanted is for God to take me. That was the reality of the moment, but I didn't have that capability in my blood, so I did what I knew best and let God do the rest. That is determination and inner strength.

Being in Taekwondo, I learned a whole lot! And I really sum up that drive and diligence to Taekwondo. If I continued to sit in my pity of being down in the dump, crying, not improving whatsoever, and turning into a hermit, that'd just blur my vision. And being that I already had double vision, it'd blur it even more. The fact that the Messiah knew exactly what He was doing when He put that spark in me to pursue Taekwondo, He was preparing me for this exact moment.

Silly as it is, no one thought I'd stick with it long enough to develop any skills, but I was persistent. When God ignites a spark of curiosity, pay attention. He might just be preparing you for the day ahead. I've come to the conclusion that the things that break your heart end up fixing your vision the most.

Eye patch pirate

Back in the day when I was undergoing eye surgeries and getting acquainted with my double vision, I was told to wear this eye patch that was supposed to help. Switching it from one eye to the other on a daily basis, it would start to confuse people as to why I was wearing it! That unappealing, pirate eye patch and I hate to break it to you, but the eye patch did not end up working at all. It was more of a social thing than anything!

When we were out and about, we would get these funny looks as to having the patch on the opposite eye the other day. Not knowing that there was a purpose for it. That's why I don't give a hoot as to those people that have a quirk of a look because I've learned overtime that others are going to have their thoughts but they're not your thoughts. You just do what works best for you in your time. Legally and ethically of course!

In Hebrews 10:19-23, the "new and living way" refers to "the way of Yahshua because He calls Himself "the way, the truth and the life." This "way" of life only comes because He "consecrated," meaning He was vigorous in the pursuit of opening your eyes to see all of the many possibilities and lifting the veil from one's eyes'. That is, His flesh. In verse 23, He says that we must cling onto our hope without wavering. It's the spark that ignites our resilience, creativity and determination.

When we hear to lift the "veil," literally meaning gaining new insight through His flesh and awaken to deeper understanding of Yahshua. It's like shedding our old beliefs and perspectives and stepping into a new light of awareness. It brings us to a new interpretation of our perception and relationship with Christ. When that "veil" is lifted, it's as if our thoughts come into direct contact with Yahshua and what He desires for our life.

Subsequently, finding our way in life takes effort and works on our behalf. But then again, it doesn't have to be a struggle. As Philippians 3:21 states, He will transform our lowly bodies. Meaning that, because we struggle and we confront difficult times, we are safe with Yahshua. Although we get ourselves into some sticky situations, He'll never leave you there to where you're stranded.

At the time, you might think so because of the complete agony that you're in, but just remember, He's either building up your character, or you got yourself in this circumstance that needs to be endured to where soon, Christ will help you through it. Reliance on the Father is key in life. And as I lose things in life that weren't mine in the first place, help us to understand that they were created by You to which they are owned by You.

See, when a person has deeper knowledge of Adonai, it helps to better cope. It doesn't make it any easier, but it helps to get to the root of it. "I lose things, that I may gain the knowledge of Christ Jesus." As it states that our citizenship is in heaven, we are made by Christ and through Christ, resulting in the mindset of Christ Himself. While it says that we are residents of Heavenly atmosphere, we need to live in it and walk like it.

Sometimes the cares of this world can get to us affecting our behavior and actions that can end in turmoil. But if we keep the mindset of Christ-like confidence, we will see Fatherly transformation. Conforming with the Father to be used in His duties in this world. Help us to continue to be used by You throughout life and not to be torn down by the devices of the enemy but to be built up by You.

In spite of having countless flaws and ailments myself, going through the layers of healing has not only been an expedition but an adventure. Because when I allowed the Father to take the reins in life and to drive the ship, I began to have a brighter outlook, incremental progression, was a more enjoyable human being to be around. And when an individual is awakened to the fact that Yahshua is King, there's divine interpretation and guidance. The thought of doing life myself brought on fears. Fear and anxiety over the future crippled me. It brought on uncomfortability and disturbances in life. That's when God said, step aside.

As we read in 1 Peter 2, we are hand-picked by Yahshua and precious in His sight. Often times, following God means that we are going to be rejected and talked down by men. And although it hurts, it might be God 's way of protecting you and saying that you are His and no one can touch you. It's His protective hedge around you. He cherishes those who are disobedient, due to their belief. They believe because they do not see. It's a belief in your heart that can only be produced through Him and by Him. Disobedience does not come from a lack of faith, but human will.

Humans think that they can do life on their own, and that may be true to a certain extent, but then the world comes crashing in. Because disobedience is our human nature, we strive to live in a Christlike manner. We stumble and fall, but we always have to remember, we were hand selected for this exact time. To be a Christlike example for our brothers. And because we are appointed people, we have to keep the perspective that we are called out of darkness. Out of those difficult times that we were in, doing life on our own. We were hand-picked to proclaim the praises to which we were called into his exuberant love.

Don't offer a lecture to a person who needs a hug.
When you work hard on something and afterwards, you are as tired as an Olympic swimmer, don't you feel the need to look back at your efforts and get some much-needed rest. That's kind of like what Jesus portrays when He made the earth in six days and rested on the seventh day. Similar to that individual that you know nothing about, our duty is not to bombard with questions but rather to love like Christ. To offer a hug or a kind word to that person that needs a break instead of a lecture.

Bringing compassion into the eyes of humankind regarding one's work of what their hands have done made a recipe for disaster. That's where vanity comes into play. It's looking at what we ourselves have made and giving ourselves credit and glory for what was done. Not giving credit to Yahshua, He is the one that gave us the power in order to perform that task.

We do realize that Yahshua brings opportunities to us and it's up to us to either shield our eyes or follow through with the process. It's all a choice. That's where free will comes into play, when we apply humility in our actions and give credit to where credit is due, the Father directly has an impact. Just like His word says, "wisdom is more useful than foolishness."

If acting out and living for the world was praised, we would get glory and have temporary satisfaction in life, whereas wisdom is a long-lasting cycle of belief in Yahshua! And as we hear the term, "feeding on the wind," it's basically stating that there is emptiness of pursuing the world. And when we realize this, vanity and having to take matters and our own hands, becomes a thing of the past. It will most likely always be present, but when Yahshua is by your side, you can be reassured that humility is the goal in this race called life.

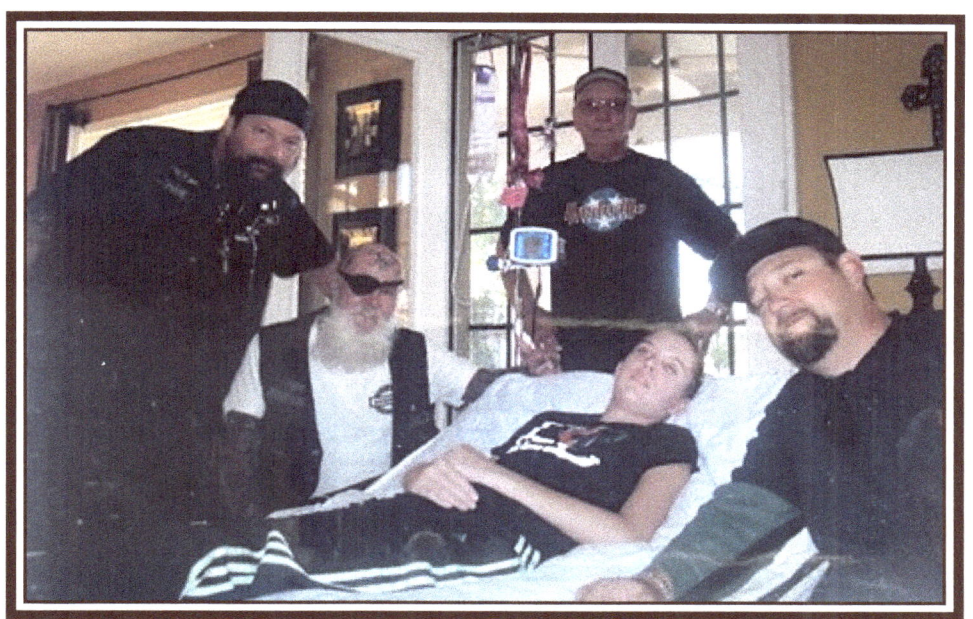

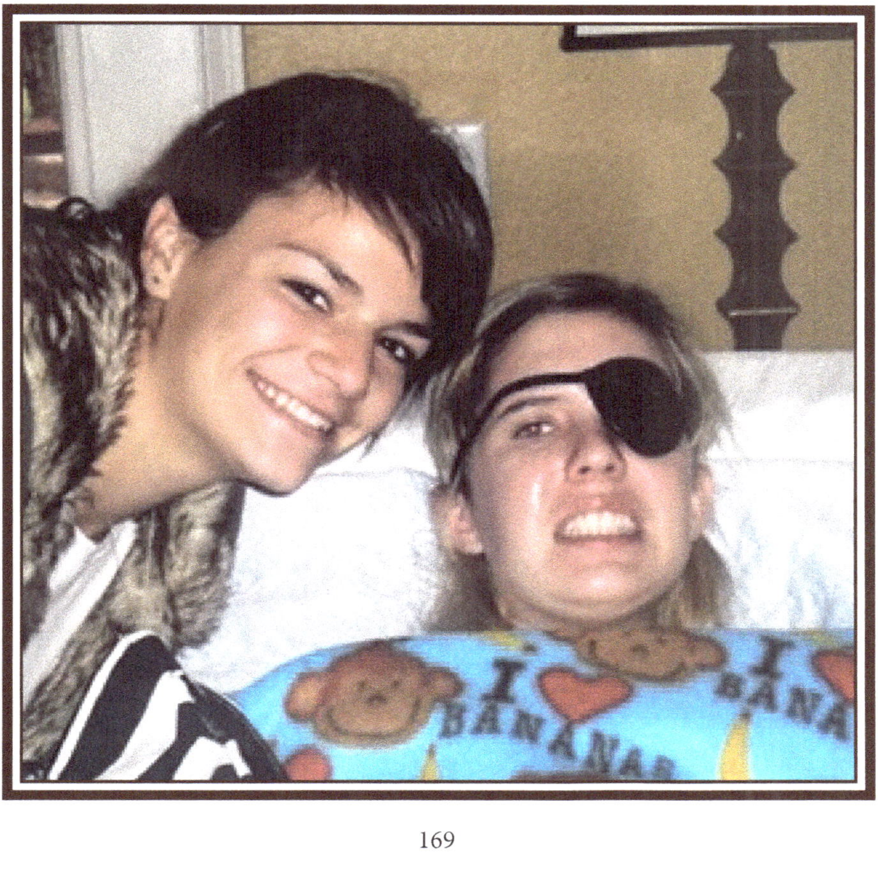

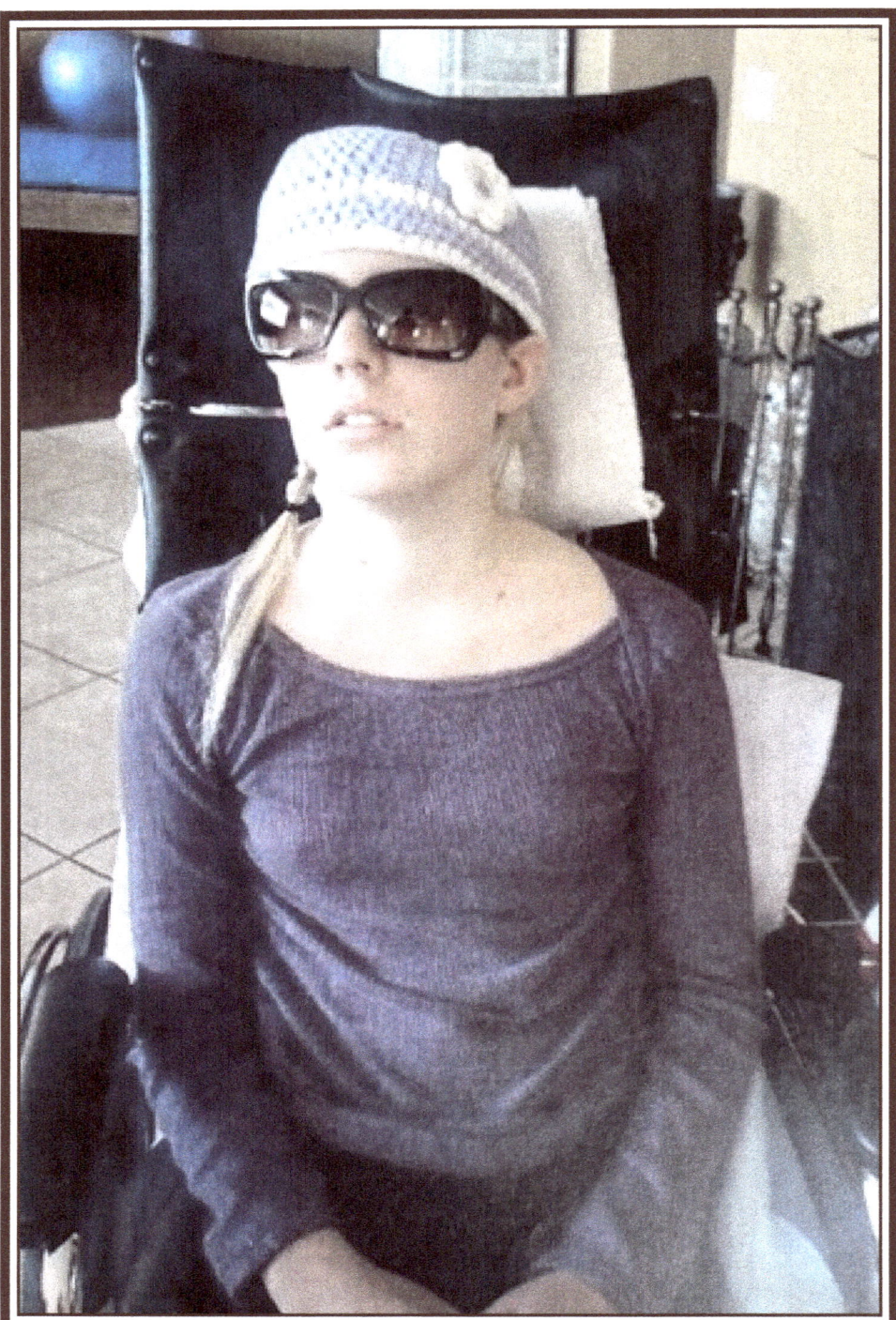

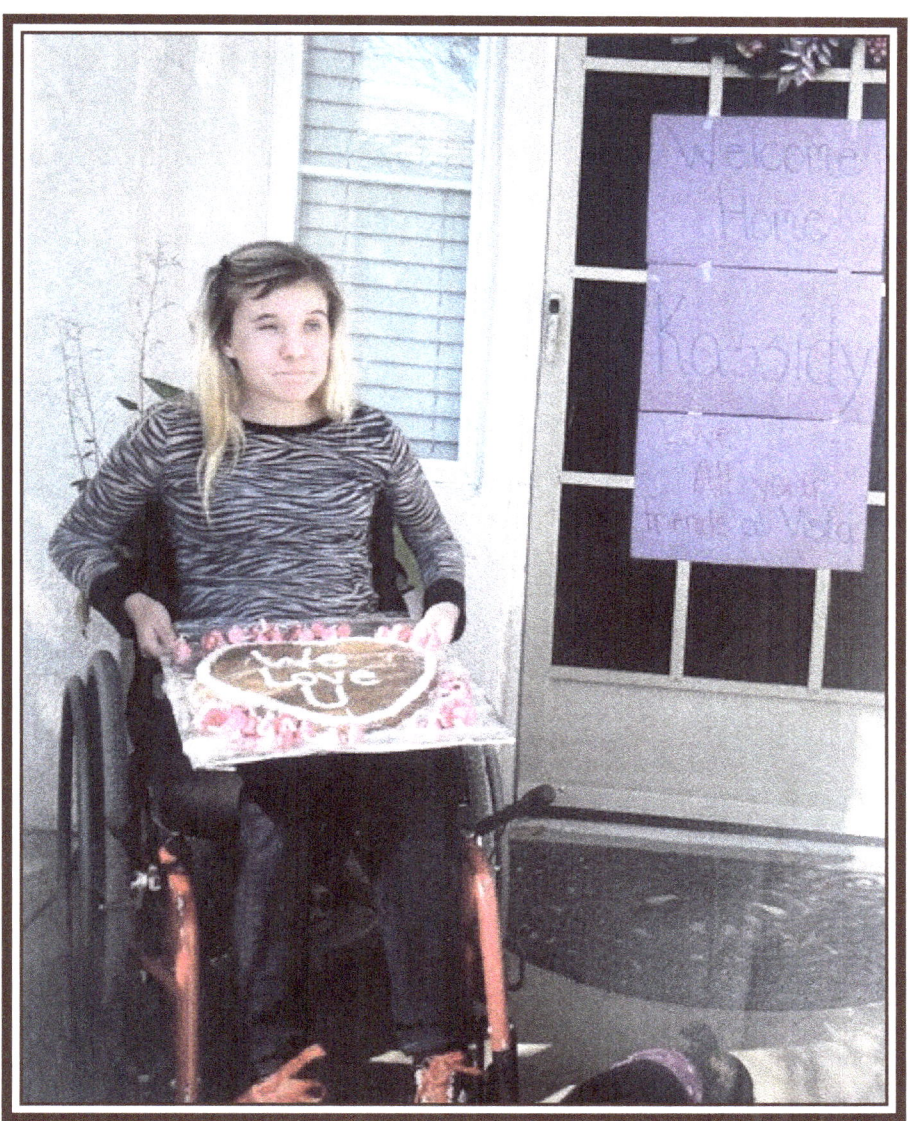

FROM THE LIBRARY OF

Kassidy
Brewer

Chapter 11

First word with Chuck

Just to be real, I did not like Physical Therapy very much. I had to get up early, exercise, and do things I was uncomfortable with. I just wanted to lie in bed. I was super exhausted, but the healing had to take place to get me to where I am today. With that, we had an in-home physical therapist, Chuck, who was absolutely incredible. It was an earlier weekday morning: it was just my mom and I downstairs with Lexi upstairs sleeping in. No one else was home; it was a therapy session kind of day. I was ready to work hard.

Not talking yet, Chuck was a past Black belt, and he understood the brain. Much like me. He knew all of what I was capable of, so we took baby steps on getting there. We had this therapy bench that was about three feet tall and about six feet long. We would sit on the edge of it, to work on some drills. If you think about a newborn baby practicing holding their floppy neck up, that's exactly the state that I was in. It was tremendously painful to learn how to relearn to hold my neck up a second time.

With that endless pain brought on annoyance and anger. Silly enough as it is, when a person gets frustrated, they end up saying either cuss words or throwing in the towel. I kind of did both in a clean way. Audibly, I said the word "no," in a really deep and low voice. It was the first word that I spoke in five months and one day! And my Physical Therapist of all people brought that out of me. When tedious frustration hits, there's no stopping you. My mom ended up yelling up the stairs at

Lexi who was sleeping in her room. She yelped, "Lexi, Lexi, she said her first words!" As Lexi came running down the stairs in a panic, they both held each other and cried happy tears. Praise be to Jesus Christ!

Chuck Bellah's' words

Kassidy Brewer is one of those rare individuals who conquers adversity with incredible courage and resilience. She is indeed one tough woman. I first met Kassidy in her mid-teens shortly after she experienced a ruptured brain aneurysm, leaving her unable to move or speak. I was her physical therapist. Over the many months of therapy, I became a witness to a deep determination within her that rivaled those who had much fewer initial physical, cognitive, and verbal challenges.

I was blessed to witness her first words since her injury as I was strongly encouraging her to push herself beyond our prior attempts with standing. (Admittedly, she was a bit cranky that day) I tried to push her beyond her tolerances a bit too far and I was met with an abrupt but very clear "NO!" For anyone that was in the room and heard her annoyance with me, it was heaven-sent music to all of our ears. From that point on, she began accelerating in her progress and providing ever more words of disagreement with me though those were rare (and usually came with a sly smile) as she appreciated the great results she was experiencing.

Those were challenging times for Kassidy, but she has translated that difficult and heart-breaking experience into a level of God-blessing compassion, that only a very few have, for others and their variety of challenges in this life. As a result of her transformational experiences, Kassidy will provide her unique insights to help others to progress to a higher level of vitality, health, and love of the life that we have all been blessed to have. On a personal note, I have been blessed to meet and know Kassidy and appreciate greatly all the periods of time that we share.

Yesha & Yahshua

Yahshua our Father, we do so because the word means salvation, as does the word Yesha in Hebrew. Yesha; generally, is construed as meaning liberty, deliverance, and prosperity: i.e., safety, salvation, or saving. Yahshua means he will save; Jeshua, the name of ten Israelites, also of a place in Palestine: Jeshua.

Never give up hope from Yahshua. He far exceeds our expectations!

Medication madness days

Still on countless medications for various reasons and in my high-back wheelchair, we lived in an area that had few cars pass by. But it was very exciting and peaceful to sit at the front door looking outside. We had a screen door and of course, Penny was right next to me. Bonus points for when someone came over to visit. We would be the first ones to greet them. Our kitchen was down a hallway and around a corner, so I was inside and safe but not supervised. My mom was typically in the kitchen, and she would periodically check on me.

Pumped up with who knows what kind of meds, let's just say, I wasn't myself. Secretly, I would try to stand up and open the screen door very quietly so my mom couldn't hear me. What

I had all planned out was to hop on top of the somewhat hard Styrofoam planter directly outside of the front door. It was going to take me "Away." Don't laugh, this was a serious problem. Medication side effects are real. I believed that it was a space shuttle that was going to take me back to my old self. That this was all a dream and that the clock could just turn back. In my medication madness days, I had a very reconstructed mindset.

Thank God those times were only temporary because they weren't only difficult on myself but everyone that had to endure it. Remember how I spoke about Job? Job wished he were never born during his difficulties in life. I guess we all have those times of doubt and disparity. Nothing like Job though. His whole life was shaken and turned upside down. I'm not idolizing Job for his automatic faith, I'm just extremely envious and deeply desire how Job turned his despair into praise so automatically. But, when he was wishing how his day of birth perished, it's understandable because that just goes to show us that he is human. Those human emotions do exist.

While the Father knows us from the inside, he knows what will come out of this heartache. So, when Job asks, "why was I not hidden like a stillborn child?" I think Yahshua was saying, "we're going to have ups and downs in life, this is a low point, but I'm bringing forth your character, just hold tight and wait and see what I have waiting." Then, to bring more insight, in verse 20, enduring any hard time, in the actual moment, I'm sure we're thinking something similar, rocky roads tend to bring out the worst in us. And while I wasn't able to control my mental health, the assortment of medications was lifesaving, providing life to these bones which I am ultimately very grateful for!

Although there were adverse effects, that time of complete denial had to happen. It's a part of the grieving process. It's actually healthy to experience all of the stages of grievances. But getting to the root cause and not only thinking about our circumstances, authorizes Christ to turn it around to use for His good. Just like in my story, Yahshua allowed this tragic ruptured brain aneurysm and stroke to happen to my mortal body but also allowed my friends and family members that watched the true battle take place behind the scenes. It's not only an ongoing process but a rowdy and messy journey to follow along on! Christ has His final say in each setting. Whether it is good or not so good, whatever it is, just remember who has the final input. The battle is never truly over until He says so.

Have you ever tried to describe yourself in one word? If you were interviewing for a new position at work today and they asked you to tell them about yourself in one word, what would you say? You want to be truthful and transparent, but you also want to speak highly of who you are. When I collided with the consequences of the medication that kept me alive, it completely jacked up my stomach to the point where I couldn't do anything but lay on the couch in agony. I didn't have any other choice but to endure the pain.

After years of this, I began to ask Yahshua why this, why now? Unfortunately, sometimes we have to go through those things that are messy, we have to make those mistakes and learn as we go. Confidence is built in those gnarly parts of life.

Perfection is the enemy of progress.
The people that seem to have it all together are going through life in two different ways. They're either drastically faking it, or

they have gone through their storm, or they've without a doubt let Christ rule over their life. The moral of the story is, they didn't wait until everything was perfect to start. Once I was on the path to helping out my gut, Yahshua led me to resources. I didn't need to be perfect; I just needed to move forward. It took too much effort to understand the whole path, but Christ is saying, just take the first step, see what I can do.

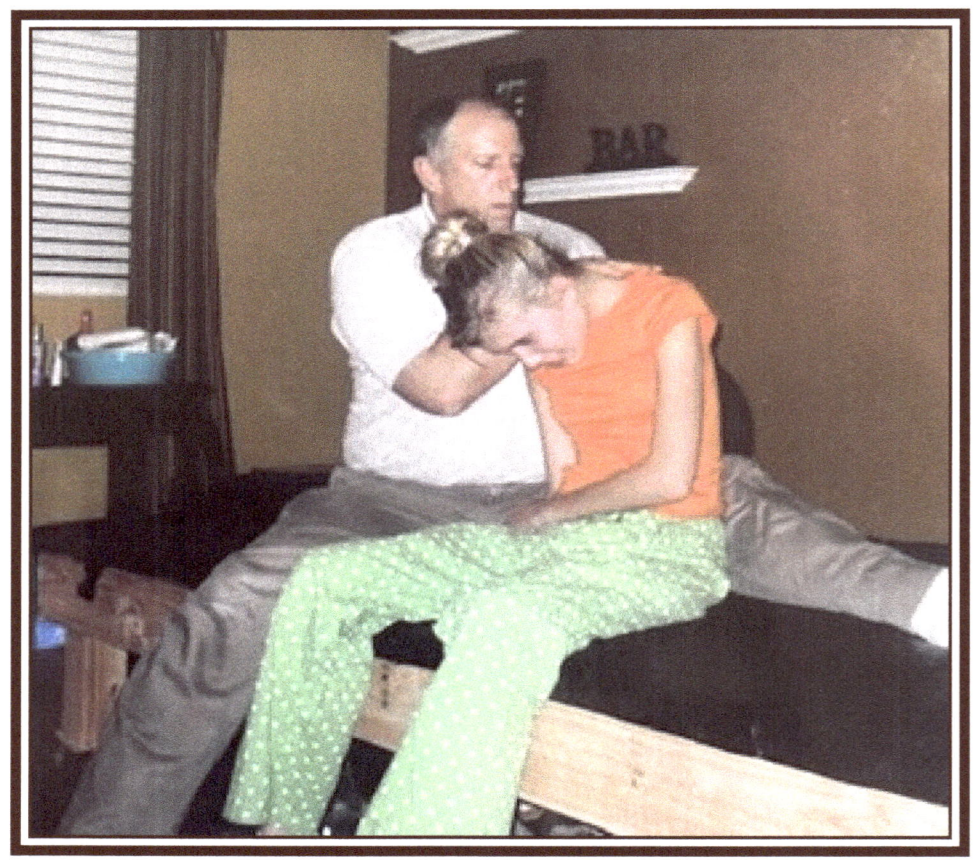

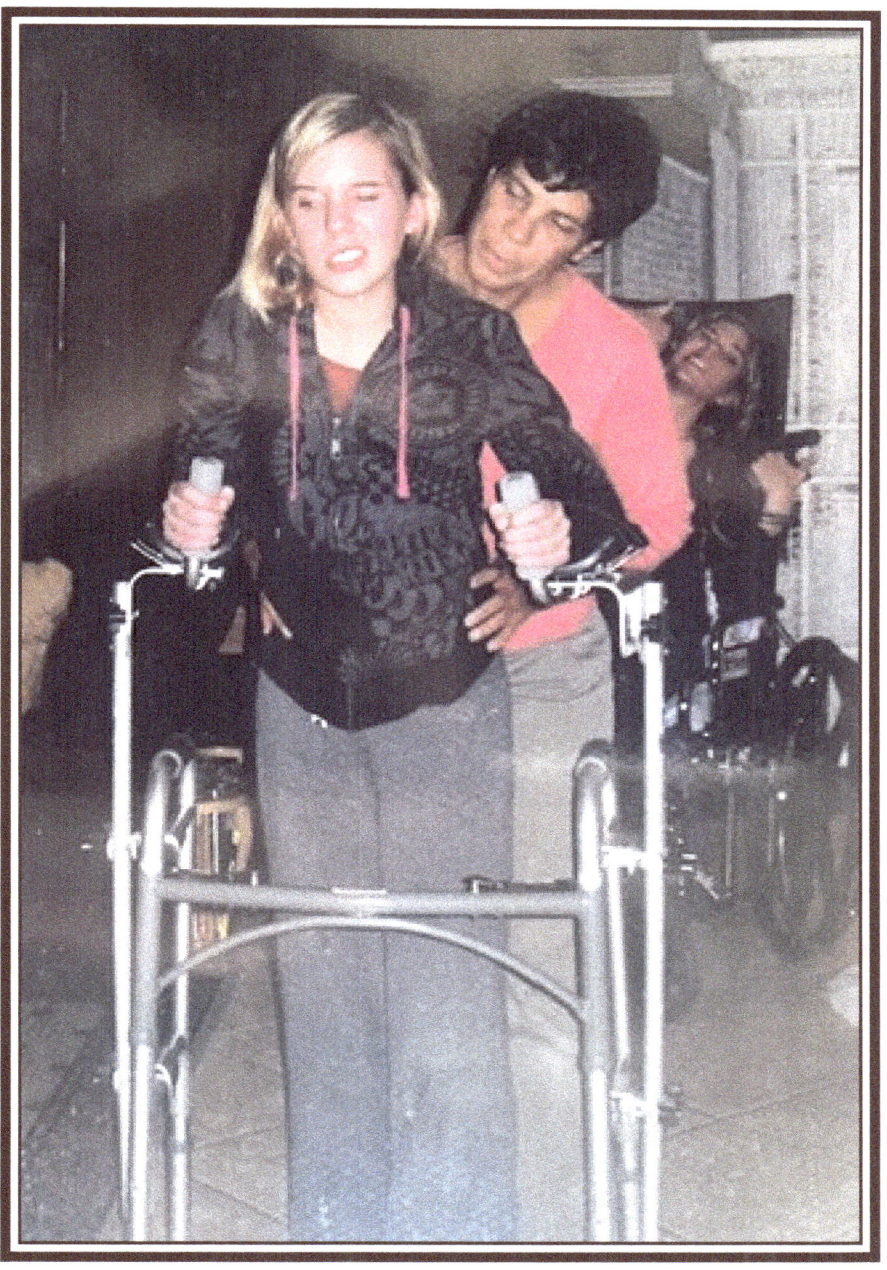

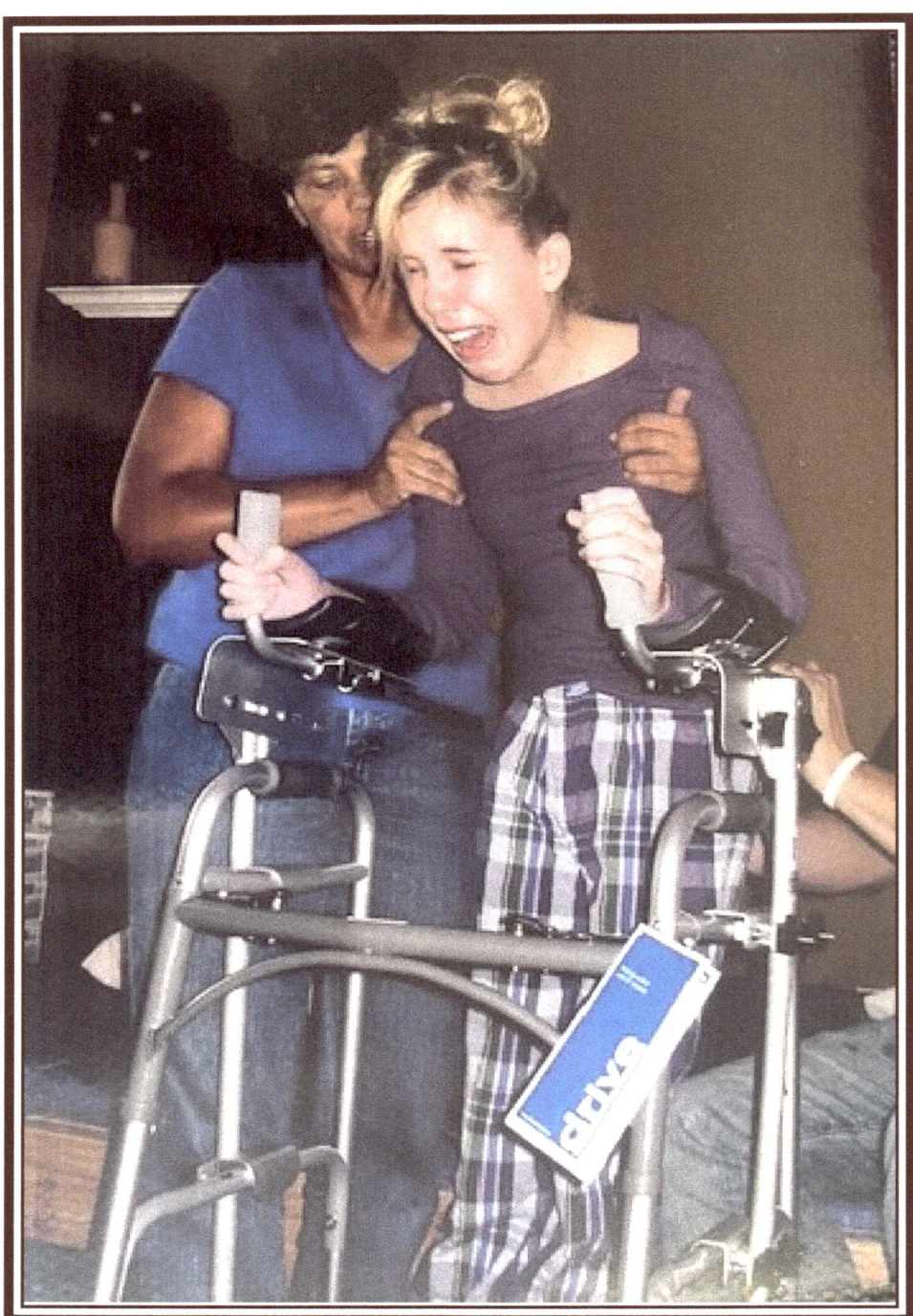

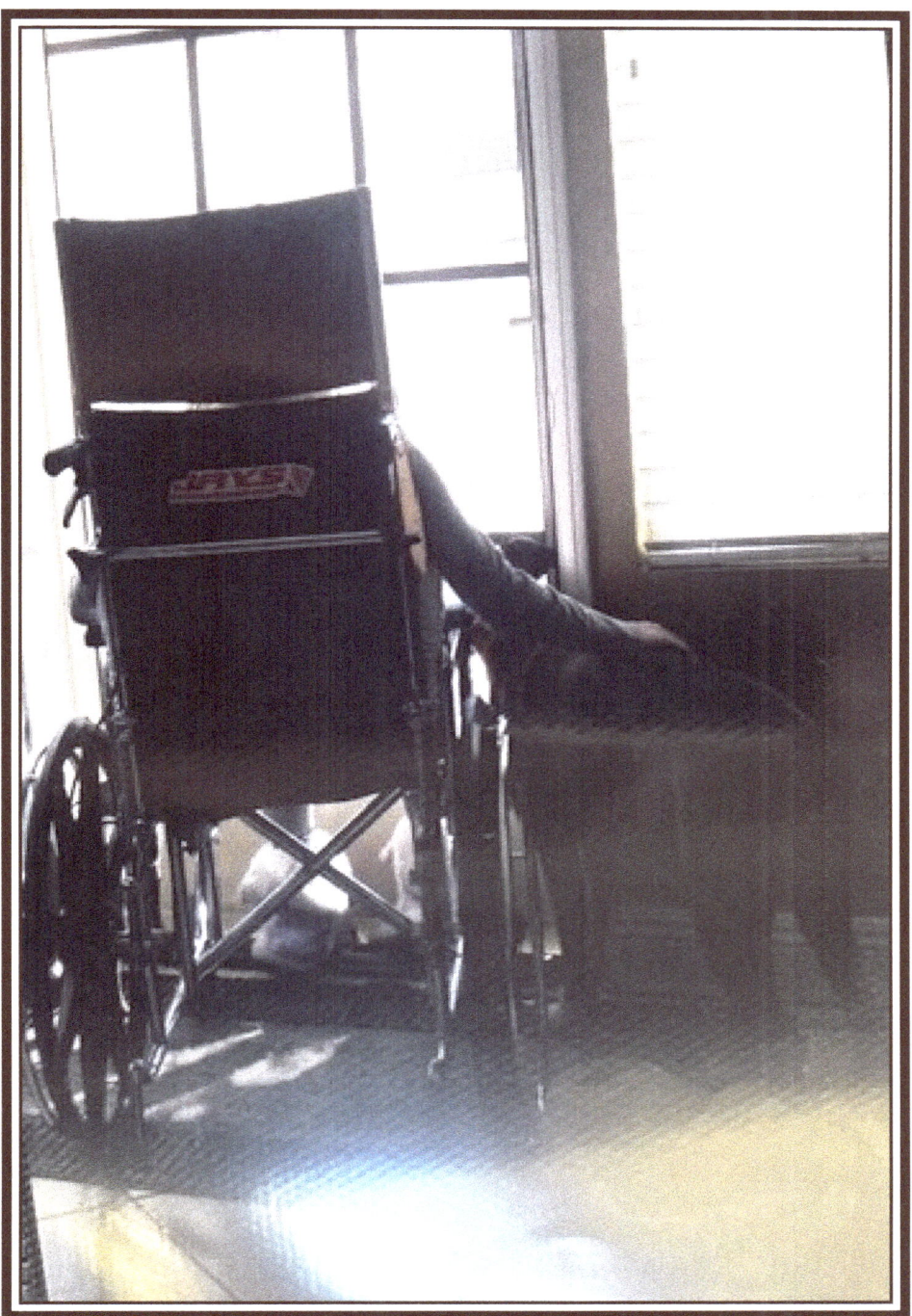

Chapter 12

Otho rehab & Cheesecake

The following week, I went into in-patient ortho rehab at Rady Children's Hospital San Diego. My mom and I stayed there for sixteen weeks for intense rehabilitation. I went into rehab in a high-back wheelchair enduring the struggle to get through the day. I was not happy with life, just to be real. I was stuck in a sad, dark, depression state of mind, but that was just the beginning of my healing process.

Setting goals was one of my passions, it was something that I always did, and it was entertaining to watch the barriers be broken down. The struggle is real with how hard the challenges were to take on, but nothing that can't be worked on and slowly progressed overtime. Once I was in ortho rehab, it was like the fundamentals and foundations of life kicked in and everything started coming back to me. Slowly but surely things started happening.

Ortho rehab basically involves a team of healthcare professionals, including physical therapists, occupational therapists, and orthopedic specialists. All working together to create a personalized treatment plan. The goal was to help the patient, myself, regain mobility, strength, and function to return to my normal self. Some people are in their short term and some long-term period, all depending on your injury or surgery. It's pretty much like an intense Physical Therapy all wrapped into one.

While I was in for rehab, I had set six goals. They're the simplest tasks, but when you're focused on recovery full-time, they seem very daunting. The goals that I set out to achieve were:
1. To walk out of camp (ortho rehab)
2. Going into the bathroom
3. School – improving on my writing/learning/computer skills
4. Using arms and hands and keeping them steady
5. Sitting cross-legged on the floor
6. No G-tube – getting all of fluids and nutrients through mouth and not feeding tube through my stomach

I'm happy to announce that I proudly hit every single one of those goals! Not only because I was determined and diligent, but because I am a daughter of the King and He was right there by my side, helping me through and pushing me on and encouraging me of all that he says that I am. In addition to those goals, every day I was presumed to participate in occupational therapy, physical therapy, school, speech, psychology… Getting back to your normal self is intense and not for wussy's!

Continuing in my endeavors, working hard round the clock was extremely tiring. As you can imagine, I felt like I wanted to throw in the towel due to learning the simplest functions. But legitimately, I didn't know any better. It was truly like I forgot how to do anything and everything. It was grueling and taxing on not only my mind but my body also.

It reminds me of Psalm 84:11, "no good thing will be withheld," many people take this out of context or read through it with the wrong motive. We have to remember, bad things come and go. It might be because He is growing your character, it might be one of Satan's tactics, it might be that your God is teaching you something in that instance, whatever it may be, what remains is the provision and protection from Yahshua Himself. But in that moment of pain and hostility, we tend to only read that verse alone, that's why reading a chapter or paragraph at a time, ties it together. Because in verse five it says, "Blessed is the man whose strength is in You."

Through my difficulties in carrying on, I knew Yahshua Elohim was with me. I would not have been able to proceed in my own strength. While miracle after miracle took place in this journey of relearning pretty much everything, I can honestly say that Yahshua was in the midst of it all.

In the course of having to do multiple vigorous therapies, during school (therapy) they would give me worksheets to work on to do the simplest tasks. I.e. Writing the alphabet, adding up single digits, anything to get my mind in motion. But, having a new brain injury and working on daily living exercises again and again was extremely difficult, let alone with double vision. The thing is, I didn't know how to vocalize it yet. So, during an eye exam is when they find an issue. When I was relearning numbers and letters, I saw two of them. Causing repetitiveness and confusion.

To help modify my schooling, the therapist gave me a pencil with a large gripper on it to hold onto my fingers. I didn't even know how to hold onto a pencil the right way. Also, my daily living skills needed to be worked on too. For example: brushing my hair, navigating the room in my wheelchair, transferring from my wheelchair to the bed, etc. I had these therapies every single day and was worked to get me back to baseline. And in addition, speech therapy kept me going strong. Practicing articulation of my words.

My mom and I were inseparable. As the rest of my family was sitting by the phone to get the phone call of the next big thing that I accomplished, they were getting back into the swing of their routines as well. During those sixteen weeks, when my mom watched me regain and win back my stamina, relearning how to do the simplest things. While we were in my ortho rehab room, we were sitting on the edge of the bed waiting for my next therapy session to take place. That's when we got creative. We started thumb wrestling or have a thumb war match out of boredom. That is the moment that I started to giggle for the first time. I finally got my giggle back. Of course, the nurses had to see it. It was truly a sight. After not talking for five months and one day, that was huge!

In my mind, I knew I wanted to get back to the usual Kassidy no matter how long it took. So, I made it my goal to get back in skinny jeans. No more of these diapers. Yes, I was in diapers for quite a while. Another challenging goal to get over was using the toilet. We made it fun and interesting. You know me by now; I am a goal setter. And just an FYI, I am motivated by money! So, we made it interesting and with every trip, I got rewarded for a quarter and we put it into a glass jar to see it. I can probably say that that goal was accomplished within four to five weeks!

However, I was still having a difficult time swallowing typical foods, and even the simplest foods were making me aspirate. I tried countless different textures from milk to pudding to Jell-O, you name it. I tried it. The only thing that seemed to be perfect consistency was cheesecake. I had cheesecake two to three times a day! And it wasn't the good for you kind of cheesecake!

But you know what, I got down to seventy-eight pounds when I was in a coma where no one stopped me from enjoying myself. It was kind of a commencement celebration kind of thing. And after eating that delicious solid exquisite piece of joy, I ended up gaining fifty pounds! That's right, you read that right!

All of my goals were extremely challenging to conquer, but I continued because that was the way of life. I didn't want these simple daily tasks to weigh me down, I wanted to hit them on the mark because they were my goals and I had it ingrained in me that goals are something to be achieved, not roadblocks. So, I quickly began putting each and every goal into action.

Imagine yourself in a mind that is just waking up in the morning after you've had the greatest night's sleep. You're probably groggy, you don't know where you are, and it feels like your body has weights on it. Now multiply that by thirty. I was in the hospital in a coma for so long, my family learned how to do so much of what the nurses were already doing. So, after quite a few attempts to get me released, I was finally brought home while still in my coma.

That was pretty much where I was. I was in the hospital, then I was taken home to be more coherent, several weeks later is when I went back to the hospital to go into ortho rehab for sixteen weeks. Thats where I learned the fundamentals of everything. Again, it was no walk in the park but that forward movement went to show me that Yahshua has never left my side despite the challenges.

Challenges are exactly what they are, difficult. But I had to take into account that there's no difficult thing unless I decide it's a difficult thing. If not, it's only another challenge to beat. See, we each have in us the free will to pick and choose. We can choose this or that in a physical sense, but God has also given us the capability to have knowledge. Knowledge of knowing when a challenge comes. Knowing whether we struggle or thrive in the situation we're in.

With the mentality I was in, I honestly didn't think twice about the challenges. Looking back, yes, they were harder than heck, but I didn't have that ability to overthink, because goal setting is in my DNA. All I knew is that I had a goal to work on.

Overthinking keeps you stuck. Focus on what you can do today and let the rest reveal itself as you go.

My mom's thoughts

Kassidy was accepted to go into Full time, In- patient Ortho Rehab at Rady Children's hospital, we are calling it "CAMP". Now that Kass is following commands and is verbal, she has met the criteria, and we are ready. Kassidy and mom will live at RCHSD for 6-8 weeks. We will pack our bags and be ready after Christmas to get our girl on her feet again.

December 20th - Kassidy had a swallow test done, we are able to eliminate one of her feedings. She is able to swallow thick consistencies, such as mashed potatoes, pudding, cheesecake, peanut butter cups, roasted carrots, scrambled eggs and bananas. We even used the magic bullet and pureed pizza, as well as, In and Out burger! She loved it! Kass is working hard to get the feeding tube out her stomach, but terrified about Doctors taking it out.

We are heading back to Neuro Ophthalmology - Kassidy is complaining about her left eye. Her double vision is frustrating... We continue to use the patch alternating each eye every 2 hours. We pray that this too shall pass. Christmas 2008 was incredibly special. We are home together as a family, we don't need anything this year, we have everything we need. Our greatest gift was God healing our girl.

Monday, **December 29th** - Kass had another breakthrough today. With all of her progress, it's very easy for us to forget that she has a couple of more coma stages to work through. Well, today she started passing through STAGE 4. This stage is punctuated by confusion, irritability and sometimes aggression. Up until today, Kassidy has been very eager to please and was totally compliant with everything that was asked of her.

Today, she became more like a teenager, Kassidy tells me that she wanted to "Go away". She's been saying this periodically, but we thought that perhaps she was trying to tell us that she was feeling trapped in her body and that she wanted to break out. As Kassidy and our boxer, Penny sits by the front door, with the screen door closed, I listen to Kass kick the screen periodically, but this time I hear the screen's soft squeak. I look around the corner and I see Kassidy out of her high back wheelchair trying to climb on the planter box.

I dash out the front door to help her down, and to make sure she doesn't fall on her head. She screams and say's "Away, away" ... She's getting a little more aggressive and stronger by the day. I ask her where she is going, where does she want to go? She screams again "away". Her cries and despair are painful to watch. I struggle to put her back in her wheelchair.

Not sure what happened, I called Kevin to come home. Something has changed, the aggression has started, and I don't know what to do, I need HELP!

Little did I know Kassidy thought the flower box was a spaceship that was going to take her away to August. Finally, Kevin arrived home from LA, Kassidy said to her dad she wanted to go to 38209 Augusta Drive, which was our old address. Her dad confirmed that it was our address, we're here now Kass. She said, "I know, but I want to go back to August. Kass continued and said, "she did not get sick". She wanted to go back to before she got sick.

It broke our hearts. We couldn't change her circumstances; we couldn't fix her. Kassidy's brain was healing; she had displayed very few signs of confusion until now. She didn't remember anything, The circuits are rewiring and finding new pathways. Kassidy feels sort of like she is in a dream, and that if she goes back to August, that we will all be there together and she will be able to undo her current situation.

We decided that it is time for Kassidy to get back to normalcy, for her to finally sleep in her bed, upstairs, with her sister Lexi right next door and mom and dad in the next room as well. We brought in a flat screen TV for her to watch her favorite shows. Here we are, almost 4 months after the brain aneurysm, life is turning around, we feel the excitement of Kass' healing, one day at a time...

We understand that Kassidy still requires diapers, she is now able to rotate in her bed by herself and use words. Life has become easier the past few months; however, we knew we had a long road ahead with therapies, surgeries, and inpatient rehab. Every day is a journey; however, we do understand the assignment from God, we have a front row seat to witnessing a TRUE MIRACLE.

Monday, **January 5, 2009,** arrives, we are off to RCHSD for Inpatient Rehabilitation (we call it CAMP Rady!). Kassidy is not too stoked on it, but she'll do fine when we get there. Well, we had a difficult time getting her into the truck today, she is suffering from temporary delusional behavior. This behavior presents itself through inappropriate behavior, confusion and passive aggressive behavior.

She's smart as a whip, and does not miss a beat, yet she'll tell you that she did not get sick, and that we (The Brew Crew) are not real. She explained to mom how to program the DVD player to sync with her new flat screen, then went on to tell us that she needs to go away, then proceeded to tell us that she would get there through a planter box on the front porch. Heartbreaking, interesting, fascinating, as she works her way through this phase.

In many ways, it's like being around a frustrated genius, someone who is so intelligent, yet perhaps out of control. Doctors tell us that this is a normal part of the healing process and again, Kassidy wakes up from her coma. We finally arrived at Rady Children's Hospital Rehab. Staff members were anxiously awaiting her arrival, you see when we left ICU back in October, Kassidy was still in the first stages of coma. Nurses and Doctors heard that Kass was making significant improvements.

Her miracle had touched the lives of more health care professionals than we had ever realized. We had an endless stream of people stopping by to say hello to Kass. We are truly overwhelmed by the outpouring of love and compassion. This in itself is amazing considering the fact that Kass has virtually NO recollection of ever being at Rady 3 months prior. Kassidy and I get unpacked in our room, ready for weeks of intense therapies. We hang lights, add purple blankets on Kass' bed and extra pillows for more lived-in-dorm room decor.

Kass had a prescheduled appointment with Dr. O'Halloran, the Neuro Ophthalmologist, Kassidy's left eye was still giving her a lot of issues, and her double vision was frustrating for her to focus. We scheduled eye surgery for the following morning. CAMP or inpatient rehab is a series of intense therapies, such as: Speech Therapy, Physical Therapy, Occupational Therapy, self-sufficiency therapy, school, Neuropsychology. Kass had little down time, but when she did, we watched movies and thumb wrestled, played games, and prayed.

January 7th - Rehab is going well, today is eye surgery day. Kass won't talk to anyone, she knows another surgery is happening and she won't have it. She repeats, with a low deep voice "NO BOTOX", "NO BOTOX". Lexi and I did our best to push Kass in her wheelchair down the hallways of the surgery center at Rady, she screamed at the time, dragging her feet. We finally arrived, as the nurses see Lexi and I struggling, they help us take Kass to an isolated room, her screams echoing through the entire Hospital wing.

Thank God Dr. O'Halloran and Dr. Khanna, our ICU Doctor came to the rescue and tried to talk Kass through the procedure, she continued screaming "NO NEEDLES". Thank God the doctors decide to use a topical on Kass' eye, no IV's or being intubated.

Dr. O'Halloran quickly administered the Botox to her eye, the procedure lasted for minutes. Lexi and I were exhausted. The Doctors were thrilled to hear Kassidy speak and make a fuss. As we watched her lay in a vegetative state to where she now was thrilling!

Ortho Rehab has been exhilarating...every day is better than the next. On day 4 of Ortho Rehab. - Kassidy learned how to dress herself, Brush her teeth, wash her face and comb her hair. WOW! They don't mess around here; no time is wasted. It's awesome! We have a meeting with Kass' Doctors, nurses, teachers, and therapists this afternoon to make a game plan for Kassidy's treatments. We will set goals, as well as an estimation of the time Kassidy will be in Ortho Rehab.

Again, we are impressed with the show of strength and unity within the "team" at Rady, each team member (therapist, Doctor or nurse) unveiling their plans to make Kassidy whole. We sit in awe of their devotion and dedication to make our girl whole. We left the room, our faith in this system at an all-time high. Let's do this...

We've been in Ortho Rehab for 7 days - One week down. Kassidy started out pretty mad at the world, but by Wednesday she was settling in and working 100% on her goals. You see, Kassidy is a goal setter. Everything she sets out to do in life was not done by accident. She thinks things through, she analyzes everything she does, so this isn't any different. Kassidy came in with 6 goals, in this order:

1.. To walk out of camp on February 5th
2. Going to the bathroom

3. School - improving on her writing / learning / computer
4. Using arms and hands and keeping them steady
5. Sitting cross-legged on the floor.
6. No G-tube - getting all of fluids and nutrients through her mouth and not her feeding tube through her stomach.

Saturday, Kassidy started her goal with going to the bathroom in the bathroom! I know we all take it for granted, and some may think it's funny, but it's pretty embarrassing when you need help in this area. We have to remember that Kassidy has to learn EVERYTHING all over again. Every single muscle in her body is being retaught how to work, her bladder included.

In Physical Therapy Kassidy is walking next to the bars, with help of course. She also hopped on a 3-wheel bike and took off in the hallways. We are blown away how quickly Kassidy's brain is healing, how her muscle memory is kicking in... Thank you, Lord, for healing our girl! Kassidy is still denying that she had a bleed in her brain, we are working with a trauma Psychologist who will be helping her with reality.

We met with the specialists from UCSD. Kassidy's embolization's have been a great success. However, they decide they need to make sure that there are no new veins that have grown from the AVM. We're not happy about it, but we have to kill off the AVM completely. Kass is terrified. Kassidy is now able to get up by herself from a lying position. She was given the O-kay to use her walker from her hospital bed to the bathroom... We are beyond excited.

Today was Epic Day, Kassidy has decided she's ready to wear her underwear and skinny jeans! No more diapers and sweats.

This has given Kassidy a new reality, nothing is stopping her with her goals or her vision! Go Kass Go!!! Kassidy had a swallow test today; she no longer needs her G-tube for feedings. All meds, liquid and food are going in her mouth! We are sooooo excited! Thank you, Jesus! Kass can finally eat, she is able to taste food and swallow with aspiration.

I can't explain how incredibly awesome today was. Kassidy asked for her cell phone, she wanted to text her friends. One of her nurses stopped into her room and I pointed to the cell phone in Kassidy's hand. She asked Kass what she was up to with her phone, Kass said, "I just want to text my friend. The nurse's face lit up; she dashed out of the room. Before we knew it, little by little, Doctors, therapists, nurses came to the room to see it for themselves.

They couldn't believe it. Kassidy's brain was healing; neurons were connecting and healing at full speed. We all witnessed yet another miracle. Her friend she was texting was overwhelmed with JOY! Speech is going very well, the Speech Pathologist said it was time for Kassidy to start singing, well, this girl hasn't stopped! We're singing in the hallways and turning up the tunes in Room 142!

Smiling was also on Kassidy's list. We're working on the muscles of her smile. It is a little forced, therefore we are working on softening the smile.... She's doing great! We reflect on God's Grace during this season. We are reminded: "Then your light will break forth like the dawn, and your healing will quickly appear, then your righteousness will go before you, the Glory of the Lord will be your rear guard. Isaiah 58:8. Thank you Lord for your words of strength and healing.

We take each day as it comes, anxiously awaiting February 5, 2009. This is the day that her life truly starts over again. She's coming home then, and we are all so very excited. She'll leave the G-Tube, most of the meds, her clunky wheelchair, and enough bad memories for five lifetimes at the door as she exits the hospital on that day.

We'll continue her healing at home, and we'll trust that the Lord is indeed our rear guard. We believe this with all of our hearts, as he has demonstrated his love for Kassidy time, and time again. There is a plan for the remaining life of this little girl that has yet to be revealed. We will wait, secure in the knowledge that the outcome of this plan has been predetermined.

Weeks have flown by, so many milestones and the healing of her brain, body and soul. Here we are on February 4th, tomorrow we go home. Kassidy and I have been working on our "goodbye" dance, complete with shoulder action! Kassidy has met and exceeded every one of her goals since January 5, 2009. Here's a recap:

1.. To walk out of Camp on February 5th - Kassidy will be walking out of the Hospital with her walker instead of a wheelchair!

2.. Bathroom - Kassidy has proudly met and achieved these goals this week 100%. Those muscles are working day and night (she also regained her dignity) Praise God!

3. School- writing / reading / math - Kassidy is working one on one with a teacher, her ataxia (shakiness) has gotten steadier, but she is well on her way. Praise God!

4. Using her arms and hands - This too has gotten so much better. She is playing catch, hitting the beach ball with a bat. Her writing is shaky, but she is writing to the best of her ability. Praise God!

5. Sitting cross-legged - This was achieved 2 weeks ago. She is becoming more flexible.

6. No G-tube - Kass is eating and drinking by mouth. We need to keep the G-tube in for a month after not using it, just to be sure. We will have that out at the end of the month.

Our Mission was accomplished, only by the Grace of God. Kassidy is still in denial about this happening and is afraid of it happening again. We assure her that she is going to be okay. God's work isn't finished yet, but every day, he continues to heal.

Thursday, **February 5, 2009** - We woke up early, ready to go home. We wait patiently for the discharge paperwork. Staff stop by to give their farewell and to let them know how proud they are of Kassidy. Pastor John walks us out the front door, we gather in a circle and Thank God for his healing hand on Kassidy. Pastor John was there praying with us from the 1st day Kassidy was brought in by Helicopter. We had some honest, heartfelt conversations about Heaven and God's will. This final farewell prayer was the Grand finale.

We are eternally grateful to Rady Children's Hospital for all they have done not only for Kassidy Dawn but our entire family. We arrive HOME, Kassidy cruises around the house in her skinny jeans and her walker! We can't believe we're home as a family with a new and healed Kass!

February 26, 2009 - We are back at UCSD for Kassidy's 4th Embolization, hopeful it's her last. Kassidy knows what is going on this time, so she's scared, she fears needles, being intubated, being back in the hospital again. I don't blame her, we all feel the same way, we have to be good at hiding it, as she doesn't understand the severity of killing off the AVM, so she doesn't have another bleed.

Again, they got a good shot of glue to a large feeder vein. The surgery was a little different this time, 2 of the Neurosurgeons arrived in the recovery room, as I stood over Kass stroking her face to wake her up from anesthesia, the Doctors started tapping at her chest telling her to "wake up". I didn't like the sound of it and became concerned. They assured me that everything would be okay, it was taking her a little longer to wake up this time.

Kassidy was taken by ambulance from UCSD to Rady Children's Hospital, back where it all began, back in the ICU fully intubated. Kassidy is resting and healing. Again, we pray and wait. Friday we fully intended on going home, but we noticed that Kassidy wasn't able to wake up, if she did, she wasn't able to open her eyes or be awake for more than a few minutes.

We are concerned and talk to the Neurosurgeon who orders a CT scan. They let us know that her brain and brainstem has swelling, as the surgeons accidentally touched an important vessel during the embolization procedure. Kassidy's entire left side, tongue, and throat are completely numb, and she can't keep her eyes open. She is lethargic and back to where she was 6 months ago. We are angry and exhausted. We want answers...

Dr. Levy orders an MRI for a closer look. The next day we received the results, as we suspected, there was a problem. During the embolization procedure, the invasive instruments caused an edema to occur near the thalamus area of her brain. In short, there is swelling in the area of the brain. It was indeed a stroke. The Thalamus controls among other things, our level of consciousness. She is resting, we are livid, sad, angry, exhausted...

It feels like we went 10 steps backwards. Kass needs a few days to heal in the ICU, finally we go home with some new challenges. God help us, we need your healing hand and Grace.

We ask our CaringBridge friends, family and followers to pray a specific prayer for Kassidy's spirit. Her brain will heal with time, but her spirit is in need of prayer. She is depressed, and she doesn't want to feel this way. She wants to be normal again, and that for a teenager is so very important. We pray that God will touch her heart, and that he will reveal to her very soon that she is normal, just not like before.

Today we'll hurt for a time, then we'll move forward, making the most of what God has given to us. We live abundant lives, made even more abundant by the journey that God has assigned to us. After a week of being home, Kass' spirits are improving, we're getting our jokester back! She still has numbness on the left side of her body, but she is strong. We are so proud of her great attitude and how far she has come.

March 18, 2009, We had our appointment with our Neurosurgeon, Dr. Levy. We are blessed to have him on our team, as he is widely recognized as one of the top Pediatric Neurosurgeons in the country. He is also a USC Football Neurologist and consults with the NFL on the long-term effects of players and head injuries.

We discussed the current situation with him and his two residents. They have determined that there is no longer the need for any further embolization's. This is a good thing. The scans indicate that the AVM, while still there, has been reduced to a manageable size. The risk of another bleed has been greatly reduced, but not entirely eliminated.

We can do nothing about the remaining AVM, just leave it there and play the odds. This decision is complicated by her age. She has many, many years ahead of her, each of those years would bring with it the chance of another AVM bleed. Or not, we have no way of knowing.

Or.... we go in and take out the remaining AVM through surgery. This would involve opening the skull and go in and remove the AVM altogether. Dr. Levy tells us that with a good outcome, she will be home in a few days. They will go in through the back of her head and essentially remove the remaining AVM, cauterize the blood vessels, re-attach the skull and call it a day. He makes it sound so routine.

We told their Team that we need to pray about it. God will give us the answer. In fact, he already has given us the answer. We just need to pick a day. Kass was in the room during the meeting, she listened intently as we discussed the options, and the potential outcome.

Neuropsychologist

After returning home, still in the course of my medication denial madness days, neuropsychology was another method of treatment that I went through. I think that was such a pivotal step because psychology was half of the battle here. How I perceived not only the situation but also how I dealt with myself. How I was coping with a change in my outlook of everything. It was unquestionably a struggle. But being that there's a therapy that deals specifically with the brain, it really helped.

The therapist asked me quite a number of questions, then went on to have me draw a house on a piece of blank paper. I did that and unknowingly, I drew a finished house that didn't have any windows or doors to it. Which signified that I was closed off on the inside. I was angry, confused, hurting. I was feeling all of the emotions, nothing set in stone that was reliable. It was like, life was quickly crumbling beneath me, and I had no control. I couldn't do a dang thing by myself. What if I was stuck in this state forever? What if I had to be dependent on other humans for everything for the rest of my life? What would my future look like?

I had to keep the sight that my triggers and emotional reactions were reminders of what still needed to be worked on. Mental health is one piece of the puzzle that no one wants to mess with but is an avenue toward functionality and necessary to health. The world isn't going to tiptoe around your triggers; it's a necessity to make it a responsibility to cope because no one is going to do it for me. But with this demonstration in therapy, we now knew how I was feeling, and we could work on helping to improve what was going on in my head. It sure didn't come easily. But what good thing comes easily. Right? It took work but step by step, it gave me assurance.

Overall, I took away that in order to become less reactive, I had to do the dirty work, the hard things. But, doing so is a huge part of growth and decreasing stress. If you let everything get you worked up, you're damaging your mind, body and spirit. This Neuropsychologist that I had was very serious, but he did a phenomenal job in what he did. And now that I've gone through that, I can relate better to others and see that they're not broken or damaged, they just need time and quality, genuine friendship.

See, maybe, not all the time, but what if these trials in life weren't only happening to me but for me? I have a hard time looking at a challenge head on and saying to the storm Mark 4:39. When Adonai says, "be still." I just know how to rely on Him to help me endure the trial. Both instances are wise. But what would happen if we looked directly to Christ at the beginning of the storm and prayed for His stillness in it? Stillness doesn't mean not moving or quietness, I find it means waiting patiently. In Hebrew the words waiting patiently is translated into the word Qavah. Meaning to eagerly expect God to act and be ready to move when He does.

Orientation to Death

My position or attitude on death has really shaped who I am today. Although each person goes about their life doing, "life," there are two ways it can go, "you beat the odds," or Christ is building up your character." Technically it's a win-win in my opinion. Furthermore, my near-death-experience has molded me because I am a more understanding, patient, bolder person. Giving grace to others because I never know what kind of struggle that person is facing in their life at the moment, so I deal with my own struggles yet continue to relate to others in an unspeakable way.

Due to just entering adolescence, I didn't quite have the sense of my own morals and values yet. However, I did have the background of structured extracurricular activities, organizational habits and respect. I still carried those throughout my healing journey and continue to do so. While we all could brush up on our skill set, respect and understanding to others should be at the top of our list. We constantly need to be reminded that the Father didn't just die to save you from sin, He died to save your soul!

However, those hopeless, dark times didn't just come and go. The thoughts of this happening to such an innocent, young, unknowing gal, was beyond me. That's partly of why I went through such a horrific grieving cycle. I speak as if it was hard on myself, but it was equally as difficult for my family because they couldn't do anything about it. This chapter of grief and anger was there for about three years. Give or take. I believe grievances are never truly over even years later, you just learn to better cope and manage them.

Within that grieving sequence, there're seven different stages that occur. First, I went through the initial shock and denial chapter to where I just didn't care about life. Secondly, pain and guilt took over. Then, anger and bargaining transpired where I'd have my crying fits and question God's goodness.

Next, that place of depression that no one likes to talk about but is necessary in order to move past it. To turn the corner, an upward turn begins to take place. I started to reconstruct myself and work through problems even more. The best step and where I'm at now, is the acceptance and hope step. Grief is quite the rollercoaster process of ups and down's, but in the end, there's purpose!

Not rushing through life

Rushing through life is one aspect in life that I try to deter because as we all have that go, go, go attitude, we tend to miss the little blessings. The little blessings that make life meaningful. The little things that make the world go round. I highly encourage you to practice walking in peace, humility and on a mission in your everyday life. Yahshua was a great example for us. He set the pace yet is humble enough not to walk into a room with authority but with humility. Humility in the fact that He recognizes and sympathizes with each and every person to the extent that He heals with words. The gentlest, loving healing is with words.

Not only receiving with gratefulness but also meekness knowing that people can be meek too. Quite often, they are looked down upon and have no influence in society. The word unimportant is the Greek word Praus, which is often translated meek. But that's because those people are loving and accepting. And that's exactly what the Father calls us to do. But on the other hand, He doesn't want us to be stepped on and trampled over so we must exercise our backbone. To stand up for ourselves and be bold. He has already given you that authority and it's in you.

So having boldness in a meek manner is a point to be said. Rather, take in faith by the power of the Holy Spirits words. See, He only has to utter the Fathers word because His will enable you to do so. It's kind of like saying, how there's power in words. Not only His words, but our words as well and when we end up using them for the glory of Christ and not for the impression of man, that is when we begin to see true healing. Healing of not only our carnal tents, but also mentally and emotionally.

As humans, we experience this crap. It's not fun by any means, but that's why we have a Savior. To speak a word into us, to satisfy and fill us. Our worth is not dependent upon our circumstances. We hear that all the time, but I always ask myself, "do I really live up to that?" Also, I had tried to remind myself to live every day with what I've already declared in me. You've spoken Your word into us and declared us to be whole, loved, mighty, righteous, servants of You. It makes me question, "Why do I bother to worry about the little things that don't go my way or to look for validation from man?"

Kass- thumb wrestling
January 2009, while in Ortho Rehab relearning how to do everything, physically, mentally and emotionally.

While waiting for physical therapy to begin, as Kass sat in her high back wheelchair, I was always talking to her, always pushing her to think and do things for herself. It was hard for her. This particular day, I decided to grab Kassidy's right hand and begin to thumb wrestle with her, little did I know this little gesture not only brought a crooked smile to her face, but it also made Kass laugh to her core, She couldn't stop laughing, with this deep laugh and crooked smile. Therapist gathered around while we all marbled at Kassidy and her ability to laugh again. Neurons were being rewired, God was restoring her brain. This was a really good day. Thank you Lord, JOY is being restored. Our girl is coming back to us slowly.

Avoidance is just prolonged suffering disguised as safety. For all those people that looked at me funny, made funny comments, and had their assumptions, it was hurtful. It was hurtful in the fact that I couldn't necessarily help this situation that I was in, but here I am. It's always hopeful to offer an encouraging word and move on with your day instead of staring and giggling at the fact that someone is doing something differently.

Come at it with curiosity rather than conviction. So, in that case, if you're avoiding a certain situation, just remember, avoidance is prolonged suffering disguised as safety. Because in the fact that when you avoid an uncomfortable situation, it doesn't just disappear in thin air. It stays in your mind, and you think about it over and over again until the issue is resolved. So, it's better to confront somebody and offer a word of encouragement as opposed to forgetting the accident happened.

"The land You have given," us is another way of saying, where we reside. Where we take up space. In Deuteronomy 4:1-6 it speaks on living in the land of wisdom and understanding. That being our place on the Earth. we need to live in the judgment of Christ and live as if He's the only one that can judge us. Not Man. Because men have their own fault and shortcomings to where Christ is the epitome of who we should resemble. Help each and every one of us to not only look at your commandments as a law but something to live by, something out of love. The love of you.

Looking to our heavenly Father, as we seek to follow Him day by day, we're not only alive because of Him, but we're thriving as a result. Going out into the world does not mean to be free-spirited and follow our heart in every case. We need to be steadfast and firm in the commandments that He has commanded us in every situation. Understanding His commandments is another form of wisdom to long for. It's a way of life that leads to wisdom. It's something that God praises and wants in life. He wants your love, your deep intimate love.

The word observe is used in this verse, I looked it up and it's an active form, "to do" or "to keep ". Sometimes we can get so caught up in the word that we forget that there is a Biblical meaning. We need to tame our tongue to what the Father states as to what the world says. Ultimately, this will catch unbelievers' attention to where they can start questioning where we get our wisdom and understanding from.

My Mom's reflections
April 27, 2009 - We're leaving for Rady Children's early in the morning, we are scheduled for 10:30 AM surgery. Today, as every day, her attitude and courage are indescribable. She brings calm to our anxiety; she steady's our hand as we once again reach out to God for his divine Grace.

The Team of Doctor's will shave the back of her head. They tell us that they will remove a sizable section of her skull at the rear of her head. This will allow them plenty of room in which to access the area of concern. They will enter the brain through the rear, and travel to the area that was affected by the AVM. At that point, they intend to remove and/or cauterize the remaining veins and arteries that were feeding the AVM. The goal is to completely eliminate what remains of the AVM, thereby preventing the chance for another bleed.

Kassidy's case was complex from the beginning, as she has close to 50 feeder veins contributing to the AVM. We're scared. She is not. We have the best Surgeon in the world in Dr. Michael Levy and his Team. We have the best facilities in the world. We have God supervising the procedure. And most importantly, we have the Prayers of the Purple Army on this day.

Kassidy's surgery took longer than expected, 10 ½ hours later, but everything is going well. A nurse came out to let us know that they were closing her up, but that she is stable and doing well. We are all exhausted and have been anxious all day. Kassidy is back in ICU - Room 335, Kassidy is fully intubated, and her face is swollen from being face down on the surgical table for over 10 hours. Dr. Levy said that everything went well. She experienced a lot of bleeding from the removal of the tissue that made up the AVM. This bleed required her to take two units of blood via transfusion. He said that there is one small vessel left that should pose no chance of any further bleeding.

What we will not know for at least a day or two is how well she is going to recover from the procedure itself. As with any brain surgery, there remains the possibility that she may lose some additional function. With God's Grace, it will be nothing. Dr. Levy has prepared us to be on the lookout for additional issues with her balance, sincere working around the cerebellum area of the brain. Again, we pray for God's protection and healing over Kassidy, we also ask for strength for our family to get through another hard day.

April 28, 2009 - Prayers are answered! Let me summarize: Kassidy was in surgery on Monday from 12 PM - 10:30 PM Monday night. Intubated and sedated. Tuesday Kass was extubated at 11:30 AM, by 1:00 PM Kassidy was cracking jokes and sending text messages to friends! The Doctors and nurses are amazed. A lot of the nurses in ICU have never heard Kassidy speak, when she left the ICU unit, she was still in a coma. They couldn't believe their eyes.

A few hours later, Kass tells us she has to go potty; she pulls herself up slowly, we help her with her walker to the restroom, she returns back to bed, grabs the remote and starts watching TV. Less than 18 hours after major BRAIN surgery with a full craniotomy, she's feeling full of energy and joy! Again, we are amazed and grateful.

We go home a few days after the surgery, Kassidy's incision is sore, as the incision starts near the base of her neck and goes about half-way up her skull. Thankfully, it's all muscle soreness. The incision looks gnarly; thank God her hair will grow back and cover the scar. For those of you who have never met her - I pray for the chance for you to get to know her. She is truly an amazing human being, and certainly one of the toughest that you will ever meet. Touched by God's hand, a living Miracle.

May 8, 2009 - Kassidy works extremely hard at walking, she doesn't want to rely on her walker. BUT, today, Kassidy took about 16 small steps - all by herself! Unaided, fully independent, since August 4th of last year. She was beaming with pride, and we were all choking back tears. She couldn't wait to get to PT yesterday to tell all of her instructors about her latest accomplishment.

May 13, 2009 - Kass is walking more and more steps without her walker, but still very unsteady. Having a railing or a wall close by to hold on to is working well for her and gives her confidence.

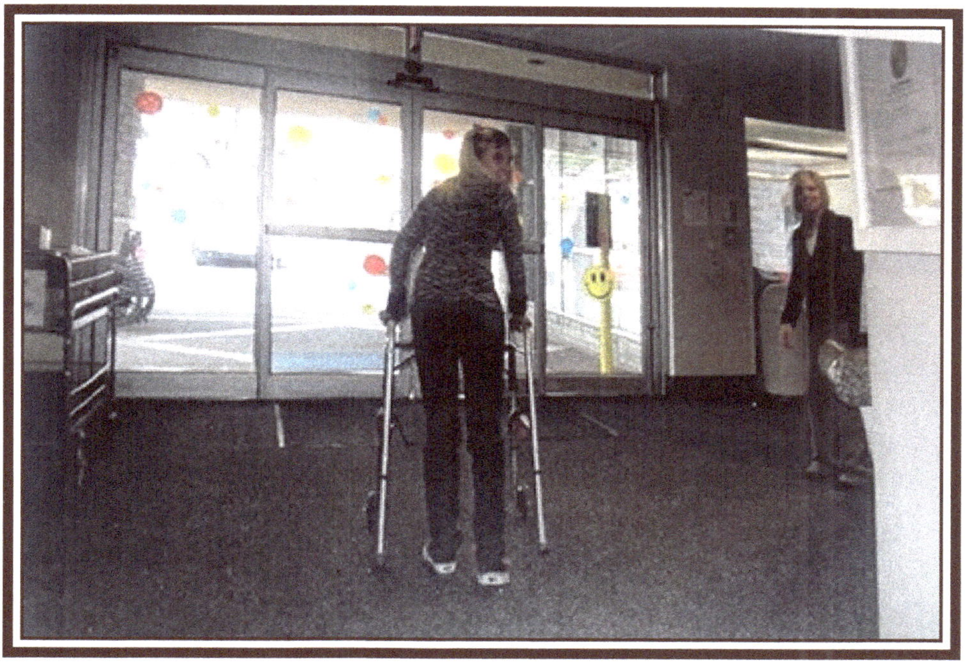

Chapter 13

Cognitive & Emotional

Believe it or not, this stage is when I really started to comprehend. I physically knew what was going on yet the connection to my brain was drastically off. It took time, God's time. With the cognitive disconnect, I really struggled with my body and what it had a difficult time doing now. Pretty much everything was an effort and a workout trying to complete a simple task like holding a pencil. My brain just wouldn't fasten to the fact that this was an ordinary action that used to naturally happen.

Now I had unlearned and needed to relearn how to do these simple straightforward gestures. Cognitively, I was just going through the motions, but it was a real struggle to say the least. Emotionally, that was another story. Like I said, my body used to do all these things that I now had to try every effort in order to make it work. It was as if I tirelessly put every inch of energy into creating some sort of result.

That was just at the beginning stages of relearning movements. Little did anyone know that the real emotional healing would further take place in the quiet times. The times of rest are when all you have to do is rest and reflect. I would not only reflect on the day and the work that I put in, but also what had just physically, mentally and emotionally hit me like a bus. To further add, when I started to live for today, the Father promises that "more will be revealed." As we learn more and more about Him and His deeds, we see that He always comes through on His promises.

In fact, through my struggles to get back to myself, the times of desperation were unbearable. And as I was reminded, "no one great has ever had an easy life." See, God has a sense of humor when it comes to trials. Even though we may be hurting and struggling, Yahshua is sitting back and saying," Don't worry, I got ya!" Keeping the mindset that, faith is built when there's a distance between promise and reality. This may be what my outer circumstances appear to be, but God promises more to be revealed.

There's a way of life that says, don't get into a pattern where you think you have to do something for the rest of your life. If we were stuck with having to do something every single day for the rest of our lives, it would become mundane and boring. We have to keep things fresh and exciting. Much like how my life was completely shaken up to turn my attention to what truly mattered. I was stuck in a pattern of trying to focus all my efforts on health and briskness that I was setting the Father on the sidelines to encourage me instead of involving Him.

I was merely informing Him. And flipping that script, was like holding a picture of health. A picture of myself on one end of the room and health on the other end. But leaving the past behind and letting God guide, brought me the picture towards the road to recovery. Through the process of slowly progressing, life seemed to only consist of therapies and making myself better to get back to the "old Kassidy". And learning how to do the simplest ordinary tasks on my own, were a big landmark.

I'll tell you what, the hardest part of my journey was the opposition I had mentally. I was not only hard on myself for not being able to do these certain simple tasks, but the reality of coping with it was another issue in itself. Throughout the process of having to overcome, time really seemed to be on fast-forward due to everything happening so fast yet at the same time it seemed so tragically slow that I was going through all this. I felt all of the emotions. But, on the other hand, cheesecake seemed to make it better!

My Recovery

While comprehending that my life is going to appear far different than what anyone or I imagined, the purpose was unclear. Yes, God has a reason and purpose for absolutely everything, and though it wasn't revealed right away, it doesn't mean that there isn't one. It just means that He's working. There are events and acts that are being worked out behind the scenes that we know nothing about. I'm not going to tell you that it was simple and a breeze and that I just jumped back into life cause that's not the case, it took denial, and grieving and asking God "why me" most of the time... And that's completely okay. You're human; you're going to have those humanistic thoughts of why things didn't go as you planned.

In this trying instance, I undoubtedly went through the hardest time of my life. Not surprisingly, I had my fair share of times that I doubted God 's purpose for me, if I had one. What I would be able to do. Why are people so uncomfortable with me? I couldn't do anything right or what's the purpose of living? All of those real self-talks that go on while tragedy strikes, and I'm not going to sugarcoat everything was OK because it wasn't. My world came crashing down. The biggest question though, "why me," was constantly overflowing in my mind of why this had to happened to me and not someone else.

Why couldn't God have just chosen someone strong enough to do this, to take on this life? But then I was reminded of 2 Corinthians 1:9 which says, "Indeed, we felt that we had received the sentence of death. But that was to make us rely not on ourselves, but on God who raises the dead. "In that moment, I cried out pleading, "This should have been a mistake." But as we learn more and more about Yahshua, we know that he does not make mistakes. There's a purpose in all things. Even this instance. For what though? I couldn't see any Hope and any light at the end of the tunnel. Zip. Nada.

I was the miss fourteen-year-old "color/neon" queen, I didn't want to be looked at as the girl with an elderly walker. No way. We had to pimp that thing out. So, we used color duct tape. Purple on one side. Orange duct tape on the other side! That was just my temporary walker until I got my more stable, support one. This colorful walker of mine did me good to get up and move, but it was time for greater intensity. So, I graduated to have a four-prong cane. And if you're inclined to ask, yes, we did make that unique too. It wasn't just a four-prong cane. My oldest sister, Dani completely blinged out the entire thing. We called it, the bling cane!

Although this ruptured brain aneurysm took place a few days before high school sign up's, I missed out on many events during that time. I don't think many people can fathom that when someone experiences a brain injury, many don't just jump back into life. It takes time. Like I say, "time does not heal, God heals in time." After completely missing a majority of my ninth-grade year, except for the last three weeks, the school did an IEP (a certain test to see where I was at cognitively).

In the end, the school put me in "special education" classes due to my recent brain injury. But we knew there had to be more. I wasn't coping well at all with this injury then throwing me into a classroom where I shouldn't be, completely threw off my level of healing where I knew I could and should be. It was a devastating process to say the least. Knowing that all my friends were out there having a good time, and I was in a different classroom being held back, my family was very receptive to the fact that I wasn't having it.

It was as if I was stuck in a place where I couldn't grow to better myself. Like I just had to live with what happened to me. So, at that point, my parents decided to homeschool me. I was in a school curriculum where I went on campus one day a week and did the rest at home. Let me just testify that could've been one of the greatest things for my healing, not only to be at home, but to thrive and grow in every area of health. I had an advocate. And in the Greek dictionary, Advocate is known as "parakletos."

Meaning, "in the widest sense, a helper, successor, aider, assistant; so of the Holy Spirit destined to take the place of Christ with the apostles (after his ascension to the Father), to lead them to a deeper knowledge of gospel truth, and to give them the divine strength needed to enable them to undergo trials and persecutions on behalf of the divine kingdom." The advocate or "the helper," was on my side, He not only believed in me, but also helped me to graduate high school on time! That was my main goal, and my amazing academic advisor Diana Miller helped me to accomplish that class of 2012!

I just want to encourage you, just because your way didn't turn out how you expected doesn't mean that God doesn't have something better for you around the corner. I just had to endure the life quacking pain for a little while for Him to reveal what He had in store. It's a continuous journey but every day I live with the mindset of pushing forward to better myself, I continue to look at challenges as gifts. Because they offer trials and trials offer us a gift. It's an opportunity to surrender to God 's wisdom, and to become more like Jesus.

In view of the fact that I was an instructor and trained at the Taekwondo studio, it was just a matter of fact that I would want to return to normalcy. The average person would think that normalcy is to jump right back in doing high kicks and grappling, but that is not what happened. Although I still returned to work on kicks and stretching and punches, it still looked very different because I was sitting in a chair or holding onto the wall mainly. But you do whatever you have to, even if it looks a little bit different. You're still out there doing it. It was one of the best therapies I could've done. Hands-down.

Of course, it's been a battle of ups and down's yet, one of the best most rewarding feelings is being proud of yourself because you know who God created you to be and you're constantly aware of who He says you are. That's, loved, whole, completed, gracious, patient, kind... All of the attributes in Yahshua because you were created to reflect His being. In addition, when you continually demonstrate Christ living inside you by constantly living beyond others doubts, some sort of determination is born due to never giving up and fighting the good fight.

The reality of living with balance issues comes with not only looking like you're drunk 24/7 with the way that I stagger when I walk, to the countless bruises all over my body. Half the time, people look at me when someone's helping me walk and they think I've been drinking one too many because they see that I can't walk in a straight line. I have fun with it! Also, 99.5 of the bruises on my body are from unknown causes!

I'm so used to hitting myself and banging myself up. It doesn't even phase me. It just comes with the territory. Like for instance, I just fell and got a bruise on my back, and I looked, and I also have three other ones on my leg. Ask me how, I have no idea. All I know is that when we get bruised and broken, the only way forward is moving past the obstacle. Not forgetting that it happened but progressing forward and learning from it.

My Family and friends perspective on my recovery journey.

My Mom's thoughts
Today, Kass made a decision that she wanted to get back into Taekwondo, as Kassidy was a 1st Degree Black Belt at the age of 12, she started with Mr. Michael Robles at Final Strike Taekwondo in Murrieta. She gave everything to her sport, but today, she wanted to surprise Mr. Robles and her black belt Team. She arrived dressed in her white Ghee, with her black belt tied with precision.

The courage it took for her to get out there with her walker and perform her black belt form was untouchable. Kassidy was faced with a forever life-changing event 9 months ago but has not let it stop her. Faith, Determination, Hope, Hard work, Goals and every other positive word is what Kassidy lives up to every day.

Kassidy continues to live her life one day at a time. Every day is a gift from the Lord, and she fully understands that God gave her a 2nd chance at life. She still faces challenges; however, she faces her challenges with expectation and joy. We know that her JOY comes from the Lord.

Kassidy's faith is strong, and she continues to be an example for others struggling in their health. She is the most selfless person I know, always helping others. I am beyond grateful to have been chosen to be Kassidy's mom, to have gone through every detail of Kassidy's journey with her. Almost losing my youngest daughter has taught me so much about myself, trusting in the Lord, believing in Miracles, witnessing miracles every single day, expectation of God's free will in my daughter's healing, accepting the good, the bad and the ugly, fully understanding that I had absolutely NO control.

I chose to surrender to HIS will for myself, but also for my daughter and my family. This journey has taught me how to trust not only in the Lord, but also in the Medical Doctors and nurses. It has also taught me that a mother's intuition is very intuitive. Being by Kass' side 24/7 allowed me to stand up to medical professionals when I felt they were not honoring our wishes or care for Kass. I became a mama bear, fully aware and present in every conversation, good or bad about Kassidy's care. I was her advocate, her voice, her Mother.

We experienced many miracles throughout the years, but then again, we look at the little things in life. We don't take life for granted, as every day is a gift. Kass has had many shunt revisions, to the point that her shunt literally stops working or a tube falls out into her stomach. Kassidy starts to dry heave and attempts to throw up, but is unable, due to her fundo. We immediately called Dr. Levy for a CT scan that shows she needs another brain surgery, a shunt revision.

Kass speaks gibberish, to the point where she doesn't make sense, due to the hydrocephalus (a condition in which fluid accumulates in the brain,) The condition becomes urgent and it's incredibly scary, to the point that it brings me back to August 4, 2008. PDSD is real. I've learned how to be calm and in control to ease Kassidy's anxiety. I've learned to hide my fear, but at the same time I've learned to give it all to God knowing I can't change anything. I surrendered, I believe 100% that Kassidy was chosen for this journey, that we were meant to make a difference in the world by sharing her story, her strength, her JOY, but mostly her FAITH in our Lord and Savior.

The Lord never left our side; He provided for us in EVERY way. I thank God for everything we went through, because it brought us closer to Him, we could feel his presence, his breath. Kassidy and I live together, and I continue to be there for her whenever she needs me. She continues to blow me away with her quick wit. She spends a lot of time researching topics including nutrition and medical research to grow in her knowledge. She also volunteers at Lily Kelly Ministries Coffee shop in Murrieta. She loves people, as well as sharing the Gospel of Jesus Christ.

I'm so proud to be your mom and I love you more than you will ever know...

My Dad 's perspective

Her determination that she displayed was contagious. Time after time, when she met new therapists, her will to win, drove "them" to be better for Kass. She never backed down from a challenge, and it was her willingness to put in the work that forced her various therapists to try their best to keep up with her. They were often amazed at this little teenager's desire to do whatever it took to keep her recovery moving forward. Kass nailed it. She had to relearn virtually everything over again – breathing, swallowing, talking, standing, walking, and more. She won!

Kenzie Gomes' perspective

As an outsider, but very close and dear friend to Kassidy, I would be lying if I said the recovery journey didn't impact me. However, I feel like there is no credit to that because I was not experiencing anything Kassidy was physically going through, but the emotional toll was certainly a challenge. I wanted nothing more than for my friend to just be better - get better - feel better so much faster than I knew it would take, and, in a way, I felt helpless in the process. That said, the hard parts for me simply could not be focused on and instead I put my energy into supporting Kass as best I could with whatever she needed. I happily chose to focus on every miracle each day presented to us because I still had my best friend Kassidy in my life.

Mr. Robles' perspective

Kassidy's recovery journey, from my perspective, unfolded in distinct phases, each leaving a profound impact on me. The first phase that stands out was when I visited her in the ICU, and her future was still uncertain. There's one moment from that time that has stayed with me, something I still can't fully explain or understand. It's hard to describe to those who didn't experience it, but when I walked into that room, there was an undeniable presence—that I can't put into words. It was almost as if something much greater than me was at work. It felt spiritual, like there was a higher power at play that I couldn't comprehend, but it was tangible in a way that transcended the physical world. To this day, I reflect on that moment. For me, it became a turning point in my own struggles with faith, a moment where I could confidently say, "There is definitely something more—there is God."

The second phase of Kassidy's recovery, which still stands out vividly, was when I was told that she had woken up. For some reason, the news of her awakening is somewhat clouded in my memory, likely due to the emotional whirlwind that was happening at the time and the overwhelming disbelief. It felt surreal, and I think my mind tried to process it in smaller, more manageable pieces. But I remember the feeling of hope that flooded in at that moment. It was like a turning point, like a door opening to the possibility of her fighting back against the odds. Even though we didn't know what the future held, hearing that she had woken up was a glimmer of light in the darkness.

The third phase of Kassidy's recovery was seeing her at home after she was released from the hospital. I'll never forget the moment when she suddenly began crying. Her mom, Donna, explained that it was likely because Kassidy had used the restroom, and simple, everyday tasks were things she had to relearn. It was such a humbling moment for all of us. It reminded me how easily life can humble you, how basic things we take for granted can become monumental when we have to relearn them. I felt a deep sadness for Kassidy at that moment, wondering how much she had already endured and how much she still had to face. But even in that moment of vulnerability, Donna's words—spoken with an unwavering positivity and strength—left an indelible mark on me. Her ability to stay upbeat and supportive through it all was a testament to her strength and love.

I continued to visit Kassidy whenever I could, and with each visit, I was amazed by her progress. Her determination was nothing short of inspiring, and it humbled me in ways I didn't think possible. Anytime I was having a difficult day or struggling with my own challenges, I would think about what Kassidy was going through. Her strength, endurance, and ability to overcome every obstacle before her gave me a new perspective on my own difficulties. It made me realize how small my struggles were compared to what she had endured, and it inspired me to keep going, no matter what life threw my way.

I watched Kassidy go through physical therapy, and there were moments when I couldn't help but feel a deep sense of admiration. I saw her struggle with basic tasks that most of us take for granted—standing, walking, talking. To be honest, one of the things that stood out the most to me during this time was the unwavering support of her mother, Donna. I can say, without a doubt, that I absolutely love Kassidy and the lessons she has taught me, but no story of Kassidy's recovery would be complete without acknowledging Donna. She is, in my eyes, the other great part of this journey.

A mother's love is a powerful thing, and it's not easily understood by those who haven't experienced it firsthand. Even as a father, I can say I still find it hard to fully grasp. But every time I saw Kassidy, Donna was there. Every time Kassidy fell, Donna was there. Through every up and every down, I witnessed Donna's constant presence and support. While this story is undeniably about Kassidy, to me, Donna is the unsung hero—the one who supported and helped shape the story and the main character. To say I have respect for her is an understatement.

As much as I loved and respected Donna, there was a time when I knew I needed to have a face-to-face moment with her. One of the most important moments in Kassidy's story, and my role in it, came when both Kassidy and Donna told me that she wanted to return to Taekwondo, to test for her second-degree black belt—a goal that, while not too far in the past, felt like it had happened so long ago. In that moment, I found my place in Kassidy's story. I had the chance to become a supporting actor in her journey again. I was able to step back into the role of Taekwondo instructor, and for that, I will be forever grateful. We got back to work, Kassidy on the mated floors of the Taekwondo studio, and Donna right there by her side, catching her every misstep. It was during this time that Donna and I had to face something head-on.

I could see how deeply Donna's love for Kassidy ran. What she had done for her daughter, while absolutely necessary and incredibly admirable, was something that, if not addressed, could hold them both back. I knew I had to step in and help Donna shift her perspective. I remember teaching Kassidy a Taekwondo lesson alongside some physical therapy, and after watching Donna catch her for what seemed like the hundredth time, I finally told her, "You have to let her go."

For a split second, Donna looked at me with what could only be described as a defensive, almost angry "mother bear" look. But I calmly said, "Donna, she's on a padded floor. If we can't let her fall here, then how can you ever expect to let her fully recover? Kassidy was like a baby again, and any parent can tell you that part of the job when your baby is learning to walk is to let them fall. You have to allow them to fail so they can build their own confidence in getting up and continuing on.

It took a moment—maybe more—but eventually, Donna relented. It was as if I saw a giant weight lift from her shoulders. She had done everything in her power to help Kassidy get to where she was, but she finally realized that her love, while necessary, was also holding her back. To move forward, she had to let go. Both she and Kassidy had been through so much, but healing requires one to release what's been in order to embrace what can be.

That moment marked a turning point for both of them, and I was honored to be a part of it. Watching Donna let go in that way was just as powerful as watching Kassidy fight her way back to health. It was a lesson in love, strength, and letting go of the past in order to build a future.

That moment has stayed with me for a long time. Working with Kassidy and her mother has been one of the most meaningful experiences of my life. The conversations we shared, the raw truth and vulnerability, and at times the frustration, are some of the most genuine and real human moments I have ever experienced. I am incredibly grateful to both Kassidy and Donna for allowing me to be a part of their journey. I have learned so much from them, grown alongside them, and had the privilege of offering whatever guidance I could, even if it was just a small piece of Kassidy's larger story.

Kassidy's journey has been nothing short of remarkable, and being a part of it has been one of the most meaningful experiences of my life. From the moment I walked into that ICU room, there was an undeniable feeling that something greater than myself was at work, a presence that helped shape my own faith and understanding of life. Witnessing Kassidy's struggle, her determination, and her unwavering spirit was incredibly humbling. I'll never forget the moments where simple tasks, like standing or walking, became monumental challenges for her. But through it all, her mother stood by her side, offering unconditional love and support every step of the way.

As Kassidy began her journey back to Taekwondo, I was honored to step into a more active role as her instructor once again. But it wasn't just about teaching her Taekwondo; it was about guiding her through the process of relearning, finding confidence, and embracing the falls along the way. In those moments, I also learned so much from both of them. Their vulnerability, their honesty, and even their frustrations taught me more about love, perseverance, and the importance of letting go than I ever expected. I'm deeply grateful to Kassidy and Donna for allowing me to be a part of their journey, to witness their growth, and to offer whatever guidance I could. Their strength has inspired me in ways I will carry with me for the rest of my life.

Felicia's perspective:

Kassidy's recovery was brutal at times. She pushed herself to limits most people would never even attempt. There were no shortcuts, no easy days, but she never stopped fighting. I was too young to fully understand what she was going through, too overwhelmed by the weight of it all to always appreciate the small victories. But looking back now, it's all very clear what was happening. Every step forward, every moment of progress— was nothing short of miraculous. Nothing short of a divine gift and privilege to bear witness to her has redefined how strength and unwavering faith are perceived by so many. And every day she continues to prove that miracles aren't just something we hope and pray for, they are something you are.

Chapter 14

Broken yet Amazing

As we realize that life is not all roses and flowers, we need to take into account the thorns that are mixed in. Those life altering beautiful thorns. They are 100% not beautiful at the moment, horrendous actually. But having the discernment to show up and be a part of the situation helps you to not only let your hair down a little bit, but to be present with others and build relationships. Because relationships are part of the equation of finding your tribe. You might be worn down, you might be bruised, you might be broken. That's exactly when we need our friends to stand by our side and push us on in our effort to completely crush the task at hand.

When I was at my lowest of lows, one of the hardest parts of getting through the day was the internal dictation that I was no good, that was broken and could not be fixed. I just wanted to be done and over with this chapter of my life despite what I meant. And because I went through that stage, it was harder than heck but again, it's all part of the grieving cycle. Looking back, I knew that was further from the truth. There's a lot to unpack in that thought. But, if I continued to live in that poor me, the pity on me kind of mindset, I wouldn't be nearly as close to where I am today.

I would be stuck in the cycle of not desiring to get better, everything would be too hard or too difficult. But guess what, life is difficult, life is hard and when you realize that and bring Yahshua into your day-to-day activities, you start involving

Him in the process, instead of merely informing Him. see, we all have physical choices of which way the game of life is going to play out. Sitting in your pain or doing something about it. That's why I always like to cheer on those that do the hard things.

Recollect what brought you from this moment of life to another moment in time. How does it make you feel? Accomplished, right? I have a tattoo on my arm that says, before you ask which way to go, remember where you've been. And although I don't need a physical reminder to recall my memory, it's a good reminder for other people when they read it. And although my Taekwondo skills have really shaped my committed, goal-oriented attitude. I believe that God has elevated my way of mind as of form therapy for not only myself, but others in addition. Like I always say, we need to help a brotha out!

My First Tattoo
With being a hardheaded and determined blondie that was recovering from a brain injury, after I got back on my feet and was on the road to recovery, my interests started to return. I was never a girly girl that was into nails and hair. I was a tomboy that wanted to ride a street bike and have tattoos! Slowly, but surely. In that case, I always wanted a tattoo growing up. I thought they were the coolest thing, But I knew I was too young, so I just let it go. I was only fifteen at that time. Jokingly, I would say to my parents, "I can't wait till I turn eighteen, I'm going to get two full sleeves! " If you don't know what full sleeves are, they're basically tattoos covering both arms.

But my parents on the other hand, knew that I had just overcome a lot. And they wanted to do something special. They contacted their friend who was a tattoo artist, and he mentioned that if my parents would sign off giving permission to move forward with a tattoo, he would do it. When I was lying in my coma lifeless, my family would pray Isaiah 53:5 over me which says, "By His stripes, I am healed, "every single day. Spontaneously, we knew that this had to be my first tattoo!

We were deciding on different places where to get this tattoo on my body. We went back-and-forth from my forearm to my back to my foot. But we ultimately ended up deciding; it was going to be in the center of my back over my spine. It looks very cool, and I am so happy with the end result. But let me tell you, the spine is a very sensitive part of the body and was not comfortable one bit. The pain was certainly worth it though! Having beautiful artwork on you forever and a wonderful story to tell that goes along with it. We all have a story to share and that's one of mine.

Within that time, I've gotten several more. They are certainly an attribute that I adore. I fully plan on getting more in the future! I'm not a big talker, so my tattoos speak for me. When people ask about them, it opens up a time for conversation of how God saved me and plays a massive role in my life. I only place tattoos on my body that have meaning and a story to share. That's why my story of triumph is number one in my life.

Life isn't fair.
Don't shoot the messenger here, I'm just saying what's on my heart. We are always faced with the question, why did this

have to happen? It's just not fair. And that's true, while I was kicking and screaming and having my down days and just not into having a prosperous life whatsoever, I consistently had to remind myself that no, life is not fair.

But these are the cards that I've been dealt so am I just going to wallow in my pity or get up and do something about it?

Obviously, I didn't speak to myself in those exact words, but that is definitely how I speak to myself now. Because just like Yahshua wants to chasten, I choose to chasten myself and apply constructive criticism to anyone, whether they like it or not. I'm going to speak the truth. The truth of Christ. However, life may not seem fair at that specific point of time, but when you take a step back and look at the big picture, there's more down the road for you to discover. We as humans tend to look at the here and now and while that's great and all, where does that lead you to where God may want to take you?

Coming back to a different era

Having ruptured my brain aneurysm and stroke at such a pivotal age of my development, I definitely see life in a whole new manner. I see things with new eyes. Things that individuals my age typically don't see. For example, the hope and perseverance of what could be and how some setbacks are typically set ups. Set ups for your future. That those setbacks may obstruct you from your path that you think you're on, but God may have a different plan in mind for you.

For the people who knew me in my middle school years, they would've called me a colorful jokester, skateboarding, troublemaker. I was that young girl that always hung out with

234

the same group of guys called friends and wore neon pairs of Ray ban shades every day with colored pants! I had them in just about every single color! I was a jokester to say the least. My friend Felicia and I would long board skateboard everywhere. I had a long board skateboard that was so tall that it went up to my chin height.

It was so freeing being on that board. I would do toes in the nose all the time and strut up and down that board like no body's business! That's another activity that brought me more joy than you would know and would love to get back to. And The troublemaker part got me in trouble most of the time. It was fun and innocent!

Having my rupture at thirteen, let's just say I had lost quite a few years of my development. In fact, some would say that I came back differently, almost like in a different era with a different mindset. Yes, this all happened in the year 2008 and I don't know why, but it seems that I came back with new passions and desires. A changed mindset, a changed outlook, similar to the 1940s–1950s era because I absolutely love everything regarding that time. Especially how they dress, their manners, their simplicity of life and the music that they listen to.

It's very strange how near-death experiences can cause one to reflect on the past, present and the future in terms of how you want to live your life. Ultimately, when we surrender our will, we have no control over our future. We do what the Father is willing. We surrender our lives to what He has for us. And certain issues can make you place your mind on one viewpoint instead of placing your mind on Christ's perspective.

You know that type of music that when you hear it, it almost takes you away. That's exactly what a live saxophone does to me. It brings me to a place of pure bliss! It makes me sway out of nowhere. It's very soothing yet on the other hand, I absolutely love swing music! Happy, fast, finger snapping music from the olden days! There's nothing like it! It just puts a smile on my face and makes me want to move my feet. We all have that kind of music that just satisfies the soul. This is it for me!

As it has been said, **"The growing of our character is a deeply personal act, it's never private because it never just affects us."**

Just look at things with a new point of view, slow down, keep life simple, enjoy the little things, and try not to take things too seriously, have fun! While my outlook for the future and my interest have changed, knowing that there are different seasons in life that come and go, is an aspect in life to always look forward to, knowing that the bad times are only temporary and that the good times come and go.

Just like trees that change color in the season.
Have you ever been in a period in life that you just didn't like and wish it could change and just fly over? I think we all have but I want to let you know that just like trees that change color in the season, your difficult chapter in life is only a season. Yes, it may last shorter, it could last longer but it's only for a time in your life. Most likely it's an uncomfortable feeling.

With what I've gone through, it's been uncomfortable, and I have had many opportunities for change and growth that have challenged my mindset and more ways than one. And because I don't want to avoid hard challenges, I want to completely defeat them and overcome them. But because life happens and seasons change, relying on God's hope to continually bring me through is all that I have. It's what I rely on.

Sue Muscarella's thoughts

We had a wonderful opportunity a few years ago to visit "Star" where he lived in Pasadena, Kassidy's healing angel from Rady's hospital who prayed over her for hours. This man exhibits the love of Jesus and even looks like him. It was a wonderful reunion. Kassidy even got Star off his feet and danced in his backyard (-:

Kassidy's story continues as she and Donna together exhibit God's love and peace to others wherever they go. Recently I was invited to share Kassidy's 30th birthday celebration at a concert at the Orange County Fairgrounds. I witnessed firsthand the generosity of strangers towards Kass as a gentleman sidled up to Kassidy at the souvenir stand and offered to buy her whatever she chose. He was so sincere and kind as he acknowledged her condition (due to her walker) and encouraged her with kind words.

We were then escorted to "first class" seats (i.e. the Handicap section). We felt like VIP's!!! It is an honor and privilege to be a part of Kassidy's story these past 17 years. God saved her for a purpose, and I believe that purpose was to be God's light to any person she meets. HER STORY CONTINUES......

How I approach life

How one approaches life is mainly determined by the way they confront trials. I'm not going to lie, I've had my fair share of medical trials, and each day does not come as a breeze, but one thing is consistent, my Father in Heaven is helping me along the way. For example, I struggle with seeing how others view my walking, my shakiness, the insecurities of my voice, what I can and cannot do, these thoughts arise on a daily basis and with each movement I make. Yes, it's exhausting, but what I've concluded, is focusing on how God sees me, just being me and letting life flow.

Life isn't a race, rather a journey to be enjoyed. Many times, I avoided doing the hard things, for fear of pain and difficulty but I've heard it said, "You will not become courageous and learn to live boldly by avoiding your fears." We need to face them and defeat them because no one else is going to do it for you. Conquer with intentionality.

This is my ultimate favorite verse; it's one that I try to live by every day,
"Count it all joy when you fall into various trials, knowing that the testing of your faith produces patience. But let patience have its perfect work that you may be perfect and complete lacking nothing."- James 1:2-3

Now, embracing challenges as they come throughout life, I see them more as a way for my character to grow as opposed to allowing it to deter me from moving forward in life. I could say that everyday life is a battle for me to overcome, but then again, I think about our Father in Heaven, and he has already overcome. I can definitely say that having this traumatic brain injury years ago has greatly enhanced the quality of my life now! My contribution of life to others wouldn't have occurred had I not had a traumatic brain injury. And now, I just want to live every day in the light of His presence, not doing what I want in life, but what His will is, in my life.

Some people call me hardheaded, and others call me easy-going but whatever you call it, it's part of what pushed me through. Through my personal experience, I've learned to not fix other people's problems and enable them, but simply to teach them. When you actively approach a situation with a genuine posture seeking a solution, pair up with the other individual and make it a team effort. Don't do it for them.

That would do them a disservice. I know that a lot of my healing was done because people would team up with me and we do it together. I mainly learned from examples. I've also learned that when you go through these hard times, you're growing and strengthening your faith in our Heavenly Father due to your dependence. Your strength does not prove anything; it's your dependence on Him that gets you through.

Deep inner thoughts

To be honest, I think that we're capable of so much more than we give ourselves credit. For example, every time I am faced with an obstacle or challenge, I have to "man up, put on my big girl panties," and just do it. If I don't, no one is going to do it for me. We have to be willing to do hard things in order to get further in life. I always am practicing the hard things in life so that those hard things will come easier. Like going to the gym and practicing squats, lunges, stepping over, under, balancing exercises, etc. Those simple, micro movements are the most challenging to overcome yet are necessary in everyday life. Another motto I live by is to get comfortable with the uncomfortable.

When I was faced with the dreadful decision to overcome or to let this disability defeat me, I didn't really have an end goal. And I still live that way. I barely ever have an end goal because who knows which path Christ is going to take you down next. It's always wise to have a general idea of what I'd like to accomplish, but I leave the ending to Yahshua. I do my part, He does His. It's the process of putting one foot in front of the other. We are built to do hard things. Apologize when you mess up but don't ever give up. That's exactly how the Father created you!

Resilience is who Yahshua made you to be. It's why we're so passionate about an issue or situation in our mind that we build upon. Fortunately, resilience is something that people can build in themselves, in ourselves, and in others. There are distinct steps that can lead to greater resilience like:
1. Reframe Negative Thoughts
2. Seek Support
3. Focus On What Is Within Control
4. Manage Stress"
Reference:
https://www.verywellmind.com/what-is-resilience-2795059

Resiliency is another way to state that a person is able to confront situations realistically. Whether it be a positive situation or a negative one. If the root of the situation cannot be pinpointed and it doesn't need to be solved at that moment, why bother thinking twice and allow it to run ragged in your mind? Subsequently, seeing problems as insurmountable. To help, micro solutions or inching your way forward is one way to strategically organize an issue. In sight of the issue at hand and entering the spiral of negativity, start seeing challenges as blessings in disguise. They're there to not only bring that character out of you that Christ already gave you, but they're there to help you develop new skillsets.

Additionally, it's always wise to seek support. While supportive friendships are beneficial in more ways than one, one of the benefits is talking through a problem. It will help you to come at it with a different perspective or to acquire validation in the eyes of another person. Discussing things with others can also help people gain insight on the challenges they are facing or even come up with new ideas for managing them.

It can be easy to get overwhelmed by things that feel far beyond our control, another way to deal with a complication, is to take note of what's inherently in our control at the moment. It's easy for the human mind to wish that there was a way to reverse the clock, but that's just not going to happen. What's done is done, there's no need to ponder on how you could've changed it because it's in the past. The only direction we're going is forward.

It might be of use to make a plan of attack whenever a certain situation comes up. This can help you to respond in a healthy mindset as opposed to reacting to the situation. When you take these realistic steps, it can drastically improve. Despite being an inch forward or an inch back, it just might help improve the situation and your mindset overall!

Finally, while you are focusing on what's inside your control, it's also imperative to build on that resilience mindset to develop your stress management habits. there is countless ways to do this. For example, the number one way that I found new habits is getting outside my comfort zone and developing habits that are new. At first, I found them dreadful and exhaustive, but overtime as I kept up with them, they have really managed stress.

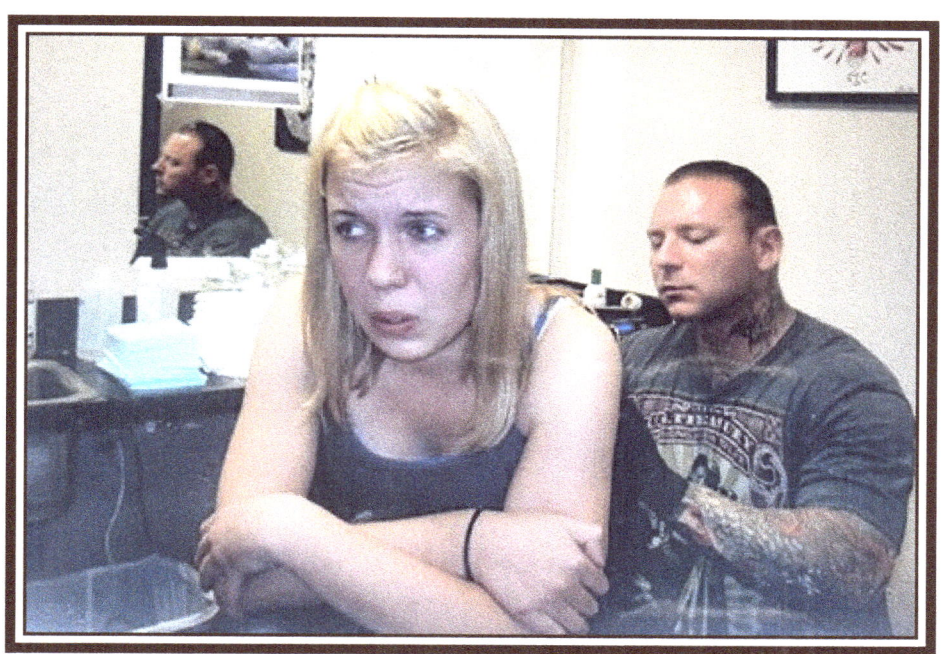

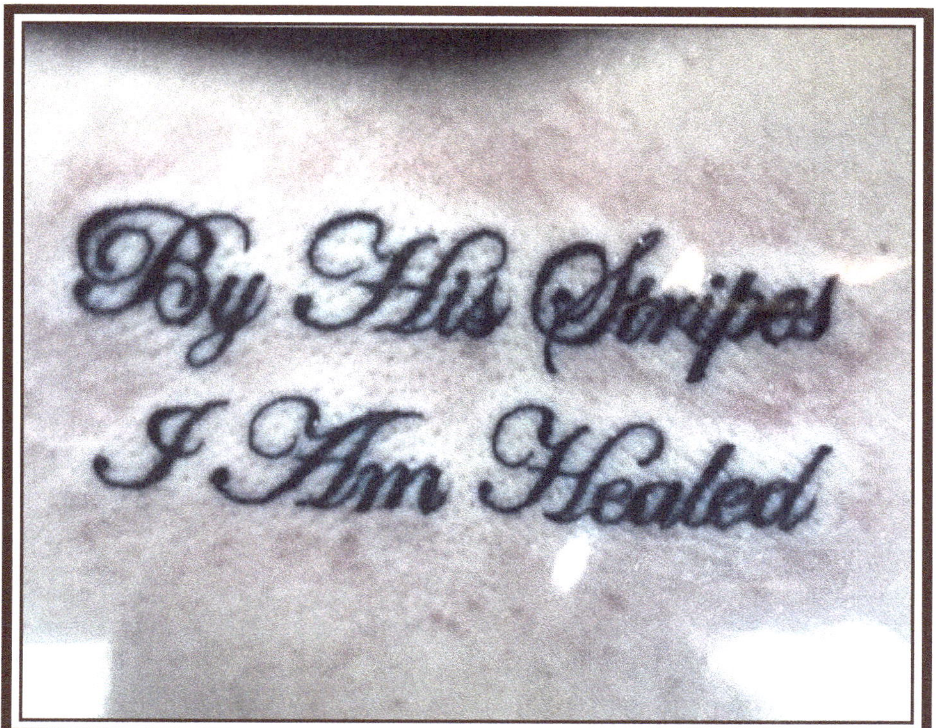
By His Stripes
I Am Healed

Chapter 15

We are like soul blues

If you've ever had the privilege of swaying to the reassuring sounds of live blues music, you've been awakened to of way of life that is easy going, friendly! And if you think about it, individuals are similar to music genres. We all relate to a type of music that elevates us and brings us joy. There are so many different types of genres, yet it's all music (despite what we think). Just like how we are all individuals with a different meaning and purpose in life, and we all are called to build one another up with brotherly love in mind.

Countless times, we are performing actions that may be fun and entertaining but is it really going to matter in the end? At the end of your life? That could be today or tomorrow or twenty years from now, we won't know. What we do know is that whatever we implement today affects our tomorrow. So similar to listening to the relaxing sounds of live blues music, while I was at my lowest of lows, I'd repeatedly ponder of why God is not healing me. But what I didn't fully understand is that I needed to turn that "why God," into "what can I do with this."

Yes, it's a change of perspective that flips the script of how I approach things. My life has been changed and transformed through this occurrence of going through these ailments and conditions all while gaining wisdom and knowledge throughout the process. It's an ongoing undertaking for one to be up for the challenge, yet 100% worth the submission! Whereas, my short thirteen years in my "old" body, some say it was cut short and that I missed out on so much. And I would agree with that comment. But again, what if that's not what God wanted me to face?

What if this was His ultimate plan for my life? See, when you constantly exercise acceptance and agreement of not knowing what's next in life, you are practicing submission. When that submission is placed on the Lord to satisfy all of your needs, wants and desires, He works like an air control tower to look out for what you don't see. Although I didn't like my circumstances at the time, years later the results have blossomed into a new and upgraded version of myself. Keeping my eyes on the hope of what is to come through our Father and Lord Jesus.

In the undertaking of these specific events, each step of my recovery process was a way to overcome in and of itself. Each step on the path was another way to defeat the odds with victory in hand. But obviously it wasn't a walk in the park, with the tireless effort that was put in, each small win was a giant step forward in my eyes. Beating the odds that were against me didn't seem to be anything special at the time, but knowing where I came from, it was huge. And that process was a slow progression, as I took things step-by-step. trusting the process and believing that there was more to come.

Blessings are inching toward you.
I stood on shore of the beach one early morning and was reflecting about where I've been, to the path that our Father has put me on. I stand there in anticipation that the sand beneath me may crumble to where I need to move inches over, relying on sturdy ground to keep me steady. Much like how Yahshua is my steady ground. I choose to build my "house," my life, His

dwelling place, on steady ground. Not wavering or tottering like the sinking sand but relying on His word to sustain me.

Father, I fully trust You to satisfy all of my needs, wants and desires. I look up to You with all I have. I desire to seek You and only You. Help me learn more and more of Your word, bring opportunities my way that I know come directly from You. I wait for Your commands in my decisions. Lord, lead me along the path of Your everlasting love, to seek You in my day to day.

Not wavering from Your truth but to look to You in all that I do. Help me to pour my heart out to You because You're the one and only that knows my true thoughts. Help me to involve You, not just to inform You of what's happening. You're my friend and You desire the best for me, help me to hunger and thirst for Your correction in every way possible. It's not condemnation, it's correction to make me a better person. A better human being to better serve You and to show others the love that only comes from You.

As I stand there with the excitement of Your peace, understanding comes to me. The understanding and insight of how when one stands in the shallow waters of where the dry sand meets the wet sand, you can just barely get your toes wet. When that does happen, the water sometimes reaches you and other times teaches you something that we may know nothing about or realize it wasn't supposed to reach that far. Much like how God can put blessings in our life. Sometimes they reach us and they're great, other times they overflow and other times they're there to remind us to keep on unshakable ground.

To realize that, in order to experience the true majesty of the beach, sometimes you go through life altering circumstances that's similar to sinking sand and come to the awareness that I needed to have the perspective of the Father. Building my "house," also known as my body, on steady ground. That's where the true miracles begin, knowing that you are phenomenal in His eyes. You are complete. You are perfect.

Then comes the waves of life, good waves, not so good waves, but as I keep my sight on Yahshua, I not only encounter these endless blessings, but I fathom that those not-so-great experiences in life were not there to try to tear me down, rather to build my character and shift my perspective. So, while sand and waves might just be a beautiful view, there's more beyond the depths. We just need to look for it. That's exactly how Christ designed it. There's something to be learned in all situations.

Different perspectives
Throughout this process of healing, I've come to the realization that my life was saved not for man's own glory but for the Father. Coming to terms that 95% of people are going to treat me unique, misunderstood, unheard, is not a quality most people have to cope with in life, but only a few are struck the good hard life. See, I strategically look for that 5% of people. Those limited amounts of individuals that see hope. That looks soul deep. Those that are there despite circumstances, despite obstacles.

I don't see my journey or obstacle in life as an affliction but rather a blessing in disguise that brought out my true character shaped from the Lord Himself that was already predestined; I just had to live it out. Each of us has strength in us that we don't even know is there. But because God created you, He already knew and believed in you. He always provides more than we ask, think or imagine. But it's up to us to look to Him to instruct us and to guide us. And when we allow Him to take the reins of life, attributes of Him shine.

For example, Phileo love. People love to love one another. It's an emotional love that conveys a strong feeling of attraction, care, respect and compassion. That's what we're designed for and called to do. A form of brotherly love. Phileo love was commonly used with reference to friendships or family relationships. For example, it was used in Matthew 10:37 to indicate love for father and mother or son and daughter. Phileo was the word used of Jesus' love for His friend Lazarus (John 11:3, 36) and His love for His disciple (John 20:2).

"I'm not intimidating, you're intimidated. There's a difference. I'm not mean, nor aggressive, I'm honest and assertive. And that can make others uncomfortable. And it's not me that makes you uncomfortable; my presence challenges your comfort. I will not be less for you to feel better about yourself."

Now, please don't mistake me when I say that caring for others is the most important thing, but sometimes people can care too much to the extent that it deters from others wanting to help because they might do things differently than you. In many cases, they're just happy that they're able to complete the task no matter how long it takes. It's always worth it to ask if an individual needs assistance instead of assuming. Sometimes it's not perfect but we try! Doing the best that you can do is all that you can, perfect or imperfect, you're trying your best. It's all about inclusion.

Including people that may not appear proficient but want to be there for moral support. That's the thing; they actually want to be there. Emphasize the word want because when people want to do something, they're eager. They might not always be sitting on the edge of their seat to help, but they genuinely want to do something for you. Take a step back and look at life through another's eyes, see how everyone has a part to play in this journey called life. We can't do life on our own, that's why God created people, friends, family to help each other along the way.

With that being said, with any disability or injury, you are implied to uptake the blue badge of honor, a.k.a. the handicap placard! Knowing that there is close parking availability, makes the world of difference wherever I go. It's not always available to be utilized, but knowing that it's there to be used helps the situation wherever I am.

Whenever I hear of people complain that parking is too far away, all I have to say is, "just bring me along and we can get front row parking!"

Pool and Horse therapy.

Recovery looks so different on each individual and there are countless different forms of clinical therapy known to humankind. Apart from your typical speech therapy, occupational therapy, physical therapy, we heard of this therapy called aqua therapy. Water therapy! Water was and is and always will be healing. "Where there's no water, there's no life." Which explains why humans are always thirsty to know more!" Not usually a destination but rather a journey in disguise.

It was a game changer for me to take on, the water. Going from my wheelchair to holding onto the side pool railings, I'd be instructed to do certain exercises, walking up and down the pool treading water and using the resistance of the water to steady me. I'd laugh; giggle be giddy due to the fact that I was on my own. I had a piece of independence I was longing for. Water of any sort is such a massive healer when used in a therapy sense. And overtime, it helped me more and more. Plus, the confidence I gained through pool therapy was beyond what anyone could've hoped for. It was a God sent and was very much a pivotal part of my healing process.

I also had heard about this form of therapy where you can ride a horse. It helps emotionally, mentally, and physically. Working on core stability and posture. With my background of having a strong bond and love for horses, I thought that it would be super constructive. Known as Hippo-therapy, I excitedly got up on the horse. It was so much fun to get back in the saddle while viewing the barren arena, it felt so freeing, like this was one step of the puzzle that I was missing to shaping the "old Kassidy" but in a new and improved kind of way.

Hippotherapy was a kind of therapy where I got structured, assisted help. I had the option to look at it as a form of freedom or view it as assisted help, either way, I was doing it! I'd do some drills on the horse, ride him then I'd have to do the occupational therapy part and brush out the horse. I'd get to brush him; bathe him, all of the necessities when it comes to caring for a horse.

Just because your pain is understandable doesn't mean your behavior is acceptable.

In all my endeavors, I completely adopted the saying, "Just because your pain is understandable doesn't mean your behavior is acceptable." Yes, there is the time in the place to have your down times, but when you're there to present yourself, God wants us to be present. Your presence is what he desires, not what you do or accomplish. Just to be present in His presence. Matt 7:15-23 is where we get the term wolf in sheep clothing. There are those false prophets that are like pruning grapes from a thorn bush. There's beauty in the midst, but first you have to get past those thorns.

It is just like a healthy tree that cannot produce bad fruit due to its' maker. Similar to these false prophets, those Jesus loving individuals are going to prophesy that Jesus is Lord, but are they truly talking about Jesus the God of Israel, Yahshua? We need to be aware of those wolves in sheep clothing. On the day of judgment, only Christ will have the ultimate say. We have to be aware of lawlessness within others' lives. And basically, because those wolves in sheep clothing will attempt to make life unbearable, remember, our pain is understandable, but it doesn't mean your behavior is acceptable. Just like having a bad day, we have to consider our surroundings and the impact on those around us.

Practice acceptance toward experience, people, appearance, emotions, ideas, and more.

Although you want one thing in life but see another, that's when it truly takes faith to come into action. To have the never ceasing hope for Yahshua's' grace. He generously gives when we are the selfish ones that only want to receive. A true servant of the Messiah does not waver to and fro. But has the mindset of one goal, and that goal is to reflect the true heart and compassion of the Lord Jesus Christ because He is the good news of the world. There is no other good news in the sight of him.

Reading through this verse, we understand that the obedience of Christ rest upon our love and passion for him. Not for what He can give us, but rather what we can give. What He has done in and through us is a clear sign of the love that he has for you and me does not disappoint. Yeah, we might not get the things that we are hoping for, but then again, that means we are getting something, but let me ask you, what are you giving?

Relatability to the Father has no end. Especially in this book venture, my desire is to not just share of You, but to share of the hope that You bring. So many people seek out the next quick fix when there's so much more to life than having to rely on pharmaceuticals and a person in order to do something. That's exactly why Jesus is so proficient at giving. He gives the final say, He encourages us to carry on, He gives us hope. Christ plays the game differently. He doesn't use a guilt factor, has no motive, looks out for the interest of you! In addition, He's looking to please your desires in His will. Within His boundaries and in His time. As we read it in Galatians 1:10.

Having your mind rest on Yahshua's hope is a way of accepting reality. Accepting the cards you've been dealt with. Not seeking approval of what man sees' but living a life of true liberty in Yahshua. However, acceptance does not mean liking, wanting or choosing something. It's basically living life with a semi colon at the end of each sentence. (;) Stating, my story isn't over. Acceptance is an active process. It must be practiced over and over again. In that case, it's like surrender. We have to die to ourselves every day, to live with Christ in control of our life.

While we live with this mentality, acceptance doesn't mean that you can't work on changing things. Throughout my recovery journey, I was met with brutal challenges to overcome. Yet because Christ enabled me to, I needed to come to terms that this is how life is right now but that could easily change. I am consistently working to better myself, physically, mentally and spiritually. Within boundaries, we can practice acceptance toward our experience, people, appearance, emotions, ideas, and more. Putting our full perception of what our life should be about in the hands of the Father with the hope of His possibilities.

Parking spaces

When we pull up to a parking spot, we fully expect to pull right in without any inconveniences. But when there are roadblocks and adversity within those parking spaces, we can't really deter them, we either have to find a new spot or avoid the event altogether. I was thinking about that and that's kind of like how Christ works, He either says yes, not now, wait, or no. Sometimes the best way to approach a situation is to have that in mind. Not trying to force your way into this situation at hand, but letting God answer and tell you that it needs to work in his ways.

Sometimes when there's many open spots available to be filled, we think that there are many possibilities. When the right one is supposed to work in your favor. It's not a matter of having the closest or the best parking spot. We're all in this race together.

Each and every part of society has a purpose. It's not about getting the closest or the best spot or thing in life. It's about being the closest and the best to Jesus that there is. Typically, we want what comes easy, but what we don't consider are the opportunities that can come from the challenge of having not only a further parking space, but a further journey in life.

Opportunities can come from the deepest parts of life; all we need to do is bring Yahshua into the forefront of our minds and let him navigate. Simultaneously, when we see that all of the convenient parking spaces are occupied, we might consider fleeing the scene because it might be too challenging to go or be in the vicinity that we need. But has God called you to a straightforward life? He may take the easy things and make them hard, but He may take the hard things and make them easy.

What he wants to do is evolve the character that He has already set in you. That He has already given each and every one of us to withdraw. And despite our hesitation to want to refrain from the environment, when we take those challenges and hard times directly, we start to notice and see changes that you didn't even know were possible. Because that's how Yahshua lives. He wants to bless you. He wants to see you thrive in this life. Much like how we might want convenience in life, that's not always the reality of the situation. Sometimes we need to face tribulation in order to get to the top.

Kassidy Brewer

FROM THE LIBRARY OF

Chapter 16

Shunts

Speaking of the recovery process, while recovering physically, mentally, and emotionally, I was hit with the most intense gut pain one can imagine. Some people think I'm crazy, but it was the kind of pain that took your breath away. I didn't want to speak except for cry in pain, the kind of pain that radiated up your back in your spine. It almost took the shape of pregnancy contractions. It was absolutely horrendous. There was only one position on the couch that seemed bearable. I definitely would never wish that on anyone. Now because I have a shunt in my brain that circulates the fluid in my brain, I don't get hydrocephalus, anything that goes on or in the gut affects my brain and that affects my shunt. It's like a hamster wheel.

It is absolutely amazing, how God intended for everything to be connected, and that there is a sense of purpose behind each and every little thing. Even the root causes of pain. With my shunt, there is a tube that goes from my brain to my belly that relieves the fluid to where everything that happens via the gut, like this pain that I was having in my stomach, easily affected my shunt because of the intense pressure being placed on it.

Due to having this immense pressure going on, a couple of times, it ended up disconnecting my shunt. And when my shunt stops working, I turn yellow, my eyes become hard to open, I become lethargic, I dry heave. I'm just not myself at all. At that time, I'd say it's an emergency. We have to get to the hospital. Not to be dramatic or anything, but whenever my shunt stops working, it's the scariest thing, not just for me but for everyone. Because I can't control what's going on.

They refer to fixing the shunt as a shunt revision. Another word for a revision is an alteration or a correction. These shunt revisions are considered a surgery because they have to put me under general anesthesia and cut a small piece of my flesh open on my skull. In addition, they have to feed the tube through my body. These shunt revisions are 100% necessary but the recovery is not the most fun. The worst part of all is having to relearn to hold my neck up, let alone washing my hair in the shower is probably just as exhausting and takes everything out of me. And to top it off, you get this new hairdo because they shaved a couple chunks of hair off too.

Extremely exhausted from the anesthesia, holding your neck up stabilizes your whole body, so without that it's pretty hard to do anything. But I did find that using one of those airplane neck pillows while resting on the couch is the ticket because it avoids the head from moving left right back or down. The things that we do. From when my incident first took place until now, I've had a total of eight shunt revisions. And with this most recent shunt revision, they brainstormed and decided to move my shunt up a few inches resulting in great impact!

Typically, a VP shunt lasts for any time period. They can last anywhere from a couple days up to decades. The previous shunts I've had didn't seem to like me very much, so I've had to have them revised. To take things in a different manner, the gym isn't necessarily my shunts friend due to the pressure that it can bring on, but it's my healthy vice. It's also the best thing for me due to how it helps strengthen my core, works on my ataxia, helps me balance, improves my mental health and so much more.

I repeatedly mention that I'm "allergic" to weights because of the pressure that gets built up in my head. I try my best to go slow, use light weight, distance myself or to greatly focus on my breath and take it very lightly. With doing weights, I've had several shunts stop working and that didn't have the best outcome. So, I mainly work on body weight and balance type moves because of that. With my Ataxia, we're thinking that my drastic movements cause some sort of disconnection. I guess I'm just too gnarly and intense for these shunts to last very long.

Resulting from this, I might do countless daily activities a little bit different than others means that the process is just another step. The process of doing these commodities gets done in the same way just in a different fashion! My own fashion. In this process, some people may view it as odd or just plain out weird, but you know what, it's the process that works for me.

That's why we should aim to do what works best for us and will make us better in the long run. And that process requires vulnerability. Vulnerability to fail and fail miserably until you get it right. That's when true growth starts to happen. You will feel it; you'll start to see it. It will make a difference to not just you but others around you as well. All of those mishaps and imperfections in my life all lead to the direction of hope.

Mineral journey

To find out the true cause of why I was having gut issues in the first place, brought me to my next step of healing. It led me to the understanding that it could've been several reasons but one of the most impactful and detrimental loops could've most likely been the medications that I was on. Remember, I was on some harsh life-saving medications. Now don't get me wrong, I absolutely love these medications because they saved my life and helped me survive. But on the other hand, they did have consequences. And that's when I started to seek relief from the gut pains that I was experiencing.

I knew that medication started all this, so I didn't want to fill myself with more of the stuff that caused this issue. So, in that case, I sought out a way of healing. But as I was researching, I started to find out that certain foods cause gut pain. That's when I started to eliminate more and more resulting in a very minimal diet. I started to fall into the trap of seeking out one diet over the other. A term known as yo-yo dieting. It got me nowhere but temporary relief.

Eventually, I got exhausted, trying to go from this diet to that diet, so I ended up searching for a deeper cause, the root cause. I started to look more into what every single ingredient meant, from what it actually was to where it was from and trying my best to avoid those at all costs. Which brought me to the next best thing, God given nutrition! I call it that because that's essentially what it is. Nutrition that was given by God himself. A lot of what our ancestors lived on.

Things that may seem unhealthy today, but when you look at it in a nutrient sense, when you fill your body with nutrients, that's how your body lives and functions from a cellular level. Food was ultimately made for us to thrive! A lot of the foods today are deprived of nutrients and minerals that our body needs and thrive on. Things today have an overabundance of additives and don't always come from the best places. Paying attention to what we eat and whatever that consumes. Because what goes into them goes into you.

Adding minerals, paying attention to gut health, thyroid health, liver health, blood sugar and brain health have greatly impacted my life for the better. Part of my mission I've set out to do is to transform actions, thoughts, and behaviors to bring wisdom and knowledge to help those that have a hard time helping themselves.

Find your tribe.
In anyone's healing journey, the number one thing I recommend is to find your tribe. Find your people, people that propel you forward to be the best you can. The ones that you can relate to the most. People in your court, individuals that you can rely on for sound advice that bring purpose to your soul. When working on you, in order to be there for others, there's a sense of purpose there.

I live by the saying; "You can't help others if you don't help yourself first." It's kind of like putting on an oxygen mask before you assist others. It sounds a little morbid but it's true. You have to be the best you, so you can make others great too. God intended for all of His children to seek, to seek and find.

And if we have a hard time finding our way, well, that's what our tribe is for, there to help us along the way.

Just like God doesn't reframe the light from the darkness, He doesn't take you out of the storm or the seas, but he contains it.

While I was in the midst of my pain and suffering, I had individuals that were by me, encouraging me along the way. Yeah, they weren't my close friends like before. But they were new and different. Much wiser to say the least. I knew for a fact that I didn't want to surround myself with people that would bring me down in life because that's not what I needed. I did have resources for extracurricular stuff, but I wasn't very interested because of the way people my age treated me.

I always tend to gravitate to people that are twice or three times my age because I can relate more to them, and they have lots of wisdom under their belts! That's my tribe, those kinds of individuals that lead you to a place of growth as opposed to a place of complacency. As I've heard before, they are my grandma's friends! And I'm not ashamed of it.

As Proverbs 17:17 states that a friend loves at all times and a brother is born for adversity. That's exactly who my tribe is and what they do. I'm not saying, go make some grandma/grandpa friends, I'm just trying to emphasize the importance of who you surround yourself with, because God can work through your friends in order to get to you. All I am saying is that it's wise to have a circle around you that will pick you up by your bootstraps, dust you off, and continue on your growth without judgment.

Not giving up on my joy

More than anything, when you pray for healing for an individual, you are expecting healing that surpasses all understanding right? Healing that comes in a physical form. But what if I told you that the type of healing that is unseen is far better. Yes, we pray for relief from pain in the flesh but what if we began to change our prayers to healing of the mind instead? Half of the battle is between our ears! If we seek acceptance over comfort, we can start to see the situation with new eyes. That's where our tribe can come in, they can help us to view obstacles as opportunities in a window of time due to the quiet moments we have to sit in our discomfort, to bring it to the Father and Lord Jesus Christ.

Pain is an attribute no one yearns for, but it can be used for His glory if we allow Him in. Matthew 7:7 states, "Ask, and it will be given to you; seek, and you will find; knock, and it will be opened to you." Many people know this verse like the back of their hand, but we have trouble with the persistence part. And giving up our own will for the will of the one who created you. It's not easy to surrender your own wants and desires but it's a characteristic that God has for you and for me. But maybe, just maybe, He desires for your mind to be healed over your body. With time and acceptance, God does His work.

I wish I had this advice when I was going through the thick of it. Although grieving is completely without a doubt a necessary part of the healing process, it can be done in a way to where it doesn't affect others. Healing between you and God. Gaining wisdom from your tribe and being on a quest for truth, not wavering but testing all instances.

That brings me to my journey of accepting that I had difficulty running. Being a runner was my joy. It was something that lit me up on the inside. It was the feeling of freedom. Knowing that a person has to relearn how to do everything again was very defeating. Defeating yes, impossible no. Impossible means that you'll never be able to. They also told me that I was never going to talk, walk, or breathe on my own but look who is doing that now.

So, there is hope! Obviously, I do these things in a unique way but I'm doing them and that's all that matters! It all begins with acceptance. Accepting what the reality of the situation is instead of only adjusting to what it is. Accepting is another way of saying, "it is what it is, but I'm not going to give up of what could be."

It's kind of like giving up your plans to involve God in your life and to start asking God to involve you in his plans for your life. I haven't fully given up running, and I never plan to. I work on the motion of jumping all the time, it's extremely difficult. Especially with Ataxia because it's either in full extension or tight against my body. It takes a lot of focus to keep those soft bends in your knees that running calls for. Ataxia is pretty much all or nothing.

I might not be able to execute the full motion of being able to run, but I am in the process of learning how to do this movement again. Like quick feet, bouncing, or jumping. It's all about progression. When we look at something in baby steps, it sometimes takes the pressure off of the big things. Step by step, little by little, we get to where we need to be. It's not always about pushing yourself to the max, God will always meet us where we're at in life and He knows how to expand our limit but never exceeds that. He knows what you're capable of because He created you.

The process of these events was quite an adventure. Speaking of my mineral journey, it was a whole voyage in itself. Around eleven to twelve years of horrendous, gut-wrenching pain on and off not knowing when it was going to confront itself and make its debut. Those times were definitely a whirlwind. And while searching for my tribe, in the very beginning stages, I was very lonely, thinking I didn't have anyone on my team. But I was far from that. I just didn't know where to look.

During my years of loneliness, I began to value safety and comfort. But slowly growing inwardly, safety in life is found by the ones that you love, cherish, and trust deeply. I found that in my church ladies, A.k.a. my grandma friends! That was the beginning process of reaching out to people and that's where my knowledge grew. I started opening myself up to different avenues of seeking Christ for answers and that led me to my mineral journey. It all trickles down and leads to growth in the long run. still, the process continues.

We're all very visual.

Think back to when you were a kid. When you were that little thirteen-year-old kid… What did you enjoy doing? Why did you stop doing that as an adult? I've found, one of the best healing mechanisms for my mental health has been getting back to what brought me "healthy joy," as a child. And for myself, that is horseback riding. Caring for them, being around them! So, let me ask you, what's something you did as a child that you enjoyed that you don't do as an adult? Focus on bringing out that childlike fun back into your life to elevate your circumstances. You'd be shocked by the outcome.

If you can imagine having a great life where all you wanted to do was to enjoy life, have fun with your friends and not have a care in the world. That's what we all long for, right? What if there was a way to compartmentalize your work- social life to incorporate fun? I'm all about taking a breather, taking a breather in Yahshua alone because in doing so you'll find not only peace but a better way to accomplish tasks and overcome them with your co-pilot!

James 1:17-25 Reflection
My interpretation of these verses, when you read it with the heart in mind, getting rid of all those judgments and evil thoughts in one's mind, we can understand that God 's word is implanted in us. Where His words are able to save our soul from the depth of whatever confronts us. Those evil things that meant harm, may actually be a vessel that God is using to get us to the next step. It's just up to us to choose to look at the obstacle, use Yahshua's promises and overcome them. And this verse directly explains why one of my main mottos is to "just do the dang thing."

This verse is saying that once we hear the word and don't put it into action, it remains complacent. Basically, it's saying just do it. That's how we need to be. Not to be on the sidelines but to be actively pursuing Faith. And we can do that by looking at the Torah with the perspective of freedom and liberty through Yahshua. Once we put his words into action and remain steadfast in his words and never back down on what he stands on, that's when we will see insight and blessing. Because there, we are actively partaking with Him and what He does.

While we're hesitant in wanting to go or to do something, we may feel reluctant to pursue. If only there was something that could take you to a whole new level of awesomeness. Wait, there is. It's called the Holy Spirit who lives inside of you helping you reach a new platform. He's there, not to push you to where you're not comfortable but to encourage you past your comfort because He already knows what you're capable of. He will help you to not only see the challenge ahead but to go forward in full confidence in Yahshua and do the dang thing!

Ecclesiastes 3 Reflection

And while Christ empowers you to a specific season in life, some things are temporary. Meaning it won't last forever to where we can have the hope and timing of Yahshua due to the season that some things may not last for a longer time than others. But some choices only last a few moments, to where we need to be prepared mentally and physically for differentiating decisions. As Solomon states in verse twelve, we just need to be happy and enjoy ourselves in the time that we do have here on earth. Reading further, we hear that God has already done the impossible in order for people to fear Him. He has already overcome it to where trust and belief in him helps to fathom His timing and not our own.

We are human, we have wants and desires, and we want them now but then again, God doesn't work in our timing. On our watch. To where looking to him helps to not only rely on Him, but to trust in His brilliant timing. We have to remember, "God seeks out what people chase after." What are you chasing after?

Does it fall in line with His timing? Does it reflect His love? And as we read on, it goes on about our intention, he mentions that there is a right time for every intention and every action. Speaking of His timing, we need to understand that His timing is perfect. Again, it doesn't happen on our watch, but His. It may not even happen in our lifetime, but that doesn't mean it's not going to happen.

Chapter 17

Black belt

Back when I was nine years old, I stumbled upon this Taekwondo studio that would soon become my second home! As a nine-year-old looking forward to getting new toys, I looked forward to setting goals and advancing to the next belt rank. I would say that I was a very motivated child and a lot of that has to do with Taekwondo. Everyone that "worked" there was like one big family. Brothers and sisters! We were all students and instructors teaching and encouraging the younger belts. Those were the days! Fridays were my absolute favorite time. We would call those Friday nights, fight nights.

We had controlled street sparring nights that would turn into a self-defense competition, but in the most fun way possible. It was intense and tiring, grappling with my brothers' and sisters'! Being this small blonde chick, I might not have had the strength to fight someone my age, but I would take on two little boys at once and downright defeated them! I thrived on Friday night fights!

But the strange part was, on our car rides to Taekwondo, I'd tell my mom, sometimes I get this weird gushing sound in my head. Nothing drastic but it's there. It's only happened about two or three times." Again, I was eleven or twelve years old, so we didn't really think anything of it. When I was a young, feisty twelve-year-old, I set out to reach my target of black belt with a hope to further advance my dreams. When a person reaches their black belt, they receive a scroll signifying their importance. I was the scroll of the Mustang horse.

This is what the actual scroll says,
"A wonder to watch as it runs through the open fields. It is a small yet swift animal, which led many to try to tame it. Although never fully tamed, as it always kept a bit of its wildness. It showed its great strength and ability to sense what someone's next move would be and could be heavily relied upon. Yet, there are always a few which can never be tamed and demand their freedom. The spirit of the Mustang running majestically through the plains is truly a sight to behold."

Well, the Lord had a different plan in mind for me, not knowing that my whole life would take a turn upside down months later. This scroll means so much more now than ever. Within those few months, I went from a new black belt to not sure if this girl would return. My instructor was like my big brother, Mr. Robles, was always looking out for the interest of his students and extremely passionate about what he does. He was the very first person that my mom contacted to tell him the news.

He was speechless and all he could do was call another black belt friend of mine that I worked with. They jumped into the car and met us at the hospital, not knowing if it would be their last time seeing me. Being some of the initial people there, they were there from the very beginning and continued for years to come. About a year and a half after my incident, is when I returned to work on some simple moves and to be back in my "normal" routine. Things obviously looked different with me not being able to spin around, to jump high, balance while I kick the pad, but I was back in the swing of things again!

Just taking it at a much slower pace and modifying a bunch, but you do what you have to. And I begun to use martial arts as a form of physical therapy because it not only helped my physical stature, but it also helped me mentally by getting back to myself, focusing on a target, hitting goals, working through things, being thorough, always trying and never giving up. In fact, achieving my black belt at such a young age definitely taught me a lot, really shaped who I am and propelled me forward in my healing journey.

At fifteen years old, I tested for my second-degree black belt. It was quite an emotional test for everyone. From watching a live miracle happen before their eyes in a hospital bed to watching in anticipation of God's work through forward movement in the "miracle mustang." We coordinated an event, that we called "Round kick for Rady Children's Hospital San Diego. Where we had a huge silent auction, food and live music, kid bouncers, a board break-a-thon, BMX-demo, local business-expos, karate demos, then my second-degree black belt test. It was a big event. It even was recorded for a TV show called "Everyday Health" Feel free to YouTube, Everyday Health – Kassidy Brewer.

With a couple hundred to thousands of people around the world seeing this, I went through over 150+ moves that had to be executed and memorized. Exhausted, then came time for board breaks. I was given three different moves with three different chances to break each one. With the first two being kicks and the last one, a punch square through the board. I punched so hard the first two times, but my hand seemed to bounce off the board. Completely wiped, I just wanted to sit on the side lines.

I had to remember Yahshua's power that's already inside of me and these people were here to experience Gods miraculous healing power. So, I gave my last and final attempt. I thought back to what I always learned growing up, "One, two and through." And that's exactly what I did. Blasting through that board on the last try. I guess I had to build the anticipation up! The entire room went crazy with excitement. After that, Mr. Robles, my instructor, said a few touching words. Remember, he was there from the beginning and saw the miracle come about.

He even saved the initial voicemail that my mom left on his phone when she called to give him the news. It's on the episode of "Everyday Health" if you're curious. What Christ can do through one person has the ability to trickle down known as the domino effect. Moving through the emotions that day, each and every person that came out to that event was there for my family and I throughout my healing process. Each and every individual are clear signs of the miraculous miracles that took place.

My Service Dogs
Another part of my healing journey back in 2010, someone mentioned service dogs. Without exception, I knew I had loved dogs so having one with me all the time was an incredible thought. After searching, we found a local organization called Canine Support Teams to where I was met by incredible individuals who have a heart for not only dogs but also their clients with disabilities too.

I was paired with a wiry golden doodle. As we were in the process of working in groups with all of the dogs, the founder/ trainer

Carol saw that one of the other dogs (a yellow lab named Chase, who was working with someone different), was eye bawling me and kind of gravitating towards me. So, Carol, switched the two dogs to see what would happen. Since that point, we have been inseparable. So, when I say that Chase chose me, I'm not kidding. He was a divine angel that played a massive role in my development today.

At the end of training, I acquired a furry best friend that came in the form of a handsome yellow Labrador retriever service dog. Chase was the best thing for me at that moment because if you consider all of what a brain injury comes with, like anxiety, worry, depression, stress, frustration... etc. It can feel isolating because you want it to be taken off your shoulders, yet you are too tired to talk about, yet you don't want anyone to speak because then you have to understand and comprehend what they're saying so it was better just to deal with it in your own way. But Chase was tremendously in tune with me. He was living proof that there are other ways to internalize your pain.

Believe it or not, Chase helped me in ways one cannot comprehend. When I was learning to speak and had noticeable Aphasia and Apraxia, I would go everywhere with him. Individuals would inquire about the dog, as opposed to asking questions and staring at me, so it took some of the pressure off of trying to perform so they wouldn't see me as a disabled body but rather asking what the dog does for me. And truthfully, I loved having a built-in best friend that didn't say much, made me laugh to the core and was always happy to see me!

Chase was brought into my life at just the right time because I was relearning a lot, but I was also was still in high school at that point. Being pulled from a regular high school to be put into home studies, strangely I didn't miss anything about regular school. I think that was particularly due to having to focus so much on my rehab, I didn't really want to spend my time reflecting.

I was paired with an incredible academic advisor Diana Miller. I told her that my number one goal was to walk across that stage without my walker, get my diploma and graduate on time. She said, "I can make that happen if you're willing to put in the work." I went to classes one day a week and did the rest of it at home with Chase encouraging me along the way. I would really like to draw attention to Diana because she was a God sent. She continually reminded me of my goal to graduate on time, but she also believed in me to make that happen!

In 2012, I did accomplish ALL of those goals. I only walked across that stage because Chase was considered a stability dog. He used a harness (kind of like a seeing eye harness but it comes straight up like a brief case instead of across the back), to where I was able to walk without my walker. Yes, it was different than I imagined but I didn't even care. Life was great, and Chase was there to celebrate every moment with me.

He was the ideal dog, unfortunately his time as a service dog was cut short due to two knee ACL surgeries making it difficult for him to jump in and out of the car. He "retired" as a service dog shortly after that. Only able for service work for around two years. Fortunately, though, he was a great therapy dog who stayed at home. He didn't go anywhere except for walks around the neighborhood and continued to be by my side through thick and thin at home.

On July 2, 2021, he woke me up, happy as usual. I then got dressed and ready for the day. Walking into the kitchen, he would typically follow me, gearing up to be fed his breakfast. But this time, he didn't. He stayed on the carpet unsure that his legs would hold him. Now I knew that something was wrong. Years prior, he was diagnosed with a degenerative disk disease in his spine, but he woke up full of life in his eyes. If you've ever witnessed someone or something you love in pain, you do whatever you can to relieve them of pain. But sometimes you're helpless.

At the vet, she did an exam on his pelvis only to find out that she might've felt a tumor. Shockingly, I had to make the devastating decision to put him down after fourteen and a half years of life. Particularly because his rear legs failed him and what was most likely a tumor pushing on his spine. We went through so much together in life and he is one of the main tangible reasons I am where I am today. God gives us the divine beings not as creatures of life but angels that are on a mission to expel the Lords' message. He was a spiritual messenger that came in the form of a fur ball. He was definitely another one of my true loves in physical form!

Four and a half dreadful months of having to wait, I had fundraised enough funds for another furry best friend through the same organization. That's where Bennett comes into the picture! Bennett was the ultimate spitfire! I was so used to Chase. Chase was very laid back and chill. I called him an Eeyore! Bennett on the other hand was like a Tigger! He knew his commands yet had ecstatic energy to please which has a characteristic known as amiable. He was a whole new level of fun! But I firmly believe that God gives us what we need, not what we want. He knew I needed a slower (Eeyore) dog for healing also known as Chase and He also knew I was at a phase of my life where I needed Bennett to bring fun and excitement into my life. God gave me these two blessings at the right time in life. No doubt.

All of a sudden, 15 short months after getting him, Bennett then became very lethargic, he wasn't eating, he was losing weight, he was shaking internally (even though it wasn't cold), several tragic symptoms. We took him to the vet. After multiple tests, he was diagnosed with Addison's disease. If you're curious what Addison's disease is, it's basically where the adrenal glands don't produce enough cortisol. He had to be put on medication for the rest of his life along with injections once a month.

At that time, after he was on meds for a few days and at the end of his Addison's crash, he was the most ideal dog! Definitely more attentive, affectionate, and goofy. But he almost needed a therapy human! Unfortunately, I had to make the decision no parent wants to make, putting your child up for adoption. I wasn't in a place to be able to give him the care that he needed so he was adopted by a couple nearby. A low stress life is exactly what he needs and I'm beyond grateful that he's in a place where he can thrive and not be held back in any way!

Being that I only had Bennett for 14-15 months, I really didn't get to go through life's ups and downs with him. However, he taught me a lot still in that short time. Now because Chase was Mr. Slow Mo and Bennett was Mr. Buzz Light-year, their personalities were completely different. I have to break it to you, I did fall into the comparison trap, but you can never compare personalities, even in a dog, that's just who they were called to be. Much like people, you can't change a dog. You just roll with the season of life that you're in. And that's exactly what I did.

Bennett was a lot for a dog, but he was so patient, and we worked so greatly together. Beyond a doubt, Bennett taught me patience and learning to pick my battles in the fact that he would have his little energy episode, while I was trying to get him dressed (he was just too ecstatic to have a job!) which I couldn't blame him for. I'd have to bite my tongue so I wouldn't correct him and laugh through it.

"Choose your battles wisely. After all, life isn't measured by how many times you stood up to the fight. It's not about winning battles that make you happy but it's how many times you turn away and choose to look into a better direction. Life is too short to spend it on warring. Fight only the most, most, most important battles, let the rest go." -C. Joy Bell C.

I'd say that Bennett really helped me to understand myself more and manage the emotional aspect of being different than other individuals. Realizing that I don't need to compare, I just need to be me because they haven't been where I've been and vice versa. "The outcome is out of my hands, the process isn't."

Getting my black belt was an achievement I will never forget and something that will always stay with me. That was a process of victory on my behalf. Not outwardly, but to expand my diligence, organization, respect, all of the above because hands-down that shaped who I am today. And while we all have stories of accomplishments that have shaped who we are today, this one stays with me!

Also, this story of my service dogs is a story of complete awe. This route that they took me down of further healing was completely unexpected, yet something that I deeply needed. Dogs just have this way of saying so much without words. And maybe that's what people need, less words, more love.

Small victories often happen behind the scenes.
Many small victories have the ability to lead you to where you want to go in life. Just like how Yahshua brought these various methods into my experiences. Being aware of those small achievements has the ability to lead nowhere, but then again, it can blossom into something extraordinary. But it's not only up to you to physically put in the work and effort, but that Christ can turn those small blessings into large opportunities in his will, and his timing.

It's my love and passion and drive for parallel fellowship with others. Leading to relatability like a brother. For instance, here's a little behind the scenes action. These multiple events that took place throughout my life were all very small ideas at the time. Because they were put into action, they were turned into milestones. They got me to where I am today.

When Christ puts an idea in your heart and you contemplate the pros and cons and get other suggestions and recommendations, those irresistible ideas can turn into mysterious miracles in their own time. It's basically like not having control of the end result, it's not in your hands. So just let it be. It's in Christs', Christ will let this happen or not, it's called surrender. We need to fully surrender the outcome to Him and not try to micromanage the end result.

Keep moving but ask questions.
Some of the best things in life require thought. Contemplation is another step to venture on due to the seeking for wisdom. I find our risk taking, the building up of faith and the movement it requires to act on faith is a direct correlation to Matthew 10:16-27. To be wise as the serpent and harmless as doves. To sum it up, we need to carry our innocence with us at all times yet have the viciousness, tenacity, wisdom, and discernment as Christ. Because He cares for us that we are able to carry out those characteristics. Just like the serpent that causes harm, those dreadful experiences can come along with a lesson in the end. Just remember, a teacher never speaks during a test.

So, while we are being tested, you may not hear from the Messiah because he is the ultimate teacher. The lesson always comes at the end of the test. To where we must use our own resources in a way that brings Him glory. But being harmless as doves refers to one's purity in God's love. Because it was the first animal that Noah released after the flood occurred and is white as snow. Spotless, blameless.

Referring to that, whenever we come under pressure, sometimes we get our words jumbled. But Christ is saying that in following and pursuing Him, He'll put His words in your mouth. And not only speak in you but also through you. We often get so caught up on what to say next that we forget to speak the right words at that moment. Therefore, reliance on the Father is a requirement and will help us use His wisdom in all areas of our life.

Understanding His word and increasing in the knowledge of Him, I pray for continual help for each one of us to grow in boldness of Yahshua and to be able to share outwardly of what you instruct us behind closed doors. In those quiet times that we have with you. Our fear of you has the ability to bring fearless attributes because we are told, "not to fear man's body because they cannot kill the soul."

Asking questions along the way helps me to grasp life better. It's a way of furthering myself in the knowledge and wisdom of You. As I was going through those extremely difficult times in the beginning of my Aneurysm, I felt like I had no choice but to cry in pity and shame of where I was in life. While my friends and acquaintances were out in the world enjoying their life, I was trapped in this broken body. But again, that was my time of grievances, and it seemed like it went on forever but was only temporary, lasting a few years. But the moral of that story is to continually keep moving forward. Whether it be a small step or a big win, you completed the task!

The Majestic Horse

Have you ever noticed that when a horse is just standing in one place that they're always content with where they are? Content in the fact that they don't have to be doing or occupied with anything. They just enjoy seeing the beauty. They're sitting back taking a break from their hectic lifestyle. It is said that horses can feel a human's heartbeat from up to four feet away, and they can easily synchronize with the human soul. That's what makes horses so beautiful.

They can sense exactly what you're going through at that moment. And because of that, horses have this majestic sense to them that certain people pick up on due to the nature of their calmness. Have you ever stopped to think that Yahshua has designed horses in His image? Much like dogs? But that's another story. Horses bring this sense of serenity to you much like Christ is able to in that exact moment. He can lift you up on your down days. He shines for his calmness and generosity toward His children.

Just ponder how the word calmness relates to the word peace on so many levels! You have to be calm to have peace, and you have to have peace to be calm. Much like a horse can bring to the table. And while I completely understand that some individuals fear horses because of how giant they are, once you understand their true character and how much they relate to Yahshua, the curiosity of peace kicks in full force. The fear starts to extinguish in the fact that genuine interest begins to take over.

My curiosity for horses began at a very young age. When I stopped riding to focus more on Taekwondo, my goals changed. I still viewed challenges as hard work but again nothing I couldn't achieve if my eyes were parallel as to perpendicular. Speaking that if my eyes looked to the Messiah for my true encouragement, it would set my mindset to parallel instead of looking horizontally to have outward conformation.

Horses have always been a love of mine and that passion is only becoming stronger. Their quietness, their stillness, their mysterious character. It's an ongoing guessing game with them though. Some are very skittish of my walker and my shakiness, yet others are very curious and social. Those are true friends! Friends that don't care about your outward appearance but want to authentically know more about you. Yes, we're still talking about horses here. I call them all friends because they all have different personalities too!

Keep your head held high in failure and low in success.
Do you want to know a secret? I think I determined the secret of life. I'm not kidding you. It has worked for me so far in my life and I would like to share it with you. But, before I do, let me ask, do you struggle with humility? Do you have a difficult time deciphering what people are saying and what you're actually feeling inside? It seems like that is the best form of therapy to understand because you're in a constant state of wonder. And that's not a bad thing.

Just think of the grape vines on the most breathtaking Autumn day. Their rows are perfectly spaced out in between each and every one in order to care for the actual bush. To nourish and to prune when the time comes. They rely on each other and other human beings to care for them. Similarly to their failure and success along the way when it comes to grape ripening. And believe it or not, their success can produce the most magnificent bottle of wine that there is. Having to be reliant on others to be cared for.

It's interchangeable in the mindset of how Yahshua designed us to be partakers in purity. To keep my head high in failure and low in success. Humility is the name of the game. Especially when it comes to seeing your imperfections and shortcomings in life. Seeing the improvements step by step. Seek the journey, not only the outcome. That's exactly how we should start viewing life. To love the process. To not only have the end goal in mind but enjoy yourself along the way.

287

289

FROM THE LIBRARY OF

Kassidy
Brewer

Chapter 18

Toastmasters

In addition to God showing us exactly what we need as opposed to our wants and the steps to getting there, I always knew that I desired for my words to come out more fluently and not so choppy. I've gone to speech therapy for years, but I just seemed to be in a "plateau." I thought to myself, "is this it, is this all? There has to be more." Healing from an injury never stops, in regard to a brain injury, there's the physical, mental, and emotional piece. Not to mention the hormonal piece as well. But that's another story!

While I'm constantly working on the mental, I'm constantly working on my balance too. That's an adventure as it is so I ended up giving the emotional piece to Christ because that's too much. In return, He has given me not only a spirit of determination but also a spirit of healing. See, healing doesn't only have to be physical, it's more emotional. Healing begins in your mind. If you see yourself the way God sees you, as a perfect mess, outcomes look different. Problems are more manageable. I'm not here to say that everything will come easy. I'm just stating that it will be a reasonable challenge, many times it's not, but with Christ, it's' possible!

In 2011, my mom and I joined a Toastmasters club in the area. Unsure of what it was, I went along. Toastmasters are said to be a speaking group for business professionals or anyone that wants to be in a growth mindset setting. "What business do I have been there?" As someone who didn't speak very well in the first place, I thought but I quickly learned that Toastmasters is a place for growth in general, a sand box to make mistakes and that everyone encourages each other to better themselves to be all that they can. It's a place for exponential growth.

This was another resource I used and still use to get more acquainted with my tribe. Those people grow me and stretch me in manageable ways. It's by far the hardest part of my recovery because I'm getting out of my comfort zone and realize that discomfort is where healing happens. It's definitely the hardest but one of the most rewarding. The first time I spoke in front of people I felt as if my legs were going to buckle out from underneath me, my face was bright red from nerves, I couldn't gather my thoughts. I stuck through that frightful feeling, with the thoughts of encouragement.

We could all use some encouragement in our daily lives, that's why Christ gave us the Holy Spirit, who lives inside of you, and ready to give you the truth. I'm happy to announce that I've been with Toastmasters now for around 12 years and continue to thrive because of the growth that all started inside my emotional healing. God continues to heal this broken, torn, stepped on emotional spirit of mine that continually seeks gratitude.

"We should be grateful when we face tests and trials, because they offer trials and trials offer us a gift. It's an opportunity to surrender to God's wisdom, and to become more like Jesus."

Being in toastmasters has not only taught me fluency of speech but also watching my "um's" and "and's" and "pause fillers."

But so much more too! I am so grateful for the life skills that it's taught me. Determination is key to pushing forward, "Once you have determined what you want, trust your instincts. God given guidance, and your decision-making ability. Don't question yourself once you have settled on a path."

That's where I continue to thrive. Words cannot describe how much I've learned from this group alone. Not only this group but this organization. Because with a brain injury, all of your thoughts are jumbled together. I've heard it before; it's like emptying a junk drawer while jumping on a trampoline. You get nowhere. And that's pretty much like it, my thoughts were everywhere, and you have a hard time understanding. Too much was too much.

Most of the time you just end up checking out and you feel isolated. But not at Toastmasters, Toastmasters teaches to organize your thoughts in a well-mannered portion. They encourage you to write speeches in a way that is comprehendible for not only yourself, but for others as well. It's what helped me to write this book and is a form of therapy to help you personally grow in an area where you feel uncomfortable.

Like I always say, we need to get comfortable in the uncomfortable. And speaking in front of people is a majority of individuals fear. This is the perfect place to practice because they are a blank canvas, they will encourage you and pick you up off the ground to try again per se. Because everyone there was in a profession, they were in a practicing profession field and wanted to enhance their communication in general. In their work environment and overall. I, however, just wanted to improve so I use it as my speech therapy alternative.

Trust me, in the very beginning of my journey there, I was definitely fighting with God about why I was there. But I've learned not to resist. Not to resist the things that could make a drastic difference in your life. After being on this voyage for some time, I really started to notice that I was quicker to answer simple questions. Once I started to give actual speeches, you get an evaluation afterwards for improvement purposes only.

It's not a time to scold you of what you did wrong but to encourage you along the path of growth. And doing this portion myself has also helped me with everyday conversations as well. There's a part of the meeting known as table topics where you get the chance to answer an impromptu question and talk about it for one to two minutes. Becoming proficient in this has been a challenge to say the least, but because it's fun and challenging and aids my growth process, it's inevitably something to work with. It's all about consistency and persistence!

During one of my shunt revisions, while I was laying in the hospital prepping for surgery. My vascular neurosurgeon, Dr. Michael Levy, walks in with his team of nurses and fellows. He conveys with my parents and I about what the plan was. As he walks away, he asks my mom "how is she talking so well? 99% of people with her injury don't talk nearly that well?" She then presumed to tell him about Toastmasters. He had never heard of that before. So, he was asking a few questions and went on to say that he was going to look it up further. Now, he recommends Toastmasters as a form of therapy to his other patients from what he's seen by my progress!

The devil thought he had me in his grasp of staying complacent and remaining in my misery, but God had another plan in store. It's almost like the story of the persistent widow in Luke 18. We have to consistently be persistent in not giving up in any circumstance that we're in. Whether we give up or keep going, they're both painful but the end result will show true colors.

My Toastmasters friend John Gants perspective

I think it was about 4 years after Kassidy had her Aneurysm and Stroke, that she found Toastmasters. She was also attending college, and I remember telling Kassidy that I had heard how beneficial Toastmasters was for Stroke recovery. In 2015 Optimal Speakers was founded, where we first met Kassidy. For the first year or so, she was just checking it out. Seeing her start to give speeches, she did shake a lot more. Along with it came her slurred, choppy, shuddering speech. You should have seen me when I started too!

I remember her trembling so badly that she almost fell. I was on the edge of my seat wanting to catch her. When she first began, she really repeated herself and jumped everywhere in her storytelling. We all began somewhere, and her structure was yet to be improved on.

Kassidy has truly impressed not only me but our members too, with humor, raw talent, and most importantly her story. She continues to bring light to her situation with humor and realism. It's truly a gift to be around Kassidy as she demonstrates strength, resilience and joy daily.

Don't get into a pattern where you think you have to do something for the rest of your life.

If we get into a mundane pattern in life, things will begin to become boring, there will be no "spark" to life. Things will become routine, like you're just going through the motions in them. Instead of looking to get things done, what if we sought opportunities to enjoy the journey? To look at events from a different perspective, to view obstacles from another angle and understand that there are always repercussions for our actions. Just like jealousy can turn into pride and shame.

To emphasize the point, that one's envy has brutal consequences. It's our job to handle them and to get them under control. we do so by surrendering our mind, will, and emotions over to Yahshua. In Job 5, it states that we may have been born into trouble but our love for Christ, or as it says, "spark of love," fly upward in the knowledge of Him. His ways cannot be sought out and is marvelous in all ways.

There're too many to count and cannot be numbered. Reading on, while Christ saw Jobs unbearable agony, Job was considered a lowly man. Unable to resolve the issue. But God elevated Him and rebuked the devices of the crafty. The enemy can affect our life in the fact, when we turn inward and try to control the situation ourselves, Christ can take those mortal feelings and turn them into hope and reliance.

Faith= risk; Risk= reaction; reaction= result

Faith is spelled R.I.S.K., and I know that's not the traditional spelling, but then again, I'm not traditional! I am me, just like you are you. We are all individuals with unique design.

If we have a dream that is too large to handle, that's exactly where faith comes in. It's having a reliance on Yahshua, to acknowledge Him, and take the risk. In doing so, we might fail, but that's exactly what draws us closer to Him. It's when we fall flat on our face yet still have the drive in us to continue in our endeavors. It's the risk we're willing to take to move on. It's the risk of either falling flat on our face, to humbly run to Him, pleading for help to fix the issue, or succeed so hard to where we are required to thank Him for this marvelous triumph.

Just like when we have the initial reaction from the risk we're willing to take. We have that reaction of, "oh no, what did I just do." Whether it is good or bad. Taking that beginning risk has the ability to bring on more effort, more work, but that's just another reason to fall back on Yahshua. Reading through Deuteronomy 4:1-6, we need to live in the judgment of Christ and live as if he's the only one that can judge us. Not a carnal human. Because us humans have their own fault and shortcomings to where Christ is the epitome of who we should resemble. Father, I pray for each and every one of us to not only look to your commandments as a law but something to live by, something to actively do out of love. The love of you. Seeking Him as we follow Him day by day.

We're not only alive because of Him, but we're thriving as a result. Going out into the world does not mean to be free-skilled and follow our heart in every case. We need to be steadfast and firm in the commandments that's been brought about in his word. Knowing and understanding his commandments is another form of wisdom to long for. It's a way of life that leads to wisdom. It's something that God praises and wants in our life. He wants your love, your deep intimate love. The word observe is used in this verse, I looked it up and it's an active form, "to do" or "to keep ".

Sometimes we can get so caught up in the word that we forget that there is a Biblical meaning. We need to tame our tongue to what the Father states, as to what the world says. To complete the triple R trifecta, after you take the risk, you get the reaction which produces the result. In my case, the result was actively doing hard work to get where I am today. Yeah, it took quite a few years but look at me now. And remember, where we are now is not where we're going to be in five or ten plus years.

We can always pray and hope for more! But I could not have acquired this journey without the hope, and the thoughts that were placed in my mind from Christ Himself. Life is better overall when someone is by your side. That someone is called the Holy Spirit. He's there to make your overall life better despite your circumstances. Despite what your naked eye sees. In the long run, your destiny resides in your hands due to free will. You are never going to be forced into following Him, but it sure does complete you. That's part of the major result of myself and pretty much sums up the story!

What has God let you to see?
Revealing hidden concepts slowly over time, I'm humbly reminded that waiting patiently means waiting on Gods' mysterious ways. But being reminded of His ways isn't a natural part of life. We have to be diligent in our study and knowledge of Him. I was refreshed by the word, "tassels" in Numbers 15:39-40. As we are commanded to continually hold fast His words, humankind struggles with what the heart and the eyes want.

But again, the Father doesn't always give us what our eyes and heart want. He gives our soul what it needs. He knows what is going to be beneficial and, in our favor, to where He has the ability to withhold specific events.

We just need to wait and trust, because He sees what we don't. Help each and every one of us to remember the "tassels" of Christ, not to have a wavering mind. He brought me to this scripture for a purpose and that is to keep His statutes in its' entirety. While looking this word up further, it means actual physical tassels in garment. And they are to serve as a reminder to keep His commandments. It's an actual, physical reminder to keep the perspective of His tassels and not fall into what the heart and the eyes want, but to keep the tassels of Your word, tattooed on my heart, forever.

Getting to that point where I was just downright frustrated with my words, really took a toll on me. It was as if I didn't even want to speak because I was so frustrated with where my words were at. Like it wasn't going to get any better. I was kind of stuck in this body that wouldn't produce the right sentences, they were all jumbled up and hardly made sense and were very slow and choppy. My mom and I were looking for different groups to get together with, we stumbled upon a Toastmasters meeting and we're just curious more than anything.

We went to our first meeting and were hooked. I don't remember what drew us in but all I know is that both of us crave growth and we desire it! As my mom got busy, I continued in the adventure of wanting to get better at speaking in general not knowing what it can turn into. What's a better place to practice than there? So basically, I went into this Toastmasters voyage, completely blindfolded, not knowing that it would change my life completely for the better. because I started this expedition in 2011, I've been in it for quite some time in the progression is continuous. But it is my speech therapy alternative, so I find it's mandatory that I keep up with it. That's where the mindset, "use it or lose it comes in."

There's really not a difficult thing unless you decide it's a difficult thing.
It's just the next thing you're trying to figure out.
Facing a life altering decision is always hard to comprehend, but when we live in the present moment with the end in mind, it seems to work out much better from a heavenly perspective. Yahshua wants those things for you that you desire. It may take some time, but you know what, great things are worth waiting for! We're so focused on the "now" portion of life, we see those events as difficult.

The keyword here is to figure out. It's just your next project that you're working on to overcome. It's very much like the wind, we can't do anything about it, but we can certainly feel it. Because we can't force and change patterns, we operate with net scope. Knowing for certain that it will lessen and grow and change within time. It's just a matter of waiting and being patient in times of change. and because wind is a natural form of beauty, realizing that the best way to fully embrace, the wind is to flow and change with it.

Not always working against it but allowing it to circulate around you. You know how they always say, dance in the rain? Another way to say it is to dance in the wind because dancing in the wind is more of a brisk free flow. Once we realize that whatever you're trying to figure out, is just another challenge in your life to better you and grow your outlook on the future. The rest of your life!

You don't need to be perfect to inspire others. Let people be inspired by how you deal with your imperfections.

Anyone else feeling tired of living in a time of perfection? Trying your best to make it through the day while forcing this "fake" smile in order to truly look like you're full of happiness when in reality, you're falling apart inside. Yes, it's always thoughtful to be kind to those around you because they're facing a battle you know nothing about, but does that mean that you have to hide yours? Being honest and being real with a person is one of the kindest things you can do. And if you're having a really bad day, sometimes I find that it's best to remove myself, clear my head and come into focus of what Yahshua desires for me. Hear me out, other people are extremely helpful in their efforts, but more times than one, it's something that only Adonai can fix.

As Christ sends out the messenger, in my opinion, that messenger is the Holy Spirit whom I seek. He is sending out the Holy Spirit and Yahshua himself. just like we hear about in verse two of the refiner's fire. When Adonai comes down from heaven, it will force us to fall on our faces in adoration of him. We will have the love of a refiner in the refiner's fire. I looked up the refiner's fire and it's basically a purification process for things like silver and gold. It's part of the whole process that must take place.

He also relates to the whole process being like a soap maker's lye. Lye is derived from clay and limestone, and is extremely alkaline, it has a very high ph. It has been used for thousands of years in order to produce the most natural soaps, deodorants, and cleaning products. To where the correlation between that, is that we cannot be used by Him without the Holy Spirit in us, much like the soap maker cannot make their soap without lye. While the soap maker cannot make their soap without one special ingredient, Yahshua cannot be used without the Holy Spirit.

And while we put our hope and trust in him, we still fall short because we are human. We still look up to him as our example, yet we fall into the trap of being a sorcerer, adulterer, perjurers, and those who take advantage of wage earners, widows, and orphans. We may not notice that we're doing those things, but that is what the Holy Spirit is there for. To point out our weaknesses and faults and to turn them over to the Father and confess them in order to repent. That's exactly where the fear of him comes into place to looking to him as our example and not turning to worldly advice. Continuing in the hope of his glory. As we read in verse seven, it says "return to me and I will return to you ".

We have walked away from Christ because we're living in this world that tells you and shows you that the grass is greener on the other side. When that is not real reality. It may be true to some extent, but that is where the Holy Spirit comes in to let us know that often times what you have is pure gold. The world is going to throw this, that, obstacles, and trials at you, but we need to put them through the refiner's fire to assess the situation with the knowledge of Yahshua. Then, in verse nineteen it states that the day of judgment is going to come and set all ablaze. The word ablaze is an ancient farming technique that was used in order to burn off any diseases or weeds planted from the old crop that would be transferred. That's exactly where the refiners fire comes in to play because that is part of the purification process of judgment.

In actuality, you don't need to be perfect to inspire others. Let people be inspired by how you deal with your imperfections. We're all humans, we have faults and shortcomings. That's what makes us relatable. Why do we hide them? Life is about being relatable and showing our true character, right? Whenever I look to the Father in whatever I'm working on, He will aid me to accomplish His will in a relatable fashion. Not deterring from my true character but living in a way that brings me comfort and edifies Yahshua overall.

Perfection is a slippery slope, we can "strive" for perfection but where does that get you? Working in your efforts, your power. What would happen if you gave that over to Adonai Elohim? To take that burden off of you. Because you don't need perfection to inspire, just seek Christ and watch what He can do in and through your life.

What is my definition of success?

If we think about it, success comes in various different forms. We might even have the perfectionist's mindset to where if it isn't perfect, we failed, it's not done right. Consider how Yahshua thinks seeing His child that may not have a perfectly functional body yet a capable mind. How do you think Christ sees His handiwork? Complete and perfect. He's always at work in people's lives but success can appear far different than others imagine. It's kind of like how He's at work in our meticulous manner of what's acceptable and not. We're all a "work in progress".

I believe He's constantly trying to get our attention because of our human nature which is to go to "the shiny objects." To always look for something to benefit. What's the best fit? Often times, we forget to involve Him in the process where sometimes we need a slap upside the head to get us back on track to realize what's important. That's where being content with the things that we have and do comes into action. Being content with what we worked for yet communicating with Yahshua to see whatever He has in store. Good or bad in our eyes, to benefit us in the long run.

Chapter 19

The Seven Perspectives & Relatability

For some people, they would call this type of experience horrific, sad, depressing, feeling bad for somebody and yes, yes, it was all of those, but I would like to call it a blessing in disguise too. It was traumatic to say the least, but trials are a part of life, and it's all based on what you ultimately do with that trial. Life alterations do shake a person up, but what are you going to do to move past that and to live your life to the fullest?

A perspective on Suffering.
The suffering that I've encountered was 100% part of God's plan. It was blameless. It happened in His timing and in His ways, not to our own. Yes, I've had to go through many obstacles that kids my age typically don't go through, but when you take your sufferings, learn from them, and turn them around to use them for the good of others, many times it has a way of finding itself back to you. Just look at the hopeless, dark, lightless days that I've had to live with. Where there was no light at the end of the tunnel, as opposed to where I am today. While tragedies like these can happen to the most random people in the most unforeseen times, keeping an outlook of thankfulness, humbleness, and gratitude helps the overall situation at hand.

"We don't develop courage by being happy every day. We develop it by surviving difficult times and challenging adversity."
– BARBARA DE ANGELIS

Healing comes in all different shades and colors. I've definitely experienced every shade and color with my quest toward vibrancy. It's an expedition to travel down because each and every day is worthwhile with the hope of miracles. It's like a night and day difference, and I could not have done that without the hope of tomorrow. The hope of having Jesus there with me every step of the way.

And while at times of suffering, we can view those times as a grudging aspect in life that we don't want to face. What I've learned through all of this is how to face challenges for what they are, another opportunity to sit in your discomfort, pray, allow Christ to take the wheel, and overcome. I'm not going to say that the journey of surrendering is an easy task to take on. It's extremely strenuous and trying at times. But when I focus on the end result of the issue and remember who's there with me in the midst of it all, it helps to relieve the tension.

The perspective of Love.
For in love, there is tribulation. And in tribulation, there is love. Something that I will always reflect on and something that remains true to this day. We could all learn from this lesson. No one likes tribulation yet everyone loves love. Although tribulation is necessary to reveal our true character, our love for one another is a mighty characteristic of Yahshua. In Galatians 5:13 it talks about serving one another in love.

Liberty is basically the freedom believers have in Christ. I posed the question, "what's the difference between liberty vs. freedom?" But what I've come to understand is that freedom is a very slippery word, it's too flexible. Some people think that they can just do whatever they want because they have freedom. Whereas liberty in Yahshua is one specific aspect, it's biblical freedom from bondage to enjoy the responsibilities of coming into a relationship with Him. Therefore, we are not to use our freedom (worldly standards), to benefit the flesh. To be a slave to your own sin is to be captivated by your own selfish desires. Remember, love is the decision to compassionately, righteously, and sacrificially seek the wellbeing of another. By this type of love, others will know that we are His disciples. And why would we do any less of how the Son set the prime example and lived to serve in love?

Love was experienced through the burning desires of wanting normalcy in my life. But normalcy was far from what the Lord imagined. I remember when I was in my denial phase of grieving my life, I always cried out; "I want to be normal, I want my old life back, "but I never got that. Instead, I got a new version. I'll take that above anything else. That's the Lord's love, and it goes far beyond what we ask, think, or imagine.

He will please beyond the imaginable. He is there to meet all our needs. That's love at its' finest. So, when we lean into failure, failing to do life on our own, that's where God's love shines forth. Think about it. What exactly is love? Love is not merely a feeling, love is action. As I've seen in my life, God will put something in front of you to exercise your faith. To stretch you to the limit of knowing that I can't do this on my own. It's very similar to receiving a gift. We all love gifts. But when we set aside the old things and look forward to the new things, love is freely given.

The perspective of Forgiveness.

I have had to completely forgive. That thought of complete abandonment and struggle raged my mind. I had no idea why this had to happen to me, but years later, I finally came into complete acceptance. Not only forgiving Christ for this happening to me, but it was also a natural cause; no one could prevent it from occurring. It was completely blameless. But also forgiving myself for the sin of my past and present and also forgiving others for the insecurities I placed upon myself that others saw. I don't blame them. I'm a sore eye!

However, I've had to surrender myself wholly to God in order to fully forgive myself of my past sins, sins of my present day, and the sins to come in the future. Because when that truly happened, that's when significant healing started to occur. Mentally, physically, emotionally, and spiritually. Even though I was thirteen years old, wrong doings still occurred in life. There were friends, boys, temptations, extracurricular fun. Temptations arose. And now I know that God was there with me through it all. Encouraging me to head down a different path in life.

People will hurt us. That's part of life. The real question is what are you going to do with it? Who are you going to turn to? And while there are various avenues to take that can lead to despair, if we choose to turn to the Father, our outlook and perspective of the situation can appear different. And while forgiveness may seem out of reach due to circumstances, that can leave the opportunity for bitterness and resentment to creep in. The Father has an abundance of love for us that one cannot fathom. And while we always hear that, truly understanding it is where the hedge lies.

If we can comprehend that He forgave those who brutally murdered Him, He set the prime example of forgiveness. Forgiveness is love. Love is action. However, we need to be vigilant in the fact that some people take advantage and use us. To where, we need to be loving and forgiving from a distance. Not interfering with one's life but noticing it and moving on. Forgiveness is one of the key aspects to not only mentally heal but can release built up animosity within.

The perspective of Presence.

Our presence in life means more than others think. I could easily say that each one of us has a purpose here on earth and that's true, but sometimes we feel lack of that. I learned that just showing up somewhere, nearly to show your support, could mean more to someone than actually being involved, due to the fact that one person knows what you're going through and that it takes a lot just to be there. Finding those people that seek presence and not perfection, those are my people! Contrary, those people that seek to get the job done perfectly are going to miss out on the fun times in life, because if you think about it, nothing in life is perfect.

Realizing that is an aspect of life that will come with maturity. Progress over perfection in things, events, and in people. While my life alteration changed pretty much everything about me, I now know that there are more things to life than being the first one out of the gate and having a perfectionistic mindset. And even though people see my walker before they see me, I don't let that get in my way, because yeah, you're going to see my walker firsthand but when you truly get to know a person, you'll start to find similarities and differences that you would like to know more about! I heard it once said before, "get to know people like they're hiding a secret." Big, amazing news!

If you asked me to describe myself in three words of who I was before the incident, I would say that I was a motivated, colorful, helpful young lady. While a majority of those characteristics remain, my outlook and presence have changed. I am more sure of myself; I see hope in those dark times. Indicating the process of aging wine. I'm aging, coming from a dark place and I am valuable within. Much like all of us, when we surrender our life, our plans, our presence illuminates into something far beyond what we imagined.

The perspective of Purpose.

As cars pass by slowly, many times individuals can sit back and watch life has passed them by. But when we take the initiative and feel that we have purpose and a reason to be somewhere or do something, it helps to get us out of our bubble. Sometimes you don't even have to be around people, It's about being there, because you are important! Just like how our presence sets the groundwork of our purpose. One's purpose and significance in this world is immense when it comes to inclusion.

Whenever people include me in their daily plans, I realize that those individuals are aware of what they're getting themselves into. I come with a walker, slow walking, doing things differently, and always ready to try new food! So, if you're not up for the battle, you're missing out! Being extroverted/introverted like myself, I love to be around people, but not necessarily interacting. So, if you're anything like me, having a purpose to help in any way shape or form means that you're committed and don't back down.

Significance is another controversy of mine. Thinking that because I can't do things typical people do, I have no significance. However, with surrendering my life to Christ, He has completely wiped away that old mentality. And although I do still battle with the whole significance condition, it's greatly diminished because I'm aware of my ultimate purpose here on this earth. For example: I had a friend ask if I'd like to deliver some drinks, yet I knew that with my walker and my Ataxia, it would be a recipe for disaster. I felt insignificant in that instance due to my shortcomings. I however know who Elohim created me to be and what He has called me to do. Maybe I'm not able to help out in certain areas of life, does that mean I don't have purpose? No way. We all have purpose; it's our significance and ego that takes the biggest hit.

The perspective of Surrender.
As wind chimes flutter in the wind, occasionally we need to take a step back to realize and fully understand how much you were made to make noise, get a little banged up and modify yourself to the environment that you're placed in all while keeping your composure. So that brings up a question. Do you look at your

life as a struggle to push through or do you triumph over it with a light at the end of the tunnel?

Just like my airplane illustration, when we have a vision, we want to take control of conditions, so it ends the way we want. But what if you completely gave up your power? To be powerless for the God who is all-powerful. Much like the air control tower at the airport. We could all use help from someone who can see what we can't see. And that's just what God saw in my stance. He saw the pain. He saw the hurt. He saw the tears. But what He also saw, was the sequel to come beyond that season of time.

"Gods' perspective is bigger, He is dynamically interacting with a whole universe of complexity when He makes decisions, that's what He calls wisdom."

Surrender, in my opinion, means to let go of control of the situation. How does one make this happen? I look to Yahshua for all that He does in and through my life. Seeking the small details of everyday life and seeing God in them. To not only praise Him for the good things in life but also the pretentious deeds as well. Because when we notice that hard times can be a blessing in disguise, our eyes become adjusted to seeing Christ-like hope despite circumstances. When I made the decision to live a life of complete surrender, that's when I began to see with new eyes. I didn't view life through my suffering but rather how I can help others in my situation and not have to experience what I have.

The perspective of impermanence

Although my presence now is slightly limited now of what I'm able to do, I hardly ever use the word "can't." Because, honestly, I can, I just don't have the knowledge, wisdom, or strength to do it right now. But God has given each one of us what we need in life. A need is described as food, water, air, etc. And our need resides inside of us until it is pulled out and discovered. That goes back to your presence in life, what YOU bring to the table. And with that, if we can't do a task on our own, or are having a difficult time, ask for help. That's why people are around us. To challenge us, help us, and lean into the Lord for further help.

"Able" bodied people, but especially "disabled" individuals have a hard time realizing their importance in life. Their importance doesn't come from what one can do or bring about; it's found in one's attitude in how they handle difficulty and tribulation. It's a mindset game, just like how life is full of impermanence, meaning only lasting for a short period of time. Our trials in life are only temporary, and the way we view obstacles at hand determines our outlook.

Although life can seem long at times, we have to remember, our time here is very limited. We aren't positive about the last hour we have left on this earth. Being prepared ahead of time for where our soul will reside when our earthy bodies are done here on earth. And that's a permanent forge. It's kind of like a here-today-gone-tomorrow kind of decision. Kind of like our bodies have an impermanent factor here on this earth. If you think about moving houses several times, the house you currently reside in may be an impermanent household. Or living with change. Changes in life are going to happen; they can be permanent or impermanent.

But it's times like those that we don't need to become stressed to the max, all we need to think about is how our Father thinks and look to Him for guidance on the right path. He will lead you. And that's a permanent fact of life. However, when we feel it emotionally from a place of self, it's already attached to itself and feels bad about its own impermanence. Meaning that because these changes that happen throughout life come and go may or may not be long lasting, we need to remember the end result. The end result of our life and what it consists of. The true meaning behind everything.

The perspective of Hope.
I continually have to remind myself that He's inviting us into His glory. It's an invitation to everyone to follow after His heart. And while He's powerful enough to move the mountains, He gives us a choice and free will to let us make the choice. He is able to forcibly change our heart, yet He gives us the option to obey or disobey His calling on our life. He doesn't need your goodness, holiness, or positive attitude in you to plant seeds in other people to have them look to Christ, but He admires our effort and honors that.

While I was going through my pain and anguish in my life, I was constantly reminded to let Him be the light in me. Because you truly can't shine unless you heal. Being a broken soul, my mind, body, and soul had to be unconditionally restored. Once you have been broken, your hurt, has to heal in order to shine your light for our Heavenly Father. And I like to work on that by working on my response time to Christ. Not letting hours or minutes go by without involving Yahshua in my choices to move forward.

We are alive through Christ and because of Christ. However, Yahshua has the authority to destroy the ones that follow false God's. Much like us carnal humans can make Godly gifts idols, He is able to retrace our steps to put Him above those gifts. Like Moses said in Galatians 4:1-9, "But you who have remained faithful are alive today." Due to that, our obedience is a fact that we must always follow through with. Obedience brings life and blessing; but disobedience brings death and destruction. God's statues and laws were to teach Israel to be the light. To be the light in the darkness whenever we are facing hard times.

After all, doing so pointed to Christ' love as opposed to their make up because of what was in them. And due to acquiring this changed mentality and gestures, those who see something different within you, will be curious to seek it out themselves. That's why He commands that we do not forget what we've seen. Because forgetting Gods goodness, faithfulness is a recipe for disaster and can lead us down the path to sin again and again. And when we remain obedient, He is the expert at not only blessing our situation but blessing it in unknown ways in order to shape us into better characters. It's all our choice.

The relatability

Complacency was not my friend when it came to growth. Growth of the mind, the soul, the emotions, and the physical aspect. All of it together shifted my perception of what truly mattered most. That wasn't this physical, outward exterior that we first saw, but rather looking at the soul. What our Heavenly Father created. And according to the Bible, that's what counts most. In addition to seeing the human soul for what it actually is, you start to see hurting people, people just like you and me.

Not looking at people for what they can do or what they have but viewing them in a way that a father or mother views their own child. If you can imagine that, how do you think your Heavenly Father views you? Imperfections are a way to catch people's attention. Just like Moses in Exodus 4:10-14 regarding how Moses had a ginormous speech impediment to where his brother Aaron spoke very eloquent. But God chose to use Moses in his struggles because that caught more people's attention than perfection. He uses those struggles that we have and makes them new and causes them to far exceed our expectations. Like Christ said to Moses, "who has made man's mouth?" And "… go, and I will be with your mouth and teach you what you shall say." So, Moses spoke with his brother Aaron who was eloquent in speech. But the Father said to Moses not to worry because He will "teach him what to do." He actively made our voice and mouth physically, He can also do far above what we ask, imagine, or think. He has the ability to not only produce words in us but is able to put the words that He wants to share inside of our mouth. To speak His Words for His purposes.

We are able to be, to do, and say in the perspective from Christ. And because Moses had a large speech impediment, he had an advantage over the people because they had a hard time understanding him with his efforts over speech, to where they were forced to hone in and listen. But Christ did that for a purpose. It was because he appointed Moses to be the spokesman for the Heavenly Father himself. During my intense altering life change, I was faced with countless difficulties and setbacks along the way. When I took two steps forward, I always seemed to jump back about five steps.

Obviously, the journey with any health scare results in some sort of setback, but we have to remember that a step back typically results in a set up. A set up for something greater, something you'd never expect it to be. The numerous times that I was rushed into an emergency surgery brought me to where I am today. Yes, it was devastatingly scary at the time for my family, but then again Christ doesn't work on our clock. It took countless years to get me to where I am today, but you know what, I wouldn't trade it for the world. This is my testimony. God chose me to take on this life. And you know what, because He's by my side, helping me find the way, I'm doing a pretty good job at this thing! This thing called life!

Chapter 20

Deciding to testify

During this difficult time, I am so thankful for all the people that kept in touch. All the people that were willing to check in on us. All the people that just wanted to hear our voice and hear how we were doing. All those people that were patient enough to spend a few hours with us meant the world. Fortunately, being that thirteen-year-old, I was in the thick of it with my friends. Everyone was changing; everyone was growing up and finding their way in life. I had a couple friends that stuck by me through the thick and thin. Everyone was focused on extracurricular sports and their activities that typical high school students would take part in.

Still in my hospital bed on the living room floor, we would have some consolation. Every Friday, one of my mom's best friends, Sue Muscarella (who is like a second mother to me and friend), would come over and spend the entire day just to help where needed and hang out. I think that's what gave my mom something to look forward to, her visits on Fridays.

One of my very vivid memories was when she came over, and I was in my high-back wheelchair, unable to talk . She made this whip cream cake. Her and my mom are like silly sisters together, so they took a small finger of whip cream and put it on my tongue just to taste. It was fun and exciting, but they didn't want me to aspirate so that's all I got. It was innocent and amusing. One of many times we'll never forget. And we are still very connected till this day.

At the time of my incident, I was learning to play the guitar. As a new player, I met some true friends. One of those friends being a friend of a friend, Merrick McCorkle actually continued playing his guitar and while I was in my hospital bed on the living room floor, he would come over and just practice the guitar in front of me for hours. He doesn't know this, but that was very healing for not only me, but I can bet it was for him as well!

I also had countless visitors from not only school, but from several charities and motorcycle crews and churches, and many more. It's truly the little things that make the biggest impact. Those people simply just came to show their support and love. Letting us know that they were praying for us and that they have spread the word. They cared not only for the little girl in distress but also the whole family. Although this may sound a little down, living every day as though it's your last has the ability to help not only you, but also others around you due to the gratitude that you exude.

In those moments, you feel like there is nothing waiting for you. It might be good, it might be painful, but in the end it's an event to look back on and acknowledge that I did. Despite what you go through, it can be a teacher to you or to others or to both. Learn from your past; try not to always look at challenges as something that needs to be overcome at that moment. Maybe it is a part of your future. Maybe it's something to look back upon and be able to relate it to another's processes. It's not always an aspect in life that needs to be figured out as soon as possible but rather to be thought on.

Nonetheless, when we ponder upon those specific life events, I'm always careful not to halt or quench the spirit in its' tracks. Giving thanks to our Heavenly Father on a continual basis is a characteristic worthy of developing. Just read first Thessalonians 5:18-23 and you'll learn all about this. In the good times, in the bad times, the trying times, the testing of times, all is edified because it all has the ability to result in growth of your spirit. Your growth of faith. Having a relationship and to be unified with the Messiah is what Christ wants for you. He desires for us to live in His image and to fully rely on that. He wants the best for us and that's what He's going to deliver, only the best. It may be nothing of what you had in mind but it's part of the equation.

While those times come where we're going to be tempted to quench the spirit and be led by this world, we are called not to shake off those thoughtful, moving God winks. A massive percentage of messages we hear come from inspiration of some sort to where our attention and motivations are likely to be reconsidered and put into perspective. Interestingly enough, we are going to come into contact with spirits of all sorts. Some that are good, countless that are harmful but that's where we need to not shy away but to test the wounding spirit with prayer and to remain in the sight of Yahshua.

Consider that you have a good thing going when it comes to being level with Christ. Take into account that when a good thing comes about, often times we must gently hold onto it with the mindset that Christ entrusted us to care for this. Thats why, when He states to keep away from every form of evil, He's referring to what He's put in our path. To test those yet to keep your distance. In doing so, you'll see one's true character reside.

In verse 23, it talks about Shalom. After looking this word up further, "the concept of SHALOM brings us to realize the perfection in our holy God, reinforcing the profound significance of this word in understanding the character of our Creator. In the Hebrew language, SHALOM signifies "wholeness," "completeness," "perfection," and more." That one word signifies so much and has the boldest counterparts! In turn, we don't emit Shalom when we're quenching the Spirit. Much like we don't portray completeness and wholeness when we're following the world, we can't fully represent the Father in His entirety and perfection.

So, if you ask what helped my recovery process the most, I'd say all of it because it all synchronized together to set me in motion. It is kind of like in Hebrews 4:15. "He sympathizes with our weaknesses and was tempted just as we are yet without sin." In the repetition of recovery, my weaknesses were very apparent, and it was vastly grueling to carry on, yet it had to be done.

It's obvious that certain breeds of hard work is a particular part of life that some procrastinate or put off due to the struggle. Doing so, one takes the easy way out. It's almost a way of taking it on in your own hands. That's when we fail miserably. But when we remember that our Heavenly Father already conquered our lack, we begin to see sympathy. Our lack brings on His love.

On the other hand, I got to a point in my therapies where therapy greatly improved my life, but it was becoming mundane, and I wasn't achieving my maximum growth. See, Yahshua the God of Israel, calls us to be so much more than average. He calls us to be whole, to be set apart, to distinguish yourself as a Child of the King. In those times of deep thought, I always thought about normalcy. I wondered if I would ever have a normal life and typical job. The standard life, but then again, we're called to be set apart. Who lives and desires to grow up to be ordinary?

I can't emphasize that point enough because coming from a place of lack to a place knowing my worth in Christ, my outlook of the future has slowly transformed into a place of abundance. So, in regard to coming from a place of lack, I did these multiple therapies that seemed to help for some time and then the repetition of it all, got me to a place of a plateau.

What I learned is that I wasn't the one that plateaued, it was actually the therapists. They were the ones that were out of unique ideas to challenge me. And in that sense, I had to find my own way of challenging myself where needed. My family and friends and I would always encourage different avenues and exercises to look into. Challenging not only my body but also my brain too.

Airplane illustration

Life is kind of like an airplane, taking off the ground. We must hold on tight and trust that the pilot has it all in control. We don't have any control of what is going to happen in our lifetime. So, we must give all control to our heavenly pilot who navigates our steps and already has our future planned out and trust the process. It's a characteristic of a human to be exercised and not nearly thought about. The practice of surrender needs to be lived out every single day and not just in the moment.

And when we do that, we are going to get backlash from others. They're going to tempt us with anything that won't bring eternal joy. Things that bring temporary satisfaction. As an airplane leaves the ground when it takes off for flight, surrendering our temptations and will of life to God leaves our life in the eye of the beholder. He created you, he created me, so leaving my life in his hands is a quality that he desires. He will drive the plane; He will take us a flight.

Truthfully, I felt the need to share this with you because although we all go through our own struggles in life, even though they all come in different shades, we can all relate to the pain that we felt during that time. It is the type of pain that people run from but during times of adversity, we need to remember that pain is there to grow us. It's not all bad. And when you realize that you're awakened to how that was specifically placed in your life to evolve you into a stronger, wiser version of your soul. We have to keep the perspective of how our relationship with our Heavenly Father is more important than the issue at hand.

I truthfully pray that my story has not only helped you to face trials with comfort, knowing that Yahshua has already come to defeat the issue at hand. You're not alone in this struggle. Much like He was with me through the thick and thin. He's not going to leave you. You're made in his image and made to have relationship with Him, if you open up your heart to do so. It's all about surrendering to His will. Giving up your own, in order to fulfill what He has for your life and what his words say, He will do. Surrendering is not an easy process. It's probably one of the hardest things that I've done but it is one hundred percent without a doubt worth every single struggle. We ALL have a purpose here on this earth, and we can't do that without Yahshua the God of Israel.

The human soul is similar to rustic wood.
We enter the world, flawless babies, and overtime, we start to get rustic, we begin to experience life. Not in a bad way or anything, we accumulate knowledge and wisdom. And to be honest, when we attain that knowledge, sometimes it can turn out better than we expected. It's all about changing and adapting to our circumstances. Living up to your morals and values but adapting in times of reconstruction.

Enduring through the hardest of hard times, there were countless instances where I thought this was as good as it's going to get. That my healing time is over and not much more can be completed. I thought that I've done all that I can do and that God was done with His work because He saved me and performed a miracle. What I've come to realize is that you can't put a limit on our Heavenly Father. His time is not synonymous with our clock. I had gone through being in a non-induced coma for four and a half months, unable to do anything for myself, to explosive expansion throughout time. Don't limit Yahshua's timing in everything.

Open your mind.
Due to my lack of ability, I fully understand that I'm not like an ordinary individual. I require more than the average person regarding my balance problems. And because of that, it requires vulnerability like no one's business. That embryonic time of trying to understand pain, hardship, emotional regulation, accessibility and everything that goes with a destructive brain injury, I had a very closed mindset. Nothing seemed to support my physical needs other than pleading to God that I wanted my

old life back. But, with all of these therapeutic methods, my old life is something that I cringe at.

**"If any man be in Christ, he is a new creation: old things have passed away; behold, all things are becoming new."
- 2 Corinthians 5:17**

Due to my physical challenges that overtook me, a new mindset, a new outlook was exactly what I needed. Not only physically but also mentally. Maybe even more mentally than anything else. Coping with the inability to do ordinary tasks like normal people really put a damper on my vision of myself and Christ's promises for me. But over the years, I've come to this incredible place of growth. Not only mentally but also spiritually. Just like 2 Corinthians 5:17 promises.

And believe it or not, I know He's not done. Yeah, I talk funny, I walk funny, I constantly shake, I have faults and shortcomings but who doesn't. We're all human, we all mess up. Give yourself grace in the fact that you have these imperfections. I say, they're our natural imperfections or that they're God given. Remember, you are human. One's emotional expansion or growth is solely reliant on exposure and vulnerability. Before everything happened, I was a go with the flow kind of person. After my Aneurysm, I was extremely closed off from the world and any possibility to thrive.

Now, I'd say I'm slowly returning to a better, improved "old me," with a new perspective. A perspective of possibility, opportunity, growth, love, encouragement, etc. What I'm trying to say here is that I had to put in hard work in order to thrive. See, when you put in the hard work and take the first step, the Holy Spirit will meet you where you are in your struggles and direct you down the path that He has for you. Whether that is a path you like or not, if we look for the blessings in each situation and look at the point of view, more times than none, you'll get a new reference.

That brings me to the next point that I've learned to take on. That is, "to do the dang thing!" Not to hold back. That's one of my mottos in life. Something that I continually remind myself. I overthink a lot. Forcing myself to do the dang thing has not only brought growth but it's brought on Christ-like confidence like no other. My shortcomings in life are just a way to grab people's undivided attention to be able to share the message of hope. The Fathers hope. It's synonymous to how Christ came to meet Abraham when he was in Mesopotamia and said to him there, that he must go out of the land.

God not only called him into unknown territory, but He called him to a specific land where he wanted to bless him unconditionally. The link between my story and his story was that Christ may not physically show you the blessing that is to come, but if we're patient and obedient in our suffering and struggle, He promised to provide all of our needs. And with that, He likes to show off, He likes to exceed our expectations.

He likes to go far beyond what we ask, seek, or imagine. And with that, He provided Abraham a son in his old age. It was a promise that God made to Abraham despite his age limit. In this scripture of Acts 7:5, the word "promise," means to make an intention or to pledge to something. We need to follow through with our promises and not take them for granted, because when we do, we resemble Christ. Love does not consist of words, love is action.

This experience helped me.
Obviously, we look at our circumstances as unfortunate yet there's always a way to view it from a different angle. Just like when Elohim calls you somewhere you're not familiar with. Obedience is His first course of action, but due to human nature, that doesn't always happen. In Abraham's case, he stepped out in complete faith, not knowing where he was going as found in Hebrews 11:8. Kind of like how our tribulations in life are going to lead us into unknown territory but keeping our eyes on Yahshua is all that we can aim for. Our pursuit to chase the Father is something we should strive for with the expectation of knowing Him and growing in intimacy with Him.

When we're compelled into the unknown, many times, our brain gets shaken up to the point of paralysis, but those narrow roads don't lead anyone to greatness. We need the Father to walk with us through those hard times and show us what He has in store. Very much like how I had to go through my trials to lead me to where I am today. He not only strategically put me in that circumstance to demonstrate His love and miraculous healing, but He also worked through other individuals that witnessed this event as well.

Hands down, I think I am a much better person because of this. If it weren't for this, I have no idea where I'd be at in life. At only thirteen, I didn't have much to envision because anything could've happened. We already knew that I was respectful and a big goal setter, but I did enjoy concerts and hanging out with friends. So, who knows where I'd be. All I know is that I don't want to reflect on the past. The past is the past and I'm not heading that way anytime soon, so I'll just keep pushing forward in my knowledge of Yahshua and bettering my character day by day.

As mentioned in Hebrews 10:39, when we're believing to the saving of our souls, we're believing for the just, the ones that are right with God. And those, only just when they live by faith. So, when we hear the word perdition in this verse, He's referring to hell. We don't sympathize with those who hold themselves back and ponder on the things in their past. Take the past into consideration, learn from it and move forward. Not drawing back to return to your own vomit.

Ecclesiastes 3

1 For everything there is a season, and a time for every matter under heaven:
2 a time to be born, and a time to die;
 a time to plant, and a time to pluck up what is planted.
3 a time to kill, and a time to heal;
 a time to break down, and a time to build up.
4 a time to weep, and a time to laugh;
 a time to mourn, and a time to dance.
5 a time to cast away stones, and a time to gather stones together;
 a time to embrace, and a time to refrain from embracing.
6 a time to seek, and a time to lose;
 a time to keep, and a time to cast away.
7 a time to tear, and a time to sew;
 a time to keep silence, and a time to speak.

8 a time to love, and a time to hate;
 a time for war, and a time for peace.

Holy Bible Reference

Straight and narrow roads

There are no straight paths in hard decisions. Do you notice that? They're all narrow and windy. And truthfully, as confrontation or trials come, the easiest and first thing that pops in my head is, "run away!" But is that going to get anyone anywhere? I don't think so... So, what I took on is to modify in a way that suits my abilities while maintaining life for others too. Our roads are hardly ever going to be a straight path.

Heck, they may just be a walking path where you get to brisk fully and enjoy your options. Whether it be a fast paced, narrow, windy race or not, choosing everlasting joy with the hope of the Father is what I hold on to. Does anyone else get tired of noticing that if people changed one thing in their life, those circumstances would turn out far differently than what they came to the conclusion of?

What if we came together to ignite the fire within, to stand up and direct each other to a way of improvement. To improve our life in order to see Christ not only in what we do, but also in who we are. I like to seek out circumstances that are so big, it's bound to fail without God in it.

Chapter 21

Celebrating GOD

Do you ever notice that the simplest questions are the deepest? Maybe that's how we should communicate with one another. Simple questions with deep answers. With that, I think stepping out and taking risks. That's definitely a way to show your celebration for Yahshua. Living in the power that He has given each one of us specifically, because in some people it comes more naturally than others.

Many people have to trust and rely solely in You to provide that. And that's 100% okay, sometimes just living in His power is all that we can do. It takes perseverance, practice, and persistence in order to live in His will. Just read 2 Samuel 6:12-22 and you'll see the persistence it took! Yes, Christ is praised when we pinpoint on His beauty, but He takes delight just as much when we live in Him and through Him giving all glory to Him. Because we have to remember the life of Paul in the Bible.

Paul correlates the ability to be wise with the knowledge of God. The first step to wisdom is purposefully giving Him glory in all instances. So, the craziest thing I've done is not anything physical, but is more mental. Believing in the fact that there's more beyond what the naked eye sees. The eyes see limitation whereas You see possibility. Like Your word says, anything is possible in You. That's where trust and faith in Yahshua come into action. We need to take into account that due to reliance on the Father, the hard things can become less hard when done in His name and with practice.

Kaleidoscope metaphor

Just like a kaleidoscope that morphs and changes, I was that kaleidoscope that had to grow and change into something greater. Although it set me back for quite some time, Yahshua definitely knew what He was doing when He bewildered my physical body to challenge me to elevate my mindset. To elevate it to a place of full repentance and surrender to His ways. Seeing every new opportunity as a way to overcome it while maintaining integrity, perseverance, and loyalty!

Focus on the path ahead, the end goal.

Viewing the path ahead of me did not seem like an easy road to follow. But it was something that had to be done. Something not to just endure but to overcome and conquer. A battle does not come to an easy hand, but rather to those ones that are blessed to understand that there's more to come than what's in front of the naked eye.

Something I wish I knew earlier in life is that doubt is not a decision, it's a normal part of life. Whenever we're faced with these challenging winding roads ahead of us, we have to remember not to only focus on the path ahead, but to look to the end goal and you'll start to see the various blessings step-by-step along the way. Always keep in mind, you are going to encounter many trials and temptations. You're not going to be sure what to do next. Just keep your focus on Yahshua, He'll help you out.

If you doubt that this crazy lady (myself), follower of the way, the truth and the life, thinks this, it's because it happened in my life and continues to happen, day in and day out. This invisible savior works his miraculous miracles every day and He can help you too. Despite what you've been through, what you've done doesn't matter. He's not about who you've been but rather who you can be.

Orientation to Life

As you see, my ethics are tied up to progress in life. Viewing life for all that can be as opposed to what it may appear. Yeah, my physical features may not appear how I desire all of the time. Am I going to let that stop me from going after what Yahshua wants for me? No way. So why do we? Because it's hard, but a lot of things in life are hard. God created us for battle, not to just live and let life happen. Get out there and live, despite your circumstances. "Boasting in your faults." Not to be embarrassed but to flaunt them because that's who the Father created you to be. You are original baby, original!

If you love something, let it go, and if it comes back to you, it was meant to be.

You know when you hear something, and it doesn't fully register in your brain until you hear it again and again and start to wonder? Just me? Well, I heard this quote again that said, "If you love something, let it go, and if it comes back to you, it was meant to be." If you think about it, many of us hear that and think that letting something go is another way of saying that you gave up. But that's where we need to take into consideration the second part. "If it comes back to you, it was meant to be." It's a way of embracing and being content with what you do have.

This quote got me thinking about how Yahshua had His Son enter the world. Gave Him a great life, then was brutally beaten and died a criminal's death. Then was put in a tomb and was raised three days later. Talk about letting go of something you love. Jesus was the ultimate bearer in the fact that He didn't criticize yet He gave His Heavenly Father all the adoration that He could. He even chose forgiveness for those that were blood-thirsty and cruel, putting Him on a cross to die. And in that, Yahshua had it all under control. He knew that His Son, Jesus, would be coming back to Him.

Basically, Christ set the ultimate example of "letting something go." And that goes for almost everything in life. I think about my service dogs. For one, Chase was at the end of his life to where I had to let him go. But that's the cycle of life. Then I got Bennett, and he got sick. I had to let him go to another family to further care for him. I had to make that decision for his best. But this next service dog is going to be exactly what I need. When tough times come, trying to emulate the Father in whatever situation we're in, puts the circumstances in perspective.

Having to let go of something you love is never fun or easy to do. But when you completely trust and believe that Christ will bring all things in standpoint, that's when hope becomes tangible. Having hope in Yahshua that it will come back to me. Not physically, but in an improved kind of way. In His will, His time, allowing Him to lead the possibility of His will to be done. If that thing that you love doesn't come back to you, there's a purpose that we may know nothing about. But again, His will be done.

In all my efforts of wanting normalcy back and fighting and rebelling, He had a greater plan in store. One that I personally knew nothing about, yet I continue to move forward in the hope of Yahshua because that's what each of us was called to do. To live in the light of Him. Living in authenticity and God given power.

Being in a nearly 5-month coma, there is so many things that drive me crazy for not knowing. I'm that type A kind of person that wants to know everything, is very curious of the unknown and lives in complete surrender to Christ knowing what He has for me is far greater. I still would love to know, but what if Elohim caused the unknown in order for me to consistently be on the search for Him? To sacrifice my own ways to see what He has beyond the suffering. I had to have a near death experience to trigger a turnabout in the direction of my life. Point my thoughts and actions to Him and live out of my own desire.

FROM THE LIBRARY OF

Kassidy Brewer

Epilogue

I wanted to sum up these tragic events that ended up revealing my true identity and character in Christ. Yahshua created us all with the character of Him, it's up to us to unveil what's inside. We can get stepped on, bruised, or broken, but what you ultimately do with your pain and sufferings reveals what is to come about.

Much like how I wanted, a normal pattern or a daily routine in life, each and every day seem to have its own specifics that came with treacherous challenges. So, let me ask you, have you wanted something so bad, but it was out of your grasp? That's exactly what a dream feels like. Something out of your grasp. Something that makes you feel that it's impossible to reach, yet we're commanded to pray about the things that we desire. They're in the Fathers hands. In His timing and His will, He will deliver.

I'm not going to give you the fluffy version that I don't make mistakes, that I have everything in order and the future looks bright. I'm positive it does look bright but good things don't come without a price. Thats why Christ took the blunt of it all for me, for you to thrive. I can confidently say that I'm ecstatic with who Christ has made me to be. Flaws and all!

I fully plan on continuing my dreams of being around horses and riding for therapy purposes and for enjoyment, to continue in my efforts to seek what You have in store for me, continue the hope of having my own service dog (BFF), to keep moving forward in my knowledge of You and love despite what I'm facing, to look for new ways of how to do things with one hand so I can be entirely independent.

"In everyone's life, at some time, our inner fire goes out. It is then burst into flames by an encounter with another human being or beings. We should all be thankful for those people who rekindle our inner Spirit." - Albert Schweitzer

REFELECTIONS

In which ways are you stopping your growth because you just don't want to feel fear?

_____
_____
_____
_____
_____
_____
_____
_____
_____
_____

What types of stressful events hold you back and not harness you forward? How can we adjust the situation and modify it?

_____
_____
_____
_____
_____
_____
_____
_____
_____

How can I take the time to really see the suffering people?

_____

_____

_____

_____

_____

_____

_____

_____

_____

_____

_____

The humanistic mindset can push authority aside and say, "I can do this all on my own," what if we practiced what "the teacher" says on command. Speaking of the one in charge. Not doing it in our own control but living up to what the teacher wants. How can we shift our mindset to be more of a "go with the flow" kind of person?

_____

_____

_____

_____

_____

_____

_____

_____

_____

_____

Are you that type of person that just wants to get the job done so you can move on? How can you help other people with complicated baggage to be more comfortable in their own skin?

_____

_____

_____

_____

_____

_____

_____

_____

Occasionally, life is about saying "yes" and figuring out "how" along the way. So how can you comprehend how to say yes and follow through with it?

_____

_____

_____

_____

_____

_____

_____

_____

_____

_____

_____

How much does God see in you that you don't see in yourself? In what way can you change your perspective to meet His?

_____
_____
_____
_____
_____
_____
_____
_____
_____
_____

In what way can you challenge yourself? Keep the mindset that you were created for battle! Spiritual battle!

_____
_____
_____
_____
_____
_____
_____
_____
_____
_____
_____
_____
_____
_____

How can I ease the tension that would make a transition difficult? Because yes, transitions make us nervous, but Christ never changed. He will always be there to help you.

_____

_____

_____

_____

_____

_____

_____

_____

_____

_____

_____

_____

_____

How do you react to suffering? Yours? Someone else's?

_____

_____

_____

_____

_____

_____

_____

_____

_____

_____

_____

Kassidy Brewer

FROM THE LIBRARY OF

Acknowledgments

Each and every person that is in my life has meaning to me! They are part of my journey. I thank our Heavenly Father for putting all of these individuals into my life. He knew I needed them, and He strategically placed them, when I needed them. Thank you all for doing the impossible and walking along side of me to build me up to be a better person. Because of you, I took a farther adventure than most!

As I reflect on my friends and families love, I'm humbled by the fact of your words. They're not only touching but elevating due to your generosity to express your thoughts. Seeing and hearing your multiple kind words and testimonials, I am in a state of awe by your love. Thank you. Thank you. Thank you from the bottom of my heart!

I would also like to express my sincerest gratitude for all who have donated and helped this book come to fruition and for your continuous support listed below and the countless others.

Bryan smiley, Charity For Charity, Sandra Stormer Simm, Denise Hernandez, Kim Woody, Rachel Woody, Sharon Griffin, Candi Jones, Daniel Fried, Debbie Vu, Leland Rolling, Melanie Assuama, Melissa, Vinciguerra, Christina Kelly, Corinne Rice, Mark Wells, James Yanoschik, Don Lloyd, AJ Twiss, Justin Kenton, Jacob Brighton, Kimberly Amos, Sue Muscarella, Mahlon Tobias, Jace Skramstad, Kevin Skramstad, Kim Ebersole, Aimee Hall, Karen Robertson, Mike Sullivan, Bruce Burns,

Lynnae Hoff, Sinead Copley, Gloria Wolnick, Janet Gay, Donnie Bishop, and Janelle Paulsrud.

Kassidy Brewer

Testimonials

Karen Robertson

I met Kassidy Brewer in the winter of 2023. She greeted me at the door of Chapel Coffee, where she volunteers weekly. Besides being slim, trim, and beautiful, she moves to a rhythm the rest of us can't totally comprehend. I was attracted to her immediately. Why? Because I could see she was special. I have a grandson whose brain cancer has caused him to be wheelchair bound, and a daughter who is recovering from a stroke. I knew Kassidy would be an encouragement to both of them.

Kassidy uses a walker to get around, but she can single-handedly throw that thing in the back of her car and drive off without assistance. She doesn't let anything slow her down. Her calendar is full, as well as her heart and mind. She has the determination of a stampeding buffalo, and she will not be denied. Her sense of humor is sharp, and she can dish it out as well as take it in. She hungers after knowledge and with this book project, she is just hitting her stride. Kassidy has a strong faith in Jesus that keeps her upright. Watch out world.

Grant Sealock

Kassidy, you have taught me the importance of perseverance. We all go through difficult situations; we either let them consume us or we confront them. You are an example of someone who confronted your situation and didn't let it hold you back.

Laura Reyes

Kassidy, you have been an inspiration for me since the first day I met you at the Toastmasters meetings. Your public speaking is amazing, and you always strive to do better. You are a strong-willed young lady that goes after dreams and does not take life for granted. I thank God for having you in our lives as a friend.

Pam Buck

Kassidy, you have inspired me to persevere in my trust in God. I know God brought you into my life for this very reason!

Taralee Layton

Kassidy, when I think of when you were in Rady Children's Hospital for weeks, no one knowing if you were going to live or die, and how there were so many, many, many people praying for you, I think of how God performed a miracle and allowed you to move forward and make a difference in so many people's lives. Your perseverance and true grit are to be envied. You inspire so many people including me, all of my family, and Isabella in particular.

She was just a little girl when you had your traumatic brain injury, and I remember the compassion that she felt toward you. Since that incident you have risen above the obstacles that you face on a daily basis. You have a determination that is beyond the norm. I believe that comes from the Lord, I believe that your faith and your positive spirit is given to you by the Lord. I believe that your trust in him and your love for him is magnified in everything you do.

If you want to do something, you try over and over and over again until you accomplish it. Those of us that have never had anything happen to us need to learn from that. I think that is the most important thing that I want to stress here, is that those of us that are considered "normal" lack the perseverance that you have.

Taralee

Kass, you are a fighter, you are respected and everything you put your mind to, you accomplish. That is so admirable. You take care of your body by feeding it well by cooking creatively. You are always learning new things about nutrition & putting it into action by your recipes. I feel that you have an extra desire, above average, to eat healthily. This is another admirable trait that you possess.

Kass, I truly believe that God allowed your incident to happen to you for a reason. He gave you the will, the strength and the determination to affect other people to set an example of what true grit looks like in overcoming the battles that many people that have injuries like yours face. I am truly humbled when I'm around you, dear one. You've always inspired me to be better & to "never" take for granted the abilities I have.
God bless you sweetheart! I love you!

Star

It is a generally accepted fact that Kassidy Brewer is alive today because of the efforts of several individuals who, in 2008, made efforts to bring her back to life from a coma. I was one of those individuals. I was brought into the situation at a critical moment. As I understood it at the time, she had been in a coma long enough and tragically enough that the medical staff advised the family that they should consider taking her off of life support and letting go of the hopeless situation.

One of her close friends was aware of my history of interventions into other dire situations that seemed to cause miraculous results. I got a call from him at midnight of the day that Kass eventually began her assent from death back to life.

When I entered the hospital room it was probably 3am and Kass was surrounded by family and friends. In the dim light they appeared to be apparitions of saints and angels. Kass was hooked up and wrapped up in various hospital equipment intended to keep her body functioning, even controlling her body temperature artificially. In spite of the dim light and equipment, Kass' beauty shined forth.

However, the equipment did present an obstacle that placed a limit on my freedom to act spontaneously under guidance from heaven. The second limiting circumstance was the presence of friends and family who I assumed had certain expectations for my actions. I tuned out as much as I could and focused on the task at hand. I found or created a bare shoulder so that I could get direct contact with her with my hands. I closed my eyes and began to internally recite my prayer as a mantra to still my mind from thoughts and got down to work. The work was to believe in the possibility that my action could promote healing and recovery.

The "work" was to feel the energy flowing from me and through me into her body, heart, mind, and soul. The "work" was to follow guidance from above. I whispered encouragement into her ear. I sang a few words from one of my healing songs, "Hold On". All the while my eyes were closed. There was a brief time when I opened my eyes to ask her family to remove the mechanical wrappers from her legs and I asked them to massage and move her legs. Then I closed my eyes and went back to prayer.

Time passed....15 hours I am told. I was not aware of time at the time.

Suddenly Kass responded. I am not sure what the initial response was that cause her friends and family to gasp or shout in a way that brought me out of my "Zone". Kass opened her eyes and made an effort to lift her head. ...and then went back down to the pillow. There was an immediate rush to action and in the blink of an eye hospital staff came into the room and took over the situation. I was not done. They did not seem to get it. Within minutes we were all out in the hallway. And before long, I was on my way back home disappointed that I did not get to continue healing Kass.

I accepted it, for now, and presumed that I would be invited back soon to follow up and follow through. That never happened. The rest of her recovery fell into the hands of the medical profession and fortunately for Kass they did an amazing job of restoring much of her functions. A few months or years later, Kass' mom told me that her progress had stalled. I offered to pray for her progress to have a breakthrough. I immediately went on a retreat to pray for her mom to see a sign that Kass' healing was progressing. Of course there is more, much more, to this story.

Charity Prestifilippo
Founder/President
Charity for Charity
"It's About Hope!"

Kassidy was nominated to be a beneficiary for my wish fulfilling organization, Charity for Charity, in July of 2015. The gentleman, Jay Oneil, who nominated her, owned a medical equipment supply company that Kassidy and her mom, Donna, frequented as a result of her TBI. In Jay's letter, he mentioned Kass's incredible personality, determined spirit and overall incredible attitude towards life, even after what had happened to her. Our Board of Advisors ended up selecting Kassidy as our 2016 beneficiary for our Stars of the Valley event.

Kass had been living with her new normal after her miracle survival, for several years when we met her in person. To beat the odds of not only surviving an AVM, but then to walk into our office with only a walker, fully cognitive and most importantly, with a giant smile. We couldn't believe our eyes! It was at that moment that she WOWed us, and she's never stopped.

Kass has become a very special part of our Charity for Charity family, involved in all of our events and activities, somewhat of a spokesperson for us if you will. Before the dreaded days of COVID, Kass was a part of our UNSTOPPABLES, a team of our beneficiaries who were motivational overcomers. We brought them into schools around the Southern California area and hosted presentations from an audience of one grade level to the entire school. In this presentation, Kass showed the kids her humor, her positive attitude and even that she can still kick boards, as she was a black belt before the incident.

Kass handled herself with grace, love and just the right bit of sass! She inspired hundreds of students, and many want to meet her, take pictures with her, and follow her on social media. They listened to a girl, who, although her words come out a little different than ours, had an attitude of "be yourself". Kass's message was about being yourself, loving yourself, and not letting others define you. For a young girl, then young woman, whose TBI changed the way she walked and talked, it's incredible to see her inspiring outlook on life! Many young girls start off self-conscious and, if something changes them that is visible, it makes it worse. Well not Kass!

This girl knows who she is from the inside out! She embraces the second chance that God has given her and understands her purpose. Kass does not just inspire me, she inspires everyone who meets her. She is magnetic! She is loveable! She is determined! She's someone who you want around and who constantly reminds you that life is precious and to be grateful for it. That it's just not that bad, no matter what. I am honored to know Kassidy Brewer. She has had a great impact on my life, and I will always keep her close because life just wouldn't be the same without her!

Kim Amos
I'll never forget the morning I asked Kassidy about her story. I was amazed at the strength, endurance, and faith from such a

young age. It's no wonder she is a beam of light at the ministry where we get to serve together (and everywhere else she goes I'm sure). It fills me with so much joy to know that she will be sharing her heart and her hurts with the world SO THAT we can all experience God's love through her.

Kenzie Gomez
Kassidy Dawn Brewer was the coolest gal I knew. Her older sister was friends with my older brother, which is how I got to know her. Kassidy was one grade older than me in school and everything I aspired.

From my perspective, Kass had an incredible group of friends, she was funny, outgoing, and incredibly driven to be her own person. She was edgy, she had a way and spirit the exuded more like her brand than her sense of style; she was the most fit and athletic girl I knew, ruling the soccer field and kicking anyone's a** in karate; yet, she was so humble, helping others around her, never saying a negative thing to someone else and living proudly in the word of God. She was beyond her years, always thinking ahead about trying new things, becoming more, and having an entrepreneurial mindset. Whether it be exploring new places to ride bikes, or selling golf balls, Lemonade, and Otter Pops out of the fence on the golf course; there truly was never a dull moment in the life of being Kassidy's friend and I am forever grateful to have made those memories alongside her.

I still don't quite know how I got lucky enough to enter the world of Kassidy Brewer, but I think it was a summer pool party that caused the rest to be history. I was lucky enough to live a few blocks down the road from Kass and from then on it was days full of pool hopping via bike rides between houses, golf course popcorn snack breaks followed by a race down the hill, cartwheel sessions in the golf course sand trap and on the green outside the gate of her house, and concert/photobooth sessions from the Apple Desktop computer at the Brewer household. Kass pushed me to be braver than I thought, believe in a higher power, and be a good person from the whole heart. Kass became my best friend fast and someone I still admire to this day.

Denise Schile

I have been thinking a lot about you since we spoke and have been reflecting a lot about you, our conversation, your AVM and your journey. I am old now, so my memory is foggy sometimes. What I do remember is that the CHET (Children's Hospital Emergency Transport) line rang in the afternoon for a transport to Rancho Springs. I think it was early August. Like the 4th maybe. It must have been 2008 as I was already a nurse practitioner, but it was before I had kids. (now my life's events are cataloged as before kids or after kids!) I would have typically gone on the call to come get you, but the PICU fellow went.

I think it was Dr. David Nathalong, I could be wrong. I think we had plans that evening so he volunteered to go so I could keep my plans. I remember hearing the details of your presentation. I think it was something like "was at home, not feeling well, had the worst headache of your life...mom drove you to the ER and I think you became unconscious about the time your mom pulled up to the ER entrance. The surgeon who placed your EVD in the ER saved your life that day! I remember meeting you in the PICU the next morning. You of course were in a non-induced coma. I remember sitting in XRAY rounds and we all reviewed your CT scans and Angiograms.

I remember being blown away by how huge your AVM and surrounding hemorrhage were. We all sat there thinking "Wow! This is bad! It's huge and in the Posterior Fossa. Bad news. She probably won't survive and if she does, she will likely be vegetative." I don't remember how long you were hospitalized or all the exact details, but I do know that was the beginning of a very long and sometimes harrowing PICU stay. I think you must have been in the PICU for a few months. During that time, you spent many weeks completely sedated. We kept you completely comatose for several weeks to manage your ICP (intracranial pressure) and give your brain and body time to heal.

I remember spending weeks getting to know your family. I think you even celebrated your 13th birthday at the PICU. You had so much love surrounding you in the PICU. I remember being so in awe of your amazing family and community. Especially your mom. That is one strong woman! I know now where you get it. At times it seemed like she was holding everyone up. Sometimes even the medical team. It didn't seem to matter whether we came up with good news or bad news, she was like a rock. She was a force!

I remember one time though, after you had been transferred out of the PICU and you were on the surgical floor, you were not yet able to speak or follow commands, not able to move purposefully and had already gotten your G tube placed. I walked out to see you with Dr. Khanna (Sandeep) You were not as "awake" as you had been and to us seemed like something was up. I remember sending you for a stat CT of the head as we were worried. Your mom, who was always so strong and so positive, looked and me and said something to the effect of "F@*k! What now?" That was the only time I think I ever witnessed her ever break down.

I think you had what we suspected which was Obstructive Hydrocephalus. You got a VP shunt after that and stuck around for a bit longer. I remember you going home and you were still total care at that point. I have a photo of us (you, me, your family and Sandeep) with you strapped in a transport gurney as you left for home via ambulance. I don't remember the exact timeline with regard to how long you were home before you came back for rehab, but I remember being amazed at the progress you made at home. It was such a privilege to hear your voice for the first time. Wow, thinking about that reminds me how far you have come.

Your mom always sent me Christmas cards with updates, and we would catch up when you came for appointments, or you know, a shunt revision! I remember coming downtown to the Vespa dealership after Devin was born to see you. You held him. I still have that photo. I remember watching you learn to walk, talk and eat again. I remember your mom bringing you to the PICU to see us all and share with us all of your triumphs and accomplishments and thinking to myself, dang she's unstoppable. I LOVE, LOVE, LOVE walking by your photo in the hallway of the PICU.

It makes me remember why I love doing what I do, and it reminds me that my patients aren't just a diagnosis or a room number, that they are someone's everything. Taking care of you and actually taking care of your family as well was such a gift to me as a fairly new nurse practitioner. I learned a lot from all of you. You continue to amaze me with your strength and grace. I am glad I had a little part in your amazing journey! You truly are inspiring Kass! I can't wait to see you realize the dream of writing this book and to witness all you have instore for us! Give all my love to the Brew Crew!

Michael Robles

Ms. Brewer has a huge and impactful story in my own personal book of life. Ms. Brewer was the very first student I remember seeing when I walked into the Taekwondo studio in Murrieta. As best as my memory serves me, she was a blue belt. She was a beautiful petite young girl with a beautiful smile and a determined yet playful attitude. She holds the distinct and esteemed place of being the only female in my 30 years of martial arts training to give me a black eye, but that is a story for another time.

Truth be told I don't remember much before her incident, I remember her dedication, she would help in classes and was well liked by not only myself but by all, she was actively training towards the goal of her 2nd degree black belt, and I could always count on her to be there when she said she would with a cheerful attitude and sometimes a bit of a "spicy" attitude. Sitting here reflecting on "who she was" and "what she was like" really makes me ponder, I knew her as a fun loving and dedicated student but her incident really marks a point for me where through it and after it I believe I really got to know her, to understand her, to admire her, It is my opinion that so many of the traits I saw and understood about her after her incident were always there, but perhaps through her trials and tribulations were brought to the forefront in a way I certainly would have never seen before.

Mike Sullivan

From what I remember of Kass before the incident, she was full of life, vibrant, somewhat quiet, shy, very competitive, and willing to help anyone. She actually taught my 1 yr old daughter how to swim in her backyard pool. They look like sisters. It's uncanny!

Martha Ettinghausen

I first met Kassidy several years ago at Toastmasters and I've had the privilege of witnessing her transformation into a remarkably confident young woman. Despite facing significant challenges from a stroke at such a young age, Kassidy has embraced these obstacles with an inspiring determination and passion. Her ability to view adversity not as a barrier but as an opportunity for growth has always impressed me. She approaches each challenge with a resolute spirit and through her resilience, she has truly become a stronger woman. Kassidy's journey is a testament to her strength and unwavering spirit. It's an honor to watch her evolve into the incredible individual she is today.

Lynnae Hoff

Kassidy, for years I've watched you walk into the gym regardless of any physical limitations. What mental and physical strength it must take to get yourself there; I will never know. I knew there was a story behind seeing you walk with the assistance of a walker and shadowed by a beautiful service dog. I was confident that I saw you on the wall at Rady's Children's. I never got the chance to connect.

I believe in God divine appointments. One day our paths crossed, and I had the courage to ask if I could interrupt you at the bathroom sink. I knew it was the day I would build the courage to connect. Your smile, beautiful eyes. kind heart, and warm personality was most powerful immediately. Your desire to share your story vulnerably and your desire to know why I was at Rady's immediately wreaked empathy and compassion. The more you shared, the more I was intrigued at just how beautiful of a woman you are. God has only begun with your story, and I can't even imagine how many lives you've positively impacted thus far and will impact as you continue to use the hard parts of life to glorify HIM and help others. May you continue to lean into God and all he has for you, beautiful. Your sweet, warrior spirit is SO inspiring.

Your gym friend Lynnae Hoff

Barbara Wise

I first came to know Kassidy five years ago. She joined my women's Bible study group at our church, and I was immediately drawn to her. I would discover that the struggles she has endured in life have created a deeply committed Christian. The illness that left her with significant physical handicaps also produced a woman of thoughtful, spiritual maturity. Kassidy 's insightful contributions to our study group discussions have blessed each of us. Her life demonstrates trust, joy, peace, faithfulness, and patience which are some of The Fruits of the Spirit.

Love you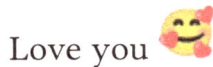

Don Lloyd

I grew up with Kevin, Kassidy 's dad to where I've known all three of his daughters their whole lives. I found out about Kassidy 's incident through another family friend via email that was absolutely devastating.

Words from a friend to inform me of what happened on August 06, 2008:

Kassidy is still physically unable to speak; I'm only getting text messages. Needless to say, the rest of the family is taking this very hard. Kassidy (age 14) had a birth defect that was virtually undetectable called a Cerebral Arteriovenous Malformation at the base of her skull. Punch in AVM into any search engine, click on the Wikipedia link with the above diagnosis to get more info. This caused a Massive Cerebral Aneurysm at the base of her brain shortly after cutting the lawn on Monday afternoon. The rupture was in her main Aorta (back of the neck) going up to the brain. This is the main blood flow conduit to the brain. She virtually immediately lost all blood flow to the brain. To my knowledge she has had no brain activity since and is on life support. She is at Children's Hospital in San Diego. No corrective procedures are scheduled. I'm led to believe that there will be a life support disconnect on Friday or shortly after. "

Hearing that Kassidy was in the hospital on life support to having to cope with the news that she could be taken off of life-support in three days. I knew the faith that her family held, and this was definitely going to be a battle with their faith. But they held it together! I cannot be prouder to call them family. I consider Kassidy to be my hero with all that she's had to go through, in the fact that her little body held through all that trauma. I came for a visit once a year to make my rounds to people in southern

California, but the Brewer family was definitely my priority! I stayed at their house in order to keep in touch and lend a helping hand.

CaringBridge was a huge support system for not only me but everyone keeping in close contact with her story. Beyond hearing of her progression over time, I was thrilled to hear of the success in her day-to-day movements and wins. She continues to live every single day knowing where she's come from!

Sierra Richards

We were about to go into our freshman year of high school when Kass got sick. It was one of the scariest things that had ever happened to someone in my life. I felt so lost that something so awful could happen to someone so wonderful, young, and vibrant. I remember being told that it wasn't looking good for her and I began to grapple with the thought of never being able to see her again. I leaned on one of our best friends and my mom for support. Then, slowly out of the blue, a miracle happened, and she began to wake up. The improbable was happening. It awakened a part of me that began to believe in something bigger than myself.

Watching Kassidy make a huge recovery from such a traumatic event that happened to her at an impressionable and important time in her life has never, ever stopped being inspiring. The strength she has shown to prevail through the hardships she has faced makes me feel like anything is truly possible. She lives her life with such an adventure in her heart and such a feisty spirit. There isn't anything she won't be able to accomplish if she wants to do it. Because of Kassidy, I have hope in the world.

Because of Kassidy, I know miracles are possible. And because of Kassidy, I am grateful for every beautiful minute in this life.

Kenzie Gomes

When I was informed of Kassidy's prognosis and recovery process, I could only imagine how long the road to recovery would be, but I didn't fully comprehend it. Relearning everything she was already a master at seemed like an impossible task, but I know if anyone could do it, it would be Kass. Even today, I remain impressed with the recovery milestones she still makes. From the first independent breath, to sitting up, talking, walking, then competing in Karate again, graduating, public speaking, baking, mentoring - the list goes on and on - The journey Kassidy has had is nothing short of absolutely incredible and I couldn't be more proud of how she has silenced every single person who may have doubted her along the way.

Felicia Gonzales Coyle

Kassidy, you were my hero when we were kids, and you're my hero now. You have shown me what it means to fight, to live, and to never give up. Even though life has changed in ways we never could have imagined, one thing never has: you are still the strongest person I know, and I am endlessly grateful to call you my best friend.

Your forever partner in crime.

About the Author

Hey, Kassidy Brewer here, the voice behind the creator of the book. Like you've read, I'm that type of gal who doesn't give up when times get hard. Relying on Christ is my only lifeline. Knowing and understanding that life can be destructive and devastating at times but when Elohim is in the picture, life doesn't fail us.

I enjoy seeing life for what it truly is, beautiful, hard, challenging, encouraging, testing, fun! I saw my circumstances and thought, well this is going to be impossible. But then I thought, hey, I have Jesus Christ in me. He's the powerful one, the mighty one, the one with all authority and He's in me. Why wouldn't I step aside and let Him take over? In the day-to-day battle, I look to faith to get me through. Not in a false sense of surviving to get through but to hand over my hopes and give them to God of how He wants me to thrive in my weaknesses.

Nowadays, I view weaknesses as a form of a person's story. It's a part of their story that's hard, that they might not like but it's part of em' whether they like it or not. Adonai enabled me to see this horrific event that was supposed to kill me as something I've fully accepted and learned to flourish with what I've been given. I was picked and pruned from all of the things I thought would fulfill me and was set to only be on the path of life.

My story is far different from your story but in a way, we all have struggles. It's just a matter of who guides your ship, who's in the storm with you?

Cover design by Travis Rosene

www.ingramcontent.com/pod-product-compliance
Lightning Source LLC
Chambersburg PA
CBHW050445150626
46551CB00029B/1701